19世纪有两位伟大的人物，一位是拿破仑，一位是海伦·凯勒。

——马克·吐温

人类的精神之美一旦被认识，我们就永远不会忘记。海伦·凯勒小姐的生活和生活乐趣，给我们这些没有那么多困难需要克服的人上了永远难忘的一课——我们希望这本书有越来越多的读者，并让她的精神传播得越来越广。

——罗斯福夫人

海伦·凯勒自传
假如给我三天光明

THE STORY OF MY LIFE
THREE DAYS TO SEE

[美]海伦·凯勒⊙著

徐 杰⊙译

群言出版社
QUNYAN PRESS

·北京·

图书在版编目（CIP）数据

海伦·凯勒自传：假如给我三天光明 /（美）凯勒著；徐杰译. - 北京：群言出版社，2015.12
ISBN 978-7-80256-935-5

Ⅰ.①海… Ⅱ.①凯… ②徐… Ⅲ.①凯勒，H.（1880～1968）-自传 Ⅳ.① K837.127=533

中国版本图书馆 CIP 数据核字（2015）第 253541 号

责任编辑：	朱前前
封面设计：	同人内文化传媒·书装设计
出版发行：	群言出版社
社　　址：	北京市东城区东厂胡同北巷1号（100006）
网　　址：	www.qypublish.com
自营网店：	https://qycbs.tmall.com（天猫旗舰店）
	http://qycbs.shop.kongfz.com（孔夫子旧书网）
	http://www.qypublish.com（群言出版社官网）
电子信箱：	qunyancbs@126.com
联系电话：	010 65267783　65263836
经　　销：	全国新华书店
法律顾问：	北京天驰君泰律师事务所
印　　刷：	北京市燕鑫印刷有限公司
版　　次：	2016年6月第1版　2016年6月第1次印刷
开　　本：	787mm × 1092mm　1/16
印　　张：	16
字　　数：	287千字
书　　号：	ISBN 978-7-80256-935-5
定　　价：	22.00 元

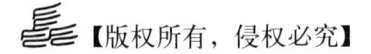

【版权所有，侵权必究】

Preface

IT is with a kind of fear that I begin to write the history of my life. I have, as it were, a superstitious hesitation in lifting the veil that clings about my childhood like a golden mist. The task of writing an autobiography is a difficult one. When I try to classify my earliest impressions, I find that fact and fancy look alike across the years that link the past with the present. The woman paints the child's experiences in her own fantasy. A few impressions stand out vividly from the first years of my life; but "the shadows of the prison-house are on the rest." Besides, many of the joys and sorrows of childhood have lost their poignancy; and many incidents of vital importance in my early education have been forgotten in the

序 言

当我提起笔来，记下从出生到现在的生命历程，真觉得惶恐不安。童年往事犹如笼罩在雾一般轻柔的薄幕下，现在要把它掀开，的确让我疑虑重重。写自传本身是件很难的事，更何况童年早已久远，我已经无法分清楚哪些是事实，哪些只是我的幻觉想象。不过，在我的大脑记忆中，有些事情仍然鲜明生动地闪现出来，虽然某些画面只是片断的、零碎的，但对于我的人生却有或多或少的影

excitement of great discoveries. In order, therefore, not to be tedious I shall try to present in a series of sketches only the episodes that seem to me to be the most interesting and important.

Helen Keller

响。为了避免冗长乏味，我将节选一些最有趣和最有价值的情节，来讲述我生活的故事。

——海伦·凯勒

目录 Contents

第一篇　我生活的故事

THE STORY OF MY LIFE

第1章　早期的光明 …………………………………………… 2
第2章　童年的记忆 …………………………………………… 8
第3章　寻找希望 …………………………………………… 17
第4章　重塑生命 …………………………………………… 21
第5章　认识大自然 …………………………………………… 26
第6章　领悟"爱"的真谛 …………………………………… 30
第7章　沐浴知识的阳光 …………………………………… 35
第8章　欢乐的圣诞节 …………………………………… 44
第9章　波士顿之旅 …………………………………… 47
第10章　和大海亲密接触 …………………………………… 52
第11章　山间秋季 …………………………………… 55
第12章　洁白的冰雪世界 …………………………………… 61
第13章　我要说话 …………………………………… 64
第14章　《霜王》事件 …………………………………… 70

第15章 世界博览会 …………………………………… 81
第16章 学习拉丁文 …………………………………… 87
第17章 客居纽约的学习生活 ………………………… 90
第18章 剑桥女子中学 ………………………………… 94
第19章 冲出困境 ……………………………………… 101
第20章 实现大学的梦想 ……………………………… 108
第21章 爱书如命 ……………………………………… 118
第22章 享受多彩的生活 ……………………………… 134
第23章 永远的朋友 …………………………………… 149

第二篇　假如给我三天光明

THREE DAYS TO SEE

珍惜每一天 …………………………………………… 162
  第一天 …………………………………………… 167
  第二天 …………………………………………… 171
  第三天 …………………………………………… 176

附　录

第一篇　从黑暗走向光明 …………………………… 182
  大学后的生活 …………………………………… 182
  结识马克·吐温 ………………………………… 190
  永不言输 ………………………………………… 195

登上演讲台 …… 199
和贝尔博士交往 …… 201
投身反战运动 …… 206
好莱坞的多彩生活 …… 210
马戏团的客串演出 …… 214
慈母离世 …… 216
为残疾朋友募捐 …… 219
从黑暗走向光明 …… 222

第二篇 安妮·莎莉文老师的故事 …… 230
厄运降临 …… 230
救济院的生离死别 …… 231
向往光明 …… 233
我要上学 …… 235
第二次生命 …… 236
新的转折 …… 237
艰辛而伟大的教育 …… 238
毕生的奉献 …… 240

《大美百科全书 海伦·凯勒传》 …… 241
译后记 …… 243

第一篇
我生活的故事

THE STORY OF MY LIFE

CHAPTER I

I was born on June 27, 1880, in Tuscumbia, a little town of northern Alabama.

The family on my father's side is descended from Caspar Keller, a native of Switzerland, who settled in Maryland. One of my Swiss ancestors was the first teacher of the deaf in Zurich and wrote a book on the subject of their education-rather a singular coincidence; though it is true that there is no king who has not had a slave among his ancestors, and no slave who has not had a king among his.

My grandfather, Caspar Keller's son, "entered"large tracts of land in Alabama and finally settled there. I have been told that once a year he went from Tuscumbia to Philadelphia on horseback to purchase supplies for the plantation, and my aunt has in her possession many of the letters to his family, which give charming and vivid accounts of these trips.

My Grandmother Keller was a daughter of one of Lafayette's aides, Alexander Moore, and granddaughter of Alexander Spotswood, an early Colonial Governor of Virginia. She was also second cousin to Robert E. Lee.

My father, Arthur H. Keller, was a captain in the Confederate Army, and my mother, Kate Adams, was his second wife and many years younger. Her

第1章　早期的光明

1880年6月27日，我出生在亚拉巴马州北部的一个小镇塔斯坎比亚。

我的祖先是瑞士人，移民到美国后定居在马里兰州。我的瑞士祖先中竟然有一位是苏黎世最早的聋哑人教育专家，他曾写过一本关于如何教育聋哑人的书。谁能料到，他的后人中竟然会有一个像我这样又盲又聋又哑的残疾人，这不能不说是一个神奇的偶然。每当想到这里，我就不得不相信所谓"国王的祖先也可能是奴隶，而奴隶的祖先中也可能诞生国王"的正确性，命运真是无法预知啊！

我的祖父，也就是卡斯帕·凯勒的儿子，到了亚拉巴马州这片广袤的土地之后，就定居下来。我曾听说，那时候由于塔斯坎比亚地处偏僻，祖父每年都要特地骑马，从塔斯坎比亚镇跑到760英里远的费城，去购买家里和农场要用的各种东西。每次祖父前往费城的途中，总会写信给家里报平安，信中对西部沿途的景观，以及旅途中所遭遇的人、事、物都有清楚而生动的描述。姑妈至今还保留了许多祖父的家信，这些信就好像是一本历险小说，令人百读不厌。

grandfather, Benjamin Adams, married Susanna E. Goodhue, and lived in Newbury, Massachusetts, for many years. Their son, Charles Adams, was born in Newburyport, Massachusetts, and moved to Helena, Arkansas. When the Civil War broke out, he fought on the side of the South and became a brigadier-general. He married Lucy Helen Everett, who belonged to the same family of Everett as Edward Everett and Dr. Edward Everett Hale. After the war was over the family moved to Memphis, Tennessee.

I lived, up to the time of the illness that deprived me of my sight and hearing, in a tiny house consisting of a large square room and a small one, in which the servant slept. It is a custom in the South to build a small house near the homestead as an annex to be used on occasion. Such a house my father built after the Civil War, and when he married my mother they went to live in it. It was completely covered with vines, climbing roses and honeysuckles. From the garden it looked like an arbour.

海伦的父亲亚瑟·凯勒，曾任南方联盟军上尉

我祖母是拉斐特一位官员亚历山大·摩尔的女儿，又是弗吉尼亚早期殖民政府总督亚历山大·斯波特伍德的孙女，她还是罗伯特·李的堂姐。

我父亲亚瑟·凯勒曾是南北战争时的南军上尉，我的母亲凯蒂·亚当斯是他的第二位妻子，母亲比父亲要小好几岁。母亲的祖父本杰明·亚当斯娶了苏珊娜·古德休，住在马萨诸塞东北部的纽伯里波特，他们生了儿子查理·亚当斯，然后又迁到了阿肯色州的赫勒拿。南北战争爆发后，查理·亚当斯代表南方参战，后来升为准将。他和露希·海伦·艾弗雷特结了婚，她与爱德华·艾弗雷特和爱德华·艾弗雷特·黑尔博士属于同一个艾弗雷特家族。战争结束后，他们搬到了田纳西的孟菲斯。

在我还没有失去视觉、听觉以前，我们住的屋子很小，总共只有两间，一间正方形的大房子和一间仆人住的小房子。当时，按照南方的习惯，人们往往会在自己家旁边再加盖一间屋子，以备不时之需。南北战争之后，父亲也盖了一所这样的小屋子，他同母亲结婚之后，就住进了这个小屋。这屋子虽小，但是爬满了葡萄、爬藤蔷薇和金银花，从园子里望去，像是一座用树枝搭成的凉亭。这里的花儿成了蜂鸟和蜜蜂的乐园。

我家的老宅子离我们的蔷薇凉亭没有几步远。由于我们家被茂密的树木、绿藤所包围，所以邻居们都称我们家为"绿色家园"。这个旧庭院是我

The little porch was hidden from view by a screen of yellow roses and Southern smilax. It was the favourite haunt of humming-birds and bees.

The Keller homestead, where the family lived, was a few steps from our little rose-bower. It was called "Ivy Green" because the house and the surrounding trees and fences were covered with beautiful English ivy. Its old-fashioned garden was the paradise of my childhood.

Even in the days before my teacher came, I used to feel along the square stiff boxwood hedges, and, guided by the sense of smell, would find the first violets and lilies. There, too, after a fit of temper, I went to find comfort and to hide my hot face in the cool leaves and grass.

What joy it was to lose myself in that garden of flowers, to wander happily from spot to spot, until, coming suddenly upon a beautiful vine, I recognized it by its leaves and blossoms, and knew it was the vine which covered the tumble-down summer-

海伦的母亲凯蒂·亚当斯，年轻时代是孟菲斯市的美女

童年时代的天堂。

在我的家庭老师莎莉文小姐来之前，我经常独自一人摸着围成方形的黄杨木树篱，慢慢地走到庭园里，凭着嗅觉寻找刚刚开放的紫罗兰和百合花，深深地闻着那清新的花香。有时我心情不好，也会独自来这里寻找安慰，我总是把炙热的脸埋在清凉的树叶和草丛之中，让烦躁不安的心情平静下来。

置身于这个绿色花园里，真是令人心旷神怡。我高兴地从这里漫步到那里，直到忽然间来到美丽的葡萄藤下。我靠抚触它的叶子和花来认识它，并且知道这是缠绕在花园另一端的摇摇欲坠的小凉亭上的葡萄藤。这里有在地上蔓延的卷须藤和低垂的茉莉，还有一种十分罕见的蝴蝶荷花，因为它那容易掉落的花瓣很像蝴蝶的翅膀，所以名叫蝴蝶荷，这种花能发出一阵阵香甜的气味。但花园里最美丽的还是蔷薇花。我在北方的花房很少见到这种令人心醉的蔷薇。它到处攀爬，长长的绿枝倒挂在阳台上，散发出芳香，没有一点儿尘土的气息。每当清晨朝露未干时，它摸上去是那么的柔软高洁，令人陶醉不已。我总是禁不住想，即使是上帝御花园里的曝光兰，也不过如

house at the farther end of the garden! Here, also, were trailing clematis, drooping jessamine, and some rare sweet flowers called butterfly lilies, because their fragile petals resemble butterflies' wings. But the roses-they were loveliest of all. Never have I found in the greenhouses of the North such heart-satisfying roses as the climbing roses of my southern home. They used to hang in long festoons from our porch, filling the whole air with their fragrance, untainted by any earthy smell; and in the early morning, washed in the dew, they felt so soft, so pure, I could not help wondering if they did not resemble the asphodels of God's garden.

The beginning of my life was simple and much like every other little life. I came, I saw, I conquered, as the first baby in the family always does. There was the usual amount of discussion as to a name for me. The first baby in the family was not to be lightly named, every one was emphatic about that. My father suggested the name of Mildred Campbell, an ancestor whom he highly esteemed, and he declined to take any further part in the discussion. My mother solved the problem by giving it as her wish that I should be called after her mother, whose maiden name was Helen Everett.

But in the excitement of carrying me to church my father lost the name on the way, very naturally, since it was one in which he had declined to have a part. When the minister asked him for it, he just remembered that it had been decided to call me after my grandmother, and he gave her name as Helen Adams.

I am told that while I was still in long dresses I showed many signs of an eager,

此吧！

就像其他新生命一样，我的生命刚开始也是简单而平常的，我来到人世，观察这个世界，再到开始人生的旅途，和任何新生儿没有什么区别。为了给我起个好名字，大家都绞尽脑汁，费尽了口舌，因为作为家里的第一个孩子，起名字可是一件大事，家里的每个人都认为自己起的名字是最有意义的。父亲希望以他最尊敬的祖先的名字"米尔德里德·坎贝儿"给我起名，并拒绝听取任何不同意见；母亲则想用她母亲婚前的名字"海伦·艾弗雷特"给我起名。经过再三讨论，最后依照母亲的希望，决定给我用外祖母的名字。

但是后来带我去教堂受洗时，由于紧张和兴奋，再加上有别的想法，父亲在前往教堂的途中竟把这个名字给忘了。当牧师问这婴儿叫什么名字时，他只记得我用了外祖母的名字，于是说出了"海伦·亚当斯"这个名字。

家人告诉我，说我还是婴儿时，就显露出了不服输的性格，对任何事物都充满了好奇心，我的个性非常倔强，总是非常固执地模仿大人的一举一动。所以，当我只有6个月大时，就已经能发出"你好！"有一天，我还因为清楚地说出了"茶！茶！茶！"而吸引了每个人的注意力。即使是在我生病之后，我依然清晰地记得我在这最初的几个月学会的单词之一——

self-asserting disposition. Everything that I saw other people do I insisted upon imitating. At six months I could pipe out "How d'ye, " and one day I attracted every one's attention by saying "Tea, tea, tea" quite plainly. Even after my illness I remembered one of the words I had learned in these early months. It was the word "water", and I continued to make some sound for that word after all other speech was lost. I ceased making the sound "wah-wah" only when I learned to spell the word.

They tell me I walked the day I was a year old. My mother had just taken me out of the bath-tub and was holding me in her lap, when I was suddenly attracted by the flickering shadows of leaves that danced in the sunlight on the smooth floor. I slipped from my mother's lap and almost ran toward them. The impulse gone, I fell down and cried for her to take me up in her arms.

These happy days did not last long. One brief spring, musical with the song of robin and mocking-bird, one summer rich in fruit and roses, one autumn of gold and crimson sped by and left their gifts at the feet of an eager, delighted child. Then, in the dreary month of February, came

海伦出生的小屋，这里是蜂鸟和蜜蜂的乐园，也是海伦童年时代的天堂

"水"。虽然我忘掉了其他的发音，但是对于"水"这个字却仍然记得。也正是在学会了拼读这个单词之后，我脱离了只能"哇哇"发音的阶段。

家人还告诉我，我刚满周岁就会走路了。那次，母亲刚把我从浴盆中抱出来，放在膝盖上，突然我发现树影在光滑的地板上一闪一闪的，于是我就从母亲的膝盖上溜下来，摇摇摆摆地去踩那些影子。当这股冲劲消失之后，我立即跌倒在地，哭着求母亲抱我起来。

但是好景不长。春天，百鸟欢鸣，歌声盈耳；夏天，到处是果子和蔷薇花；当草黄叶红时，深秋已经来临。三个美好的季节就这样匆匆而过，在一个活蹦乱跳、咿呀学语的孩子身上留下了美好的记忆。在第二年那个可怕的2月，我突然生病了，失去了视力和听力，成为一个懵懂无知的新生婴儿。医生诊断，我得了急性胃充血和脑充血，说我救不过来了。但在一个清晨，奇迹却出现了，我忽然发高烧，但高烧又突然退了，全家人对于这种奇迹惊

the illness which closed my eyes and ears and plunged me into the unconsciousness of a new- born baby. They called it acute congestion of the stomach and brain. The doctor thought I could not live. Early one morning, however, the fever left me as suddenly and mysteriously as it had come. There was great rejoicing in the family that morning, but no one, not even the doctor, knew that I should never see or hear again.

 I fancy I still have confused recollections of that illness. I especially remember the tenderness with which my mother tried to soothe me in my waking hours of fret and pain, and the agony and bewilderment with which I awoke after a tossing half sleep, and turned my eyes, so dry and hot, to the wall, away from the once- loved light, which came to me dim and yet more dim each day. But, except for these fleeting memories, if, indeed, they be memories, it all seems very unreal, like a nightmare. Gradually I got used to the silence and darkness that surrounded me and forgot that it had ever been different, until she came- my teacher- who was to set my spirit free. But during the first nineteen months of my life I had caught glimpses of broad, green fields, a luminous sky, trees and flowers which the darkness that followed could not wholly blot out. If we have once seen, "the day is ours, and what the day has shown."

喜异常。但是，我的家人（甚至连医生）也都没有料到我再也看不见、听不到了。

  我至今还依稀记得那场大病，尤其是母亲在我高烧不退、痛苦难熬的时候，在我身边温柔地抚慰我，让我在恐惧中勇敢地渡过难关。我还记得高烧退去之后，我从半睡中被吵醒，睁开了双眼，可是眼睛却干燥灼热、疼痛怕光，所以不得不避开我以前所喜爱的阳光。后来，我的视力一天不如一天，对阳光的感觉也渐渐模糊不清了。

  那段记忆就像是一场噩梦，仿佛一切都那么的不真实。我逐渐习惯了周围的寂静和黑暗，几乎忘记了这以前的世界。直到她——莎莉文小姐——我的家庭老师到来。是她减轻了我心中的负担，重新带给我精神的自由。

  虽然我只拥有过19个月的光明和声音，但我却仍然能够清晰地记得那宽广而翠绿的田野、灿烂的天空、青翠的草木、争奇斗艳的鲜花，所有这些都一点一滴地铭刻在我心上，永驻在我心中。

CHAPTER II

I CANNOT recall what happened during the first months after my illness. I only know that I sat in my mother's lap or clung to her dress as she went about her household duties. My hands felt every object and observed every motion, and in this way I learned to know many things. Soon I felt the need of some communication with others and began to make crude signs. A shake of the head meant "No" and a nod, "Yes", a pull meant "Come" and a push, "Go". Was it bread that I wanted? Then I would imitate the acts of cutting the slices and buttering them. If I wanted my mother to make ice-cream for dinner I made the sign for working the freezer and shivered, indicating cold. My mother, moreover, succeeded in making me understand a good deal. I always knew when she wished me to bring her something, and I would run upstairs or anywhere else she indicated. Indeed, I owe to her loving wisdom all that was bright and good in my long night.

I understood a good deal of what was going on about me. At five I learned to fold and put away the clean clothes when they were brought in from the laundry, and I distinguished my own from the rest. I knew by the way my mother and aunt

第2章 童年的记忆

生病后几个月发生了什么事情,我已经记不起来了,只记得我常坐在母亲膝盖上,或者紧拉着母亲的裙角,跟着母亲到处走动。我用手触摸每一件物体,感觉每一个动作,通过这种方式,我熟悉了许多东西。我渴望与人交流,于是开始做一些简单的动作,摇头表示"不",点头表示"是",拉着别人向着我表示"来",推向外侧表示"去"。当我想吃面包时,我就以切面包、涂黄油的动作来表示。当我想让母亲做冰淇淋时,就会模仿工人制作冰淇淋的动作。我还会做出发抖的样子,表示冷的感觉。母亲也竭尽所能做出各种动作,让我了解她的意思,我也总是可以明白母亲的意思,去楼上或其他地方给她取东西。说实在话,母亲的慈爱和智慧是我在那漫长的黑夜里的光明。

我也慢慢明白了许多发生在我身上的事情。5岁时,我学会了把洗好的衣裳叠好收起来,把洗衣店送回家的衣服分类,并能分辨出哪些是我自己的。从母亲和姑妈的梳洗打扮中,我知道她们要出去,于是我就求她们带上我。当有亲戚朋友来访时,我总被叫来见客人;他们离开时,我会挥手告

dressed when they were going out, and I invariably begged to go with them. I was always sent for when there was company, and when the guests took their leave, I waved my hand to them, I think with a vague remembrance of the meaning of the gesture.

One day some gentlemen called on my mother, and I felt the shutting of the front door and other sounds that indicated their arrival. On a sudden thought I ran upstairs before any one could stop me, to put on my idea of a company dress. Standing before the mirror, as I had seen others do, I anointed mine head with oil and covered my face thickly with powder. Then I pinned a veil over my head so that it covered my face and fell in folds down to my shoulders, and tied an enormous bustle round my small waist, so that it dangled behind, almost meeting the hem of my skirt. Thus attired I went down to help entertain the company.

I do not remember when I first realized that I was different from other people; but I knew it before my teacher came to me. I had noticed that my mother and my friends did not use signs as I did when they wanted

别，我还隐约记得这种手势的意义。

记得有一次，家里有客人来看母亲，从大门的一开一关中，我知道了他们的来到。于是，我突发奇想，趁大家不注意，跑到母亲房间，学着母亲的样子在镜子前梳妆打扮起来，往头上抹油，在脸上擦了厚厚的粉，用发卡将面纱固定在头发上，让面纱垂下来轻轻地

失明后的小海伦经常陷入沉默，喜欢一个人抱着小狗坐在椅中，似乎在期待着什么

盖在脸上，低垂在我肩上。然后我又找了一件肥大的裙子穿在我小巧的身上，让那大大的裙摆拖在后面。这样打扮好后，我就帮助他们去接待客人。

我已经记不清楚是什么时候第一次意识到自己和别人有所不同了，但是我知道这应该是我的老师来之前的事。我曾注意到母亲和我的朋友们都是用嘴巴交谈，而不像我用手比划。因此，我会站在两个谈话者之间，用手摸他们的嘴巴，可是我仍然不能明白他们的意思。于是我也蠕动嘴唇，并用力做手势，想和他们交谈，可是一点用都没有。我气愤极了，又踢又叫，直到筋疲力尽。

当我无理取闹的时候，我想我自己很清楚，可是一旦我气极了，我就难

anything done, but talked with their mouths. Sometimes I stood between two persons who were conversing and touched their lips. I could not understand, and was vexed. I moved my lips and gesticulated frantically without result. This made me so angry at times that I kicked and screamed until I was exhausted.

I think I knew when I was naughty, for I knew that it hurt Ella, my nurse, to kick her, and when my fit of temper was over I had a feeling akin to regret. But I cannot remember any instance in which this feeling prevented me from repeating the naughtiness when I failed to get what I wanted.

In those days a little coloured girl, Martha Washington, the child of our cook, and Belle, an old setter, and a great hunter in her day, were my constant companions. Martha Washington understood my signs, and I seldom had any difficulty in making her do just as I wished. It pleased me to domineer over her, and she generally submitted to my tyranny rather than risk a hand-to-hand encounter.

I was strong, active, indifferent to consequences. I knew my own mind well enough and always had my own way, even if I had to fight tooth and nail for it. We spent a great deal of time in the kitchen, kneading dough balls, helping make ice-cream, grinding coffee, quarreling over the cake-bowl, and feeding the hens and turkeys that swarmed about the kitchen steps. Many of them were so tame that they would eat from my hand and let me feel them.

One big gobbler snatched a tomato from me one day and ran away with it.

以控制得住，就像我明白踢伤保姆艾拉一样，我知道她很痛，所以当我气消时，心里就会觉得很愧疚。但是当事情又不能称心如意时，我还是会发疯般地乱踢乱打。

在那些日子里，我有两个朝夕相处的好伙伴，一个是黑人女孩玛莎·华盛顿，她是我们家厨师的女儿；另一个是一只名叫贝尔的老猎狗。玛莎·华盛顿很容易就能明白我的手势，所以每次让她去做什么事情，她都能很快做好。能够让玛莎听命于我让我很高兴，她非常听我的话，甚至我的无理取闹她通常也绝对服从。她从不和我打架，而是努力完成我让她做的任何事情。

我的身体一向结实，人又好动，感情冲动时完全不顾后果。我非常自负，总喜欢我行我素，有时为了实现目的甚至不惜一战。在那个时期，我和玛莎在厨房度过了不少时光，一起揉面团、做冰淇淋、磨咖啡豆，或者为了几个点心而争吵不休，或者和她一起喂在厨房台阶上散步的母鸡和火鸡，这些家禽是如此温顺，一点儿也不怕人，它们在我手上吃食，并乖乖地让我抚摸它们。

有一天，一只大雄火鸡抢走了我手中的番茄。也许是受到火鸡的启发，我和玛莎也从厨房偷走了刚烤好的蛋糕，躲在柴堆中吃得干干净净，可是事后吃坏了肚子，这可能就是偷东西的报应，却不知那只火鸡是否也受到了同

Inspired, perhaps, by Master Gobbler's success, we carried off to the woodpile a cake which the cook had just frosted, and ate every bit of it. I was quite ill afterward, and I wonder if retribution also overtook the turkey.

The guinea- fowl likes to hide her nest in out- of- the- way places, and it was one of my greatest delights to hunt for the eggs in the long grass. I could not tell Martha Washington when I wanted to go egg-hunting, but I would double my hands and put them on the ground, which meant something round in the grass, and Martha always understood. When we were fortunate enough to find a nest I never allowed her to carry the eggs home, making her understand by emphatic signs that she might fall and break them.

The sheds where the corn was stored, the stable where the horses were kept, and the yard where the cows were milked morning and evening were unfailing sources of interest to Martha and me. The milkers would let me keep my hands on the cows while they milked, and I often got well switched by the cow for my curiosity.

The making ready for Christmas was always a delight to me. Of course I did not know what it was all about, but I enjoyed the pleasant odours that filled the house and the tidbits that were given to Martha Washington and me to keep us quiet. We were sadly in the way, but that did not interfere with our pleasure in the least. They allowed us to grind the spices, pick over the raisins and lick the stirring spoons. I hung my stocking because the others did; I cannot remember, however, that the ceremony interested me especially, nor did my curiosity cause me to wake before

样的惩罚。

　　珍珠鸡喜欢在隐蔽处筑巢，我特别爱到深草丛中去寻找它们的蛋。我虽不能对玛莎说要去找鸡蛋，但我可以把两手合成圆形放在地上，以表示草丛里有某种圆形的东西，玛莎总是一看就能明白。如果我们有幸找到了鸡窝，我绝不允许玛莎拿着蛋回家，我用手势向她强调，她拿着蛋，一摔跤就会把鸡蛋打碎的。

　　对于我和玛莎来说，存储粮食的仓库、养马的厩槽、早上和晚上给奶牛挤奶的草场，全都充满了我们童年永不褪色的回忆，也给了我们无穷无尽的乐趣。我还记得，挤奶工人挤牛奶时，常常让我把手放在奶牛身上，我也因为好奇而被牛尾打了好多次。

　　对我来说，准备庆祝圣诞节也是一件非常令人愉快的事情，虽然我不明白过节的意义，但是我喜欢家里因为节日而到处弥漫的欢快和愉悦，至于大人赏给玛莎和我的美味，更是我们所喜爱的。即使是在伤心的时候，我也会因为圣诞节的到来而心情开朗起来。过节时，家人会让我们磨香料、挑选葡萄干、舔那些搅拌过食物的调羹。我也模仿别人，把长袜子挂起来，然而我对圣诞老人的礼物并不真的感兴趣，所以也不会因为兴奋好奇而天不亮就爬起来看袜子里装了什么礼物。

daylight to look for my gifts.

 Martha Washington had as great a love of mischief as I. Two little children were seated on the veranda steps one hot July afternoon. One was black as ebony, with little bunches of fuzzy hair tied with shoestrings sticking out all over her head like corkscrews. The other was white, with long golden curls. One child was six years old, the other two or three years older. The younger child was blind-that was I-and the other was Martha Washington. We were busy cutting out paper dolls; but we soon wearied of this amusement, and after cutting up our shoestrings and clipping all the leaves off the honeysuckle that were within reach, I turned my attention to Martha's corkscrews. She objected at first, but finally submitted. Thinking that turn and turn about is fair play, she seized the scissors and cut off one of my curls, and would have cut them all off but for my mother's timely interference.

 Belle, our dog, my other companion, was old and lazy and liked to sleep by the open fire rather than to romp with me. I tried hard to teach her my sign language, but she

莎莉文21岁时照片，此时她刚到海伦家

  玛莎·华盛顿也和我一样喜欢搞恶作剧。在7月一个炎热的午后，我和玛莎坐在阳台的石阶上，肤色黝黑的玛莎用鞋带把她绒毛般的头发扎成一束束的，看上去就像很多螺丝锥长在头上。而我皮肤白皙，一头长长的金黄色卷发。一个6岁，另一个大两三岁。那个小点儿的盲童就是我，另一个就是玛莎·华盛顿。我们两人坐在石阶上剪纸娃娃，但是不久我们厌倦了，于是就把鞋带剪碎，又去剪石阶边用手够得到的冬青叶子。突然，我的注意力转向玛莎那一头"螺丝锥"。一开始，玛莎还挣扎着不肯让我剪，可最后还是屈服了。因为游戏必须公平，于是玛莎抓起剪刀剪下我一缕头发，若不是母亲及时发现并制止，玛莎很可能把我的头发全部剪光了。

  贝尔，也就是那只猎狗，是我的另一个伙伴。它既老又懒，喜欢躺在暖炉旁睡觉，一点也不爱陪我玩。它也不够精明，我竭尽全力教它手语，但是它又懒又笨，根本不懂我在做什么。有时贝尔也会突然兴奋地狂奔起来，这时它看上去就像瞄准了猎物的机敏猎狗，威风凛凛的。我不明白它为什么会

was dull and inattentive. She sometimes started and quivered with excitement, then she became perfectly rigid, as dogs do when they point a bird. I did not then know why Belle acted in this way; but I knew she was not doing as I wished. This vexed me and the lesson always ended in a one-sided boxing match. Belle would get up, stretch herself lazily, give one or two contemptuous sniffs, go to the opposite side of the hearth and lie down again, and I, wearied and disappointed, went off in search of Martha.

Many incidents of those early years are fixed in my memory, isolated, but clear and distinct, making the sense of that silent, aimless, dayless life all the more intense.

One day I happened to spill water on my apron, and I spread it out to dry before the fire which was flickering on the sitting-room hearth. The apron did not dry quickly enough to suit me, so I drew nearer and threw it right over the hot ashes. The fire leaped into life; the flames encircled me so that in a moment my clothes were blazing. I made a terrified noise that brought Viny, my old nurse, to the rescue. Throwing a blanket over me, she almost suffocated me, but she put out the fire. Except for my hands and hair I was not badly burned.

About this time I found out the use of a key. One morning I locked my mother up in the pantry, where she was obliged to remain three hours, as the servants were in a detached part of the house. She kept pounding on the door, while I sat outside on the porch steps and laughed with glee as I felt the jar of the pounding.

这样，但它不听我的指挥是肯定的。对此我很着急，但无论如何我只是一厢情愿而已。对于我的种种努力，贝尔总是无精打采地爬起来，伸伸懒腰，嗅嗅暖炉，然后又在另一端躺下，一点也不理会我的指挥。我觉得自讨没趣，便又去找玛莎玩。

我童年的记忆充满了零碎的片断，虽然孤独，但是非常清晰生动，它使我在没有声音、没有光明，甚至没有前途的情况下，仍然能够强烈地感受这个世界。

一天，我不小心把水溅到了裙子上，就把裙子摊开来放在卧室采暖炉的边上，想把它烘干。但是裙子干得不够快，我就直接把裙子放在暖炉的热灰上面。突然，火一下子着了起来，包围了我，连我的衣裳也烧着了。我发出了可怕的叫声，老奶奶维尼赶来了，用一床毯子裹住我，我差点儿窒息，但火也被扑灭了。除了手和头发之外，我其余的地方烧得并不太厉害。

大约在这个时期，我发现了钥匙的妙处，对它的使用方法表现出了浓厚的兴趣。一天早晨，我把母亲锁在储藏室里，这时仆人们都在屋外干活，结果母亲被锁在里面足足有3个小时。她一直用力地敲门，而我却坐在走廊前的台阶上，因为感觉到敲门的震动而咯咯地笑个不停。由于我的这次恶作剧，父母决定尽快请人来管教我，于是我的家庭教师——莎莉文小姐走进了

This most naughty prank of mine convinced my parents that I must be taught as soon as possible. After my teacher, Miss Sullivan, came to me, I sought an early opportunity to lock her in her room.

I went upstairs with something which my mother made me understand I was to give to Miss Sullivan; but no sooner had I given it to her than I slammed the door to, locked it, and hid the key under the wardrobe in the hall. I could not be induced to tell where the key was. My father was obliged to get a ladder and take Miss Sullivan out through the window-much to my delight. Months after I produced the key.

When I was about five years old we moved from the little vine-covered house to a large new one. The family consisted of my father and mother, two older half-brothers, and, afterward, a little sister, Mildred.

My earliest distinct recollection of my father is making my way through great drifts of newspapers to his side and finding him alone, holding a sheet of paper before his face. I was greatly puzzled to know what he was doing. I imitated this action, even wearing his spectacles, thinking they might help solve the mystery. But I did not find out the secret for several years. Then I learned what those papers were, and that my father edited one of them.

My father was most loving and indulgent, devoted to his home, seldom leaving us, except in the hunting season. He was a great hunter, I have been told, and a celebrated shot. Next to his family he loved his dogs and gun. His hospitality was

我的生命中，但我还是找机会把她锁在了她的房间里。

一次，母亲让我上楼送东西给莎莉文老师，我回转身的时候，锁上了房门，把钥匙藏在客厅角落的衣柜下。我没有说出藏钥匙的地方，父亲不得不搭了一架梯子，将莎莉文老师从窗户中接了出来，我当时得意极了。几个月之后，我才把钥匙交出来。

当我大约5岁的时候，我们从那所爬满蔓藤的房子搬到了一所更大的新房子。我们家有父亲、母亲、两个异母哥哥，后来又有一个小妹妹米尔德里德。

我对父亲最初而且清晰的记忆，是我有一次穿过一大堆的报纸，来到父亲跟前。他当时独自一人举着一大张纸，遮住了脸部。我很奇怪，想知道父亲在干什么，于是也学着他的样子，举起一张纸，甚至戴上了他的眼镜，以为这样就可以知道了。但是多年来我一直没有搞明白，后来我才知道那些纸都是报纸，而我父亲是其中一份报纸的编辑。

父亲非常仁慈宽厚，对家庭充满了热爱。除了打猎季节，他很少离开我们。有人告诉我说，他是个好猎人和神枪手。除了家人，他最爱的就是狗和猎枪。他非常好客，几乎有些过分，没有一次回家不带回客人的。

他还有一个特殊的爱好，就是侍弄果园。有人说，父亲栽的西瓜和草

great, almost to a fault, and he seldom came home without bringing a guest.

His special pride was the big garden where, it was said, he raised the finest watermelons and strawberries in the county; and to me he brought the first ripe grapes and the choicest berries. I remember his caressing touch as he led me from tree to tree, from vine to vine, and his eager delight in whatever pleased me.

He was a famous story-teller; after I had acquired language he used to spell clumsily into my hand his cleverest anecdotes, and nothing pleased him more than to have me repeat them at an opportune moment.

I was in the North, enjoying the last beautiful days of the summer of 1896, when I heard the news of my father's death. He had had a short illness, there had been a brief time of acute suffering, then all was over. This was my first great sorrow-my first personal experience with death.

How shall I write of my mother? She is so near to me that it almost seems indelicate to speak of her.

For a long time I regarded my little sister as an intruder. I knew that I had

莓是全村最好的。他总是给我带来最早长熟的葡萄和最好的草莓吃，我还记得他常常温柔慈爱地带着我在果林和瓜田中散步，他给我的快乐与关爱无论我在哪里都会伴随着我，让我感到非常快乐。

海伦和莎莉文老师到户外学习，坐在一棵树上，这是她们最喜欢的上课地点

父亲还是讲故事的高手，在我知道写字之后，他经常把许多有趣的故事写在我手上，我会高兴地大笑起来。最令他高兴的，则莫过于听我复述他讲过的故事。

1896年，我正在北方享受那怡人的夏天的最后美景，突然传来了父亲去世的噩耗。他病了很短一段时间，在经过一阵急性发作之后，很快就去世了。这是我第一次尝到悲痛的滋味，也是我对死亡的最早体验。

我该如何描述我的母亲呢？她对我来说是如此的亲近，我反而不知道从何处开始说了。

长时间以来，我一直将我的小妹妹看成是一个入侵者。我认为我被分走了母亲唯一的爱，因此心中满怀嫉妒。她常常坐在母亲的腿上，而那是我以前常坐的位置，她似乎夺走了母亲所有的关爱和时间。后来发生了一件事，

ceased to be my mother's only darling, and the thought filled me with jealousy. She sat in my mother's lap constantly, where I used to sit, and seemed to take up all her care and time. One day something happened which seemed to me to be adding insult to injury.

At that time I had a much-petted, much-abused doll, which I afterward named Nancy. She was, alas, the helpless victim of my outbursts of temper and of affection, so that she became much the worse for wear. I had dolls which talked, and cried, and opened and shut their eyes; yet I never loved one of them as I loved poor Nancy. She had a cradle, and I often spent an hour or more rocking her. I guarded both doll and cradle with the most jealous care; but once I discovered my little sister sleeping peacefully in the cradle. At this presumption on the part of one to whom as yet no tie of love bound me I grew angry. I rushed upon the cradle and overturned it, and the baby might have been killed had my mother not caught her as she fell. Thus it is that when we walk in the valley of twofold solitude we know little of the tender affections that grow out of endearing words and actions and companionship. But afterward, when I was restored to my human heritage, Mildred and I grew into each other's hearts, so that we were content to go hand-in-hand wherever caprice led us, although she could not understand my finger language, nor I her childish prattle.

使我觉得不仅被分割了母爱，而且受了侮辱。

那时，我有一个心爱异常的洋娃娃，我后来给它起名"南茜"。它是我脾气发作时无辜的牺牲品，被我玩得破旧不堪。虽然我有许多洋娃娃，它们有的会说话，有的会哭闹，有的会眨眼，但我最喜欢的还是可怜的南茜。南茜有一个摇篮，我经常好几个小时在摇篮旁边摇她玩。我以最大的嫉妒心护卫着我的洋娃娃和摇篮。一天，我发现妹妹正舒舒服服地睡在摇篮里。那时，我正嫉妒她夺走了母爱，对她当然没有任何爱心，又如何能容忍她睡在摇篮里呢？我勃然大怒，冲向摇篮，将它掀翻。妹妹掉到地上时，如果不是母亲及时赶来接住，可能就会摔死了。这时我已经既盲又聋，正处于双重孤独的低谷中，所以领略不到亲热的语言和怜爱的行为以及伙伴之间所产生的感情。后来，当我回复到人的本性之后，妹妹米尔德里德和我变得心灵相通，我们手拉着手到处游玩，尽管她看不懂我的手语，我也听不见她咿咿呀呀的童音。

CHAPTER III

MEANWHILE the desire to express myself grew. The few signs I used became less and less adequate, and my failures to make myself understood were invariably followed by outbursts of passion. I felt as if invisible hands were holding me, and I made frantic efforts to free myself. I struggled-not that struggling helped matters, but the spirit of resistance was strong within me; I generally broke down in tears and physical exhaustion. If my mother happened to be near I crept into her arms, too miserable even to remember the cause of the tempest. After awhile the need of some means of communication became so urgent that these outbursts occurred daily, sometimes hourly.

My parents were deeply grieved and perplexed. We lived a long way from any school for the blind or the deaf, and it seemed unlikely that any one would come to such an out- of- the- way place as Tuscumbia to teach a child who was both deaf and blind. Indeed, my friends and relatives sometimes doubted whether I could be taught. My mother's only ray of hope came from Dickens's "American Notes". She had read his account of Laura Bridgman, and remembered vaguely that she was deaf and blind, yet had been educated. But she also remembered with

第3章　寻找希望

随着年龄的增长，希望表达我自己思想情感的愿望开始增加。我使用的那几种单调的手势也渐渐显得少而不够用了。每当别人无法理解我的手语的意思时，我都会大发脾气。我感觉仿佛有许多看不见的手紧紧地抓着我，我拼命挣扎，想获得自由。我拼命抗争，烈火在体内燃烧，可是却无法表达出来，我只能是疯狂地厮打，直至精疲力竭。如果母亲正好在旁边，我就会一头扑在她怀中，伤心欲绝，以至于为什么发脾气都忘了。过了一段时间，由于我想表达思想的愿望变得越发强烈，以至于每天都要发脾气，有时甚至每小时就发一次火。

我的父母处于极度痛苦之中，然而却又毫无办法。我们居住的地方离任何一所聋哑学校都很远，而且好像不会有谁愿意到塔斯坎比亚镇这样偏僻的地方来教一个盲聋哑孩子。事实上，当时大家都怀疑我是否还能接受教育。然而，母亲从狄更斯的《美国人札记》中看到了一线希望。她读过狄更斯书中提到的盲聋哑少女劳拉·布里奇曼，劳拉在豪博士的教导下，学有所成。然而，当得知这位发明盲聋人教育方法的豪博士已经去世许多年，

a hopeless pang that Dr. Howe, who had discovered the way to teach the deaf and blind, had been dead many years. His methods had probably died with him; and if they had not, how was a little girl in a far-off town in Alabama to receive the benefit of them?

When I was about six years old, my father heard of an eminent oculist in Baltimore, who had been successful in many cases that had seemed hopeless. My parents at once determined to take me to Baltimore to see if anything could be done for my eyes.

The journey, which I remember well, was very pleasant. I made friends with many people on the train. One lady gave me a box of shells. My father made holes in these so that I could string them, and for a long time they kept me happy and contented. The conductor, too, was kind. Often when he went his rounds I clung to his coat tails while he collected and punched the tickets. His punch, with which he let me play, was a delightful toy. Curled up in a corner of the seat I amused myself for hours making funny little holes in bits of cardboard.

My aunt made me a big doll out of towels. It was the most comical, shapeless thing, this improvised doll, with no nose,

领悟了语言的真谛之后，海伦经常与老师用手语交谈，探索生命中更深层次的问题

他的方法也许已经随着他的去世而失传时，母亲苦恼极了。或者即使这些方法没有失传，又如何让我这样一个住在亚拉巴马州这个偏远小镇的小女孩从中受益呢？

在我大约6岁时，父亲听说巴尔的摩有一位著名的眼科大夫，他已经成功地治好了几个似乎没有希望治好的盲人。我的父母立即决定带我去巴尔的摩，看看是否有什么办法治我的眼睛。

这次旅行非常愉快，我至今依然记得非常清楚。我在火车上交了许多朋友。一位女士送了我一盒贝壳，父亲把这些贝壳都钻了孔，好让我用线一个一个地将它们串起来，有很长一段时间，这些贝壳给我带来了极大的快乐和满足。列车员也很和善，每次他来例行检查或检票时，我就拉着他的衣角。他会让我玩他检票的剪子，这可是一个很好的玩具。我会趴在座位的一角，把一些零碎的卡片打些小孔，玩上好几个小时。

我姑妈用毛巾给我做了一个大娃娃，可它不过是一个非常滑稽的、没

mouth, ears or eyes- nothing that even the imagination of a child could convert into a face. Curiously enough, the absence of eyes struck me more than all the other defects put together. I pointed this out to everybody with provoking persistency, but no one seemed equal to the task of providing the doll with eyes. A bright idea, however, shot into my mind, and the problem was solved. I tumbled off the seat and searched under it until I found my aunt's cape, which was trimmed with large beads. I pulled two beads off and indicated to her that I wanted her to sew them on doll. She raised my hand to her eyes in a questioning way, and I nodded energetically. The beads were sewed in the right place and I could not contain myself for joy; but immediately I lost all interest in the doll. During the whole trip I did not have one fit of temper, there were so many things to keep my mind and fingers busy.

When we arrived in Baltimore, Dr. Chisholm received us kindly: but he could do nothing. He said, however, that I could be educated, and advised my father to consult Dr. Alexander Graham Bell, of Washington, who would be able to give him information about schools and teachers of deaf or blind

有形状的玩意儿，既没有鼻子和嘴巴，也没有耳朵和眼睛。即使孩子最丰富的想象力，也说不出那张脸是个什么样子。极具讽刺意味的是，洋娃娃没有眼睛对我

与爱犬在一起，使海伦感到踏实和安全

来说比其他任何缺陷加在一起的打击还要大。我给每个人指出了这一点，坚持让大家想办法，但最终还是没有人能给洋娃娃安上眼睛。这时，一个聪明的想法在我大脑中闪现，这个问题立即得到了解决。我溜下座位，找到姑妈的披肩，这件披肩上缀着一些大珠子。我扯下两颗珠子，示意姑妈，想让她缝在洋娃娃的脸上。姑妈以疑问的方式牵着我的手去摸她的眼睛，我使劲地点点头。她将珠子缝在了洋娃娃合适的地方，我真有说不出来的高兴。但没过多久，我对洋娃娃就失去了兴趣。在整个旅途中，有如此多的吸引我的事情，我的大脑和手指一直忙个不停，所以一次脾气也没有发。

我们到达巴尔的摩之后，齐夏姆医生热情地接待了我们，但是他也没有办法。不过他说我可以接受教育，并建议我父亲带我去华盛顿向亚历山大·格雷厄姆·贝尔博士咨询，也许他会给我们提供有关聋哑儿童学校以及老师的相关信息。根据齐夏姆医生的建议，我们立刻赶到华盛顿去看望贝尔

children. Acting on the doctor's advice, we went immediately to Washington to see Dr. Bell, my father with a sad heart and many misgivings, I wholly unconscious of his anguish, finding pleasure in the excitement of moving from place to place.

Child as I was, I at once felt the tenderness and sympathy which endeared Dr. Bell to so many hearts, as his wonderful achievements enlist their admiration. He held me on his knee while I examined his watch, and he made it strike for me. He understood my signs, and I knew it and loved him at once. But I did not dream that that interview would be the door through which I should pass from darkness into light, from isolation to friendship, companionship, knowledge, love.

Dr. Bell advised my father to write to Mr. Anagnos, director of the Perkins Institution in Boston, the scene of Dr. Howe's great labours for the blind, and ask him if he had a teacher competent to begin my education. This my father did at once, and in a few weeks there came a kind letter from Mr. Anagnos with the comforting assurance that a teacher had been found. This was in the summer of 1886. But Miss Sullivan did not arrive until the following March.

Thus I came up out of Egypt and stood before Sinai, and a power divine touched my spirit and gave it sight, so that I beheld many wonders. And from the sacred mountain I heard a voice which said, "Knowledge is love and light and vision."

海伦的书写版

博士。一路上,父亲心情沉重,顾虑重重,而我对他的痛苦却毫无觉察,反而在从一个地方奔波到另一个地方的旅行中找到了乐趣。

虽然我当时还是个孩子,但是我一接触贝尔博士,就感受到了他的亲切和仁爱,同时也理解了他为什么能赢得那么多人的喜爱和尊敬。他把我抱在膝上,让我玩他的表。他让手表的闹铃响起来,好让我感觉到表的震动。博士懂得我的手势,我也能明白他的意思,并立刻喜欢上了他。当时我并没有意识到,这次见面将会成为我人生的转折点,使我从此由黑暗走向光明,由孤独走向友情、集体、智慧和爱。

贝尔博士建议父亲写信给安纳格罗斯先生,他是波士顿帕金斯学校的校长,请他为我找一位启蒙老师。帕金斯学校是《美国人札记》中豪博士为盲聋哑人孜孜不倦工作的地方。父亲立刻写了信,几个星期后我们就收到了安纳格罗斯先生一封热情的回信,他在信中安慰式地保证说已经找到老师了。这是1886年夏天的事,但莎莉文老师直到第二年3月才来到我们家。

就这样,我就像摩西走出了埃及,站在了西奈山的面前,感受到一种奇妙而难以言喻的力量涌遍我的全身,我眼前展现出无数奇景。从这座圣山上我听到一个声音这样说:"知识给人以爱,给人以光明,给人以智慧。"

CHAPTER IV

THE most important day I remember in all my life is the one on which my teacher, Anne Mansfield Sullivan, came to me. I am filled with wonder when I consider the immeasurable contrasts between the two lives which it connects. It was the third of March, 1887, three months before I was seven years old.

On the afternoon of that eventful day, I stood on the porch, dumb, expectant. I guessed vaguely from my mother's signs and from the hurrying to and fro in the house that something unusual was about to happen, so I went to the door and waited on the steps. The afternoon sun penetrated the mass of honeysuckle that covered the porch, and fell on my upturned face. My fingers lingered almost unconsciously on the familiar leaves and blossoms which had just come forth to greet the sweet southern spring. I did not know what the future held of marvel or surprise for me. Anger and bitterness had preyed upon me continually for weeks and a deep languor had succeeded this passionate struggle.

Have you ever been at sea in a dense fog, when it seemed as if a tangible white darkness shut you in, and the great ship, tense and anxious, groped her way toward the shore with plummet and sounding-line, and you waited with beating heart

第4章　重塑生命

我人生中最重要的一天，是老师安妮·梅西费尔德·莎莉文来我家的这一天。回想此前此后两种全然不同的生活，我禁不住感慨万分。那是1887年3月3日，当时我7岁还差3个月。

在那个多事之天的下午，我默默地站在走廊上，期待着什么。从母亲的手势以及家人匆忙地来来往往的样子中，我猜想一定有什么不寻常的事将要发生，因此，我走到门口，站在台阶上等待着。下午的阳光穿过遮满阳台的金银花叶子，照射到我仰望着的脸上。我的手指几乎是无意识地搓捻着那些熟悉的花叶，抚弄着那些为迎接南方的春天而绽开的花朵。我还不知道未来会有什么奇迹发生。当时，我经历了好几个星期的极度愤怒和苦恼，已经疲倦不堪了。

朋友，你可曾在茫茫大雾的大海中航行过，被黑暗所笼罩，紧张地驾驶着一条大船，小心翼翼地缓慢地驶向对岸，而你的心怦怦直跳，唯恐发生意外？在没有接受教育之前，我就像在大雾中航行的那条大船，既没有指南针，也没有探深绳，不知道离海港有多近。"光明！光明！快给我光明！"

for something to happen? I was like that ship before my education began, only I was without compass or sounding-line, and had no way of knowing how near the harbour was. "Light! Give me light!" was the wordless cry of my soul, and the light of love shone on me in that very hour.

I felt approaching footsteps. I stretched out my hand as I supposed to my mother. Some one took it, and I was caught up and held close in the arms of her who had come to reveal all things to me, and, more than all things else, to love me.

The morning after my teacher came she led me into her room and gave me a doll. The little blind children at the Perkins Institution had sent it and Laura Bridgman had dressed it; but I did not know this until afterward.

When I had played with it a little while, Miss Sullivan slowly spelled into my hand the word "d-o-l-l". I was at once interested in this finger play and tried to imitate it. When I finally succeeded in making the letters correctly I was flushed with childish pleasure and pride. Running downstairs to my mother I held up my hand and made the letters for doll. I did

海伦（左侧站立者）与帕金斯盲人学校的学生一起合影

我在心里无声地呼喊着。正在此时，爱的光明洒在了我身上。

我觉得有脚步朝我走来，我以为是母亲，立刻伸出双手。有个人握住了我的手，把我紧紧地搂抱在怀中。她是来向我揭示人间真理、给我深切关爱的，她就是我的老师——安妮·莎莉文。

第二天早晨，莎莉文老师把我带到她的房间，给了我一个洋娃娃。那是帕金斯盲人学校的学生赠送的，洋娃娃的衣服则是由劳拉·布里奇曼亲手缝制的，这些我是后来才知道的。

我玩了一会儿洋娃娃，莎莉文老师在我的手掌上慢慢地拼写"d-o-l-l"这个词，这个举动使我立刻对手指游戏产生了兴趣，并且模仿她写起来。当我终于能正确地拼写这个词时，我自豪极了，兴奋得脸都涨红了。我立即跑下楼去，找到母亲，拼写洋娃娃这个词的字母给她看。我当时并不知道这就是在写字，甚至也不知道世界上有文字这种东西存在；我仅仅是依葫芦画瓢地模仿莎莉文老师的动作而已。从此以后，我就通过这种并不很理解的方式，学会了拼写许多单词，例如"针"（pin）、"帽子"（hat）、

not know that I was spelling a word or even that words existed; I was simply making my fingers go in monkey-like imitation. In the days that followed I learned to spell in this uncomprehending way a great many words, among them pin, hat, cup and a few verbs like sit, stand and walk. But my teacher had been with me several weeks before I understood that everything has a name.

One day, while I was playing with my new doll, Miss Sullivan put my big rag doll into my lap also, spelled "d-o-l-l" and tried to make me understand that "d-o-l-l" applied to both.

Earlier in the day we had had a tussle over the words "m-u-g" and "w-a-t-e-r". Miss Sullivan had tried to impress it upon me that "m-u-g" is mug and that "w-a-t-e-r" is water, but I persisted in confounding the two. In despair she had dropped the subject for the time, only to renew it at the first opportunity. I became impatient at her repeated attempts and, seizing the new doll, I dashed it upon the floor. I was keenly delighted when I felt the fragments of the broken doll at my feet. Neither sorrow nor regret followed my passionate outburst. I had not loved the doll. In the

"杯子"（cup），以及"坐"（sit）、"站"（stand）、"走"（walk）等动词。但是世间万物都有自己的名字，这是老师教了我几个星期以后，我才领悟到的。

一天，我正在玩我的新洋娃娃，莎莉文老师把我原来那个洋娃娃也拿来放在我膝上，然后在我手上拼写"d-o-l-l"，想让我明白"d-o-l-l"指的是两个洋娃娃。

海伦在马萨诸塞州弗伦塔姆自家的土地上检查树木开花的情况

这天上午，我们为"m-u-g"（杯子）和"w-a-t-e-r"（水）这两个词发生了争执。莎莉文老师拼命地想让我懂得"杯子"是"杯子"，"水"是"水"，而我却总是将二者弄混淆。绝望之际，她只好暂时放下这个问题，重新练习洋娃娃这个词。我对她一而再、再而三的重复实在有些不耐烦了，抓起新的洋娃娃朝地上一摔，就把它摔碎了。当我察觉到我脚边上的洋娃娃碎片时，心里觉得特别痛快。我发这种脾气，既不惭愧，也不悔恨，我对洋娃娃并没有爱。在我寂静而黑暗的世界里，根本没有什么温柔和同情。我察觉到我的老师把洋娃娃碎片扫到炉子边，我终于摆脱了令我不开心的东西，

still, dark world in which I lived there was no strong sentiment of tenderness. I felt my teacher sweep the fragments to one side of the hearth, and I had a sense of satisfaction that the cause of my discomfort was removed. She brought me my hat, and I knew I was going out into the warm sunshine. This thought, if a wordless sensation may be called a thought, made me hop and skip with pleasure.

We walked down the path to the well-house, attracted by the fragrance of the honeysuckle with which it was covered. Some one was drawing water and my teacher placed my hand under the spout. As the cool stream gushed over one hand she spelled into the other the word water, first slowly, then rapidly. I stood still, my whole attention fixed upon the motions of her fingers. Suddenly I felt a misty consciousness as of something forgotten-a thrill of returning thought; and somehow the mystery of language was revealed to me. I knew then that "w-a-t-e-r" meant the wonderful cool something that was flowing over my hand. That living word awakened my soul, gave it light, hope, joy, set it free! There were barriers still, it is true, but barriers that could in time be swept away.

I left the well-house eager to learn.

贝尔，美国发明家，电话发明者，对语音学有专门研究，一生热心帮助残疾人，是海伦·凯勒最知心的朋友

感到很满意。老师把我的帽子递给我，我知道又可以到外面暖和的阳光里去了。这种无法用语言表达的想法让我高兴得跳了起来。

我们沿着小路散步到水井房，这里盛开的金银花芳香扑鼻，令人心旷神怡。有人正在打水，我的老师把我一只手放在喷水口下。一股清凉的水在我手上流过，她在我的另一只手上拼写"w-a-t-e-r"（水），起先写得很慢，然后写得快一些。我安静地站在那里，所有的注意力都集中在她手指的动作上。刹那间，我恍然大悟，好像记起了一件早已经忘却的事，一种神奇的感觉在我脑中激荡，我一下子理解了语言文字的奥秘，知道了"水"这个字就是正在我手上流过的这种清凉而奇妙的东西。"水"这个活生生的词唤醒了我的灵魂，并给予我光明、希望、快乐和自由。虽然前面的道路还布满荆棘，但一定能够被扫除。

井房的经历使我的求知欲望油然而生。啊！原来世间万物都各有名称，而每个名称都能启发我新的思想。当我们回到房子里时，因为我开始用一种全新的、神奇的眼光去看每一件东西，所以我碰到的每件东西似乎都有了生

Everything had a name, and each name gave birth to a new thought. As we returned to the house every object which I touched seemed to quiver with life. That was because I saw everything with the strange, new sight that had come to me. On entering the door I remembered the doll I had broken. I felt my way to the hearth and picked up the pieces. I tried vainly to put them together. Then my eyes filled with tears; for I realized what I had done, and for the first time I felt repentance and sorrow.

I learned a great many new words that day. I do not remember what they all were; but I do know that mother, father, sister, teacher were among them-words that were to make the world blossom for me, "like Aaron's rod, with flowers." It would have been difficult to find a happier child than I was as. I lay in my crib at the close of the eventful day and lived over the joys it had brought me, and for the first time longed for a new day to come.

命。进门时，我想起了那个被我摔碎的洋娃娃，于是我摸索着来到炉子边，捡起了碎片。我努力想把它们拼起来，但怎么做也无济于事。想起我刚才的所作所为，我的泪水浸满了双眼，这是我生平第一次感到悔恨和悲伤。

海伦正在阅读布莱叶文图书

那天，我学会了不少词，我不记得具体是哪些了，但我知道有"母亲"、"父亲"、"妹妹"、"老师"等。这些词使整个世界在我面前变得犹如花团锦簇，美不胜收。啊！世界上还有比我更幸福的孩子吗?那天晚上，我躺在床上，心中充满了无限喜悦，第一次盼望新的一天到来。

CHAPTER V

I RECALL many incidents of the summer of 1887 that followed my soul's sudden awakening. I did nothing but explore with my hands and learn the name of every object that I touched; and the more I handled things and learned their names and uses, the more joyous and confident grew my sense of kinship with the rest of the world.

When the time of daisies and buttercups came Miss Sullivan took me by the hand across the fields, where men were preparing the earth for the seed, to the banks of the Tennessee River, and there, sitting on the warm grass, I had my first lessons in the beneficence of nature. I learned how the sun and the rain make to grow out of the ground every tree that is pleasant to the sight and good for food, how birds build their nests and live and thrive from land to land, how the squirrel, the deer, the lion and every other creature finds food and shelter. As my knowledge of things grew I felt more and more the delight of the world I was in.

Long before I learned to do a sum in arithmetic or describe the shape of the earth, Miss Sullivan had taught me to find beauty in the fragrant woods, in every blade of grass, and in the curves and dimples of my baby sister's hand. She linked

第5章　认识大自然

1887年夏天，我的灵魂渐渐苏醒，许多往事至今记忆犹新。我整天用手去探摸我所接触到的每一件东西，并记住它们的名称。我摸到的东西越多，对它们的名字和用途了解得越细，我内心的愉悦与满足感及其对外部世界的渴望也越来越强烈。

当繁花似锦的夏季来临时，莎莉文老师牵着我的手，穿过田野（人们正在那里耕耘播种），来到田纳西河的岸边。我们坐在河边温软的草地上，开始学习人生的新课程，我也明白了大自然对人类的恩惠。我懂得了阳光雨露如何使树木茁壮成长，使粮食得到丰收；我懂得了鸟儿如何筑巢，如何生殖繁衍，又如何随着季节的变化而迁徙；我还懂得了松鼠、鹿和狮子等各种动物如何觅食，如何栖息。当我了解的事情越多，我就越感到我所生活的世界的美好。

在我学会做算术和画地球的形状之前，莎莉文老师先教会我从那粗壮的树木、那细嫩的草叶以及我妹妹的那双小手中去领略美的存在。她把对我的启蒙同大自然联系起来，使我认识到鸟儿、鲜花和人都是平等的伙伴。

my earliest thoughts with nature, and made me feel that "birds and flowers and I were happy peers."

But about this time I had an experience which taught me that nature is not always kind.

One day my teacher and I were returning from a long ramble. The morning had been fine, but it was growing warm and sultry when at last we turned our faces homeward. Two or three times we stopped to rest under a tree by the wayside. Our last halt was was under a wild cherry tree a short distance from the house. The shade was grateful, and the tree was so easy to climb that with my teacher's assistance I was able to scramble to a seat in the branches. It was so cool up in the tree that Miss Sullivan proposed that we have our luncheon there. I promised to keep still while she went to the house to fetch it.

Suddenly a change passed over the tree. All the sun's warmth left the air. I knew the sky was black, because all the heat, which meant light to me, had died out of the atmosphere. A strange odour came up from the earth. I knew it, it was the odour that always precedes a thunderstorm, and a nameless fear

海伦·凯勒端坐像

　　但是，在这期间我所经历的一件事，却让我发现大自然并不总是那么慈爱可亲。

　　一天，老师和我散步到了一个较远的地方之后正往回走，本来早上天气很好的，但现在天气变得闷热起来，我们有好几次不得不停在路边的树下休息。我们最后一次停在离家不远的一棵野樱桃树下歇息。这棵树枝繁叶茂，而且很好攀登，莎莉文老师用手一托，我就上了树，找个枝杈坐了下来。树上是如此的凉快，于是莎莉文老师提议我们就在这儿吃午餐。我答应她一定安静地待在那里，等她回去把饭取过来。

　　忽然间，天气陡变，太阳的温暖完全消失了，我知道天空布满了乌云，因为那对我来说意味着光明的热气从大气中消失了。一种奇怪的味道从泥土中散发出来，我知道这是暴风雨即将来临的征兆。我感到一种莫名的恐惧。我感觉到了孤独，感觉到自己被和朋友、坚实的大地割裂开来。巨大的恐惧很快包围了我。我一动不动地坐在那里等待，一阵恐惧袭来，心中盼望莎莉文老师快快回来。但我最希望的是从那棵树上下来。

clutched at my heart. I felt absolutely alone, cut off from my friends and the firm earth. The immense, the unknown, enfolded me. I remained still and expectant; a chilling terror crept over me. I longed for my teacher's return; but above all things I wanted to get down from that tree.

There was a moment of sinister silence, then a multitudinous stirring of the leaves. A shiver ran through the tree, and the wind sent forth a blast that would have knocked me off had I not clung to the branch with might and main. The tree swayed and strained. The small twigs snapped and fell about me in showers. A wild impulse to jump seized me, but terror held me fast. I crouched down in the fork of the tree. The branches lashed about me. I felt the intermittent jarring that came now and then, as if something heavy had fallen and the shock had traveled up till it reached the limb I sat on. It worked my suspense up to the highest point, and just as I was thinking the tree and I should fall together, my teacher seized my hand and helped me down. I clung to her, trembling with joy to feel the earth under my feet once more. I had learned a new lesson-that nature "wages open war against her children, and under softest touch hides treacherous claws."

After this experience it was a long time before I climbed another tree. The mere thought filled me with terror. It was the sweet allurement of the mimosa tree in full bloom that finally overcame my fears.

One beautiful spring morning when I was alone in the summer-house, reading, I became aware of a wonderful subtle fragrance in the air. I started up and

一阵沉寂之后，树叶哗啦啦齐声作响，一阵狂风扫过，树身猛烈地摇动起来，差点儿将我从树上刮下来，幸亏我抱住了树枝。树摇晃得越来越厉害，落叶和折断的小树枝就像雨点般打向我。虽然我急得想从树上跳下来，但恐惧很快就控制了我，我吓得丝毫不敢动弹。我蜷缩在大树的树杈处。树枝不断地抽打着我，风儿在耳边呼啸。我觉得大地在一阵一阵地震动，像有什么沉重的东西掉到了地上，这震动由下而上传到了我坐着的树枝上。我恐惧之极，就在我觉得仿佛要和大树一同走向毁灭之际，这时莎莉文老师恰好赶来了。她抓住我的手，将我扶下树。我紧紧抱着她，为自己又一次接触到坚实的大地而狂喜不已。我又学到了新的一课，那就是："大自然有时也会向她的孩子们开战，在她那最温柔美丽的外表之下，还隐藏着利爪！"

经过这次惊险的经历之后，我很长一段时间不敢爬树，甚至一想到爬树我就害怕得浑身发抖。直到有一天，当我面对那繁花满枝、香味扑鼻的含羞树的诱惑时，才战胜了这种恐惧心理。

那是春天一个美丽的早晨，我独自坐在凉亭里看书，感觉到空气中有一股奇妙的香气迎面扑来。我站起身来，决定去看看。这种香味就像是"春之神"穿过凉亭。"那是什么？"我问，马上就明白那是含羞树的花香。于是我摸索着走到花园的尽头，含羞树就长在篱边小路的拐弯处。

instinctively stretched out my hands. It seemed as if the spirit of spring had passed through the summer-house. "What is it?" I asked, and the next minute I recognized the odour of the mimosa blossoms. I felt my way to the end of the garden, knowing that the mimosa tree was near the fence, at the turn of the path.

Yes, there it was, all quivering in the warm sunshine, its blossom-laden branches almost touching the long grass. Was there ever anything so exquisitely beautiful in the world before! Its delicate blossoms shrank from the slightest earthly touch; it seemed as if a tree of paradise had been transplanted to earth. I made my way through a shower of petals to the great trunk and for one minute stood irresolute; then, putting my foot in the broad space between the forked branches, I pulled myself up into the tree.

I had some difficulty in holding on, for the branches were very large and the bark hurt my hands. But I had a delicious sense that I was doing something unusual and wonderful, so I kept on climbing higher and higher, until I reached a little seat which somebody had built there so long ago that it had grown part of the tree itself. I sat there for a long, long time, feeling like a fairy on a rosy cloud. After that I spent many happy hours in my tree of paradise, thinking fair thoughts and dreaming bright dreams.

含羞树的花朵在温暖的阳光下飞舞，开满花朵的树枝快要垂到青草上了。世上还有比这更美妙的事物吗？那些美丽的花儿只要轻轻一碰，就会敏感地卷起来，这仿佛就是从天堂移栽下凡的灵树。我穿过如雨般飘落的花瓣，走近大树，在愣了片刻之后，我就把脚伸到枝丫的空处，两手抓住枝干，开始往上爬。

青年时代的海伦虽然身体有机能障碍，但没有向命运屈服

由于树干太粗了，我几乎抱不住它，而且已经剥离的树皮还把我的手擦破了。尽管如此，我还是有一种美妙的感觉：我正在做一件不同寻常的、奇妙的事。因此，我不断地往上爬，直到爬上一个舒适的座位。这个座位是很早以前有人在树上做的小椅子，日久天长，它就成了树的一部分。我在上面呆了许久，感觉自己就像是在天空中凌云飞翔的仙女。从那以后，我在这棵"天堂树"上度过了许多快乐的时光，尽情地思考，美妙地梦想。

CHAPTER VI

I HAD now the key to all language, and I was eager to learn to use it. Children who hear acquire language without any particular effort; the words that fall from others' lips they catch on the wing, as it were, delightedly, while the little deaf child must trap them by a slow and often painful process. But whatever the process, the result is wonderful. Gradually from naming an object we advance step by step until we have traversed the vast distance between our first stammered syllable and the sweep of thought in a line of Shakespeare.

At first, when my teacher told me about a new thing I asked very few questions. My ideas were vague, and my vocabulary was inadequate; but as my knowledge of things grew, and I learned more and more words, my field of inquiry broadened, and I would return again and again to the same subject, eager for further information. Sometimes a new word revived an image that some earlier experience had engraved on my brain.

I remember the morning that I first asked the meaning of the word, "love." This was before I knew many words. I had found a few early violets in the garden and brought them to my teacher. She tried to kiss me: but at that time I did not like to

第6章 领悟"爱"的真谛

我现在已经领悟了所有语言的真谛，并且有些迫不及待地想加以应用。通常对于听力健全的孩子来说，学习语言是一件轻松的事情，只要捕捉到别人说的单词的时候，他们就可以模仿它，当然这对充满好奇的孩子来说，不仅不是一件痛苦的事，相反还是一件有趣的事情。但对于丧失听力的孩子来说，那可就是一个痛苦缓慢的过程了。但不管过程多么艰辛，结果却令人欢欣鼓舞。我们从事物的名称开始学起，一步一步地前进，最终跨过那看似难以逾越的鸿沟，从只会断断续续地发几个音节，到可以在莎士比亚的十四行诗中领略文学的魅力。

起初，当老师向我介绍新鲜事物时，我的问题很少，因为我对事物的概念模糊，掌握的单词有限。而随着知识的增长，词汇量的增大，我的问题也就越来越多，涉及的面也越来越广，常常是就一个问题一再地提问、思索，一定要打破砂锅问到底。有时候，一个新生词还可能唤醒我的某些记忆，使脑海中呈现出以前的画面。

我至今还清楚地记得问老师"爱"一词意义的那个清晨。当时，我的词

have any one kiss me except my mother. Miss Sullivan put her arm gently round me and spelled into my hand, "I love Helen."

"What is love?" I asked.

She drew me closer to her and said, "It is here, " pointing to my heart, whose beats I was conscious of for the first time. Her words puzzled me very much because I did not then understand anything unless I touched it.

I smelt the violets in her hand and asked, half in words, half in signs, a question which meant, "Is love the sweetness of flowers?"

"No, " said my teacher.

Again I thought. The warm sun was shining on us.

"Is this not love?" I asked, pointing in the direction from which the heat came. "Is this not love?"

It seemed to me that there could be nothing more beautiful than the sun, whose warmth makes all things grow.

But Miss Sullivan shook her head, and I was greatly puzzled and disappointed. I thought it strange that my teacher could not show me love.

汇量还很少。我在花园里找到了几朵早开的紫罗兰，于是拿来献给了莎莉文老师。她非常高兴，激动得想亲吻我，但我那时并不愿意母亲以外的人亲吻我，当然也包括莎莉文。她轻轻地把我搂抱在怀中，在我的手上写道："我爱海伦！"

美国总统克利夫兰（1885-1889年在任）

"什么是爱？"我问她。

她把我抱得更紧了，用手在我的心口比划说："这就是爱。"我第一次感觉到了心脏的跳动，但是对于她的话还是懵懂无知，因为任何无法触摸到的东西，对我来说都是难以理解的。

我闻着她手中紫罗兰的芳香，边比划边问她："爱，就是花儿的香味吗？"

"不，"她回答我。

我又搜索了一下记忆。此时，温暖的阳光正洒落在我们的身上。

"这就是爱吧？"我指着阳光射来的方向问，"爱就是太阳吧？"

对我来说，这世上没有比太阳更美丽的东西了，因为它滋养着万物。

但莎莉文老师还是摇摇头，我愈发的困惑和失望。我想"爱"一定是个古怪的东西，否则老师就不会无法准确告诉我它是什么了。

A day or two afterward I was stringing beads of different sizes in symmetrical groups-two large beads, three small ones, and so on. I had made many mistakes, and Miss Sullivan had pointed them out again and again with gentle patience. Finally I noticed a very obvious error in the sequence and for an instant I concentrated my attention on the lesson and tried to think how I should have arranged the beads. Miss Sullivan touched my forehead and spelled with decided emphasis, "Think."

In a flash I knew that the word was the name of the process that was going on in my head. This was my first conscious perception of an abstract idea. For a long time I was still-I was not thinking of the beads in my lap, but trying to find a meaning for "love" in the light of this new idea. The sun had been under a cloud all day, and there had been brief showers; but suddenly the sun broke forth in all its southern splendour.

Again, I asked my teacher, "Is this not love?"

"Love is something like the clouds that were in the sky before the sun came out," she replied. Then in simpler words than these, which at that time I could

海伦在莎莉文老师的辅导下学习，莎莉文老师正在用手语与海伦交谈

又过了一两天。我试着用线把大小不一的珠子均匀地串起来，先是两个大的，然后是三个稍小的，如此反复依次递加。我失败了很多回，莎莉文老师则不厌其烦地耐心帮我纠正错误。最后，我发现有一段明显串的位置不对，就决定集中注意力，冥思苦想怎样才不会串错。莎莉文老师摸了摸我的额头，带着强调意味地拼写下了"想"一词。

仿佛醍醐灌顶一般，我突然明白了这个词指的就是在我头脑里正进行的活动。于是，我第一次领悟了抽象的概念。我静静地坐了好长一段时间，并不是在思索串珠的方法，而是想从刚才的启迪中找到理解"爱"一词的线索。那天一直是阴天，间或下点零星小雨。可是突然间，太阳破云而出，发出了耀眼的光芒。

我再一次的问老师："爱难道不是太阳吗？"

"爱有点像太阳出来前天空中的云彩。"她回答我。为了便于我的理解，她用尽可能浅显的语言解释给我听，但是在当时我仍然不能完全明白她

not have understood, she explained:

"You cannot touch the clouds, you know; but you feel the rain and know how glad the flowers and the thirsty earth are to have it after a hot day. You cannot touch love either; but you feel the sweetness that it pours into everything. Without love you would not be happy or want to play."

The beautiful truth burst upon my mind- I felt that there were invisible lines stretched between my spirit and the spirits of others.

From the beginning of my education Miss Sullivan made it a practice to speak to me as she would to any hearing child; the only difference was that she spelled the sentences into my hand instead of speaking them. If I did not know the words and idioms necessary to express my thoughts she supplied them, even suggesting conversation when I was unable to keep up my end of the dialogue.

This process was continued for several years; for the deaf child does not learn in a month, or even in two or three years, the numberless idioms

话中的意思。

"你无法触摸到云彩，但是你却能感觉到雨水，体会到干涸的大地与花儿在烈日暴晒一天之后得到雨水滋润时的欢畅。同样的，爱虽然不可触摸，但你能体会到饱含着爱在其中的一切甜蜜幸福。没有爱，你就不会快活，也不会想玩耍了。"

莎莉文坐在椅子上给海伦读书，并在海伦手中拼写

刹那间，智慧的火花迸发在我的脑海之中，我感到仿佛有无数条绳索连接着我与他人的心灵，这就是人与人之间千丝万缕的情感吧！

从我学习开始，莎莉文老师就像对其他正常孩子一样不停地和我对话。唯一不同的是她把生词写在我的掌心，而不是读出来。如果我不知道用什么样的词语和俗语表达我的想法时，她就会教给我，当我不能与别人顺畅地沟通时，她也会提示我。

这样的学习过程持续了好几年，对一个失聪的孩子来说，要在一个月甚至是两到三年的时间里掌握与运用最简单的日常生活用语，毕竟是不现

and expressions used in the simplest daily intercourse. The little hearing child learns these from constant repetition and imitation. The conversation he hears in his home stimulates his mind and suggests topics and calls forth the spontaneous expression of his own thoughts. This natural exchange of ideas is denied to the deaf child. My teacher, realizing this, determined to supply the kinds of stimulus I lacked. This she did by repeating to me as far as possible, verbatim what she heard, and by showing me how I could take part in the conversation. But it was a long time before I ventured to take the initiative, and still longer before I could find something appropriate to say at the right time.

  The deaf and the blind find it very difficult to acquire the amenities of conversation. How much more this difficulty must be augmented in the case of those who are both deaf and blind! They cannot distinguish the tone of the voice or, without assistance, go up and down the gamut of tones that give significance to words; nor can they watch the expression of the speaker's face, and a look is often the very soul of what one says.

实的。正常的孩子学习语言靠不停的重复与模仿，他们在家里听到家人的交谈，容易自发形成对事物的想法以及众多的话题，同时也激发了表达自我的本能。但是失聪却阻碍了聋哑孩子与其他人的自然交流。莎莉文老师认识到这一点后，就想尽各种办法来弥补我的缺陷，激发我的语言表达能力。每一句话，她都尽可能逐字不断重复，并告诉我怎样与人交流。尽管这样，我还是用了相当长的一段时间才能够与人交谈，以后又用了更长的时间，才知道在什么样的场合该说什么样的话。

  单是听不见或单是看不见的人就已经很难体会到交谈的愉悦感，而对于那些既听不见又看不见的人来说，与人交流就更是难上加难！在没有帮助的情况下，他们无法分辨谈话者语调的高低升降、语气强弱轻重的变化，也就无从知晓其中所包含的意义；同时，他们又看不见对方脸上的表情，不能从中觉察其内心的真实想法。

CHAPTER VII

THE next important step in my education was learning to read.

As soon as I could spell a few words my teacher gave me slips of cardboard on which were printed words in raised letters. I quickly learned that each printed word stood for an object, an act, or a quality. I had a frame in which I could arrange the words in little sentences; but before I ever put sentences in the frame I used to make them in objects. I found the slips of paper which represented, for example, "doll", "is", "on", "bed" and placed each name on its object; then I put my doll on the bed with the words is, on, bed arranged beside the doll, thus making a sentence out of the words, and at the same time carrying out the idea of the sentence with the things themselves.

One day, Miss Sullivan tells me, I pinned the word girl on my pinafore and stood in the wardrobe. On the shelf I arranged the words, is, in, wardrobe. Nothing delighted me so much as this game. My teacher and I played it for hours at a time. Often everything in the room was arranged in object sentences.

From the printed slip it was but a step to the printed book. I took my "Reader for Beginners" and hunted for the words I knew; when I found them my joy was

第7章 沐浴知识的阳光

我接受教育的第二个阶段是学习阅读。

就在我刚能拼写几个字后，莎莉文老师就给我一些硬纸片，每张纸片上都有由凸起的字母组成的单词。很快我就知道每一个突起的词都代表一种物体、一种行为或一种特性。我有一个纸板框，可以用这些单词在上面摆出短句子。但我在用这些硬纸片排列短句之前，仍然习惯于用实物来表达句子。例如，我会先找出上面写有"娃娃"、"是"、"在……上"和"床"的硬纸片，把每个硬纸片放在有关的物体上，然后再把娃娃放在床上，在旁边摆上写有"是"、"在……上"和"床"的卡片，这样既用词造了一个句子，又用与之相关的物体表达了句子的内容。

一天，莎莉文老师让我把"girl"（女孩）这个词别在围裙上，然后站在衣柜里，把"is"（是）、"in"（在……里）、"wardrobe"（衣柜）这几个词放在框架上，后来这竟然成为我最喜欢的一种游戏。我和老师有时一玩就是几个小时，屋子里所有的东西都被我们摆成了各种含义不同的句子。

拼卡游戏是我进入阅读的初级阶段。不久，我开始拿起"启蒙读本"，

like that of a game of hide-and-seek. Thus I began to read. Of the time when I began to read connected stories I shall speak later.

For a long time I had no regular lessons. Even when I studied most earnestly it seemed more like play than work. Everything Miss Sullivan taught me she illustrated by a beautiful story or a poem. Whenever anything delighted or interested me she talked it over with me just as if she were a little girl herself. What many children think of with dread, as a painful plodding through grammar, hard sums and harder definitions, is to-day one of my most precious memories.

I cannot explain the peculiar sympathy Miss Sullivan had with my pleasures and desires. Perhaps it was the result of long association with the blind. Added to this she had a wonderful faculty for description. She went quickly over uninteresting details, and never nagged me with questions to see if I remembered the day-before-yesterday's lesson. She introduced dry technicalities of science little by little, making every subject so real that I could not help remembering what she taught.

We read and studied out of doors, preferring the sunlit woods to the house. All my early lessons have in them the breath of the woods-the fine, resinous odour of pine

海伦·凯勒晚年像

找寻那些我已经认识的字。一旦找到自己认识的字，我就高兴得像玩捉迷藏一样兴奋不已。就这样，开启了我的阅读进程，当时我只是阅读一些我后面将会提到的故事。

相当长的一段时间，我没有上过正规的课程。即使是我非常认真地学，依然像是在玩游戏，而不像在上课。莎莉文老师无论教我什么，都会用一些美丽的故事和动人的诗篇来解释。一旦发现我感兴趣，就不断与我讨论，好像她自己也变成了一个小女孩。一般孩子们最讨厌的事，如学语法、做数学题、名词解释等，在她的耐心指导下，我做起来都兴趣盎然。这些都成了我记忆深处最华美的乐章。

我至今都不能理解莎莉文老师对我的快乐和愿望所表现出来的特有的耐心，也许是和盲人长期接触，加上她特有的描述事物的独特技巧吧！那些枯燥无味的细节，她一带而过，使我根本感觉不到乏味和单调；她也从来不会责备我是否忘了昨天还是前天教的功课。说来也怪，在她的解释下，那些本来枯燥无味的专业术语变得生动逼真起来，我也就自然而然地记住了她讲的内容。

needles, blended with the perfume of wild grapes. Seated in the gracious shade of a wild tulip tree, I learned to think that everything has a lesson and a suggestion. "The loveliness of things taught me all their use." Indeed, everything that could hum, or buzz, or sing, or bloom, had a part in my education-noisy- throated frogs, katydids and crickets held in my hand until, forgetting their embarrassment, they trilled their reedy note, little downy chickens and wild-flowers, the dogwood blossoms, meadow-violets and budding fruit trees. I felt the bursting cotton-bolls and fingered their soft fiber and fuzzy seeds; I felt the low soughing of the wind through the cornstalks, the silky rustling of the long leaves, and the indignant snort of my pony, as we caught him in the pasture and put the bit in his mouth-ah me! how well I remember the spicy, clovery smell of his breath!

Sometimes I rose at dawn and stole into the garden while the heavy dew lay on the grass and flowers. Few know what joy it is to feel the roses pressing softly into the hand, or the beautiful motion of the lilies as they sway in the morning breeze. Sometimes I caught an insect in the flower

我们经常坐在屋外面，在阳光照耀的树林里看书和学习。在这里，我早期所学到的东西饱含着森林的气息，带着树脂的松香味，混杂着野葡萄的芬芳。坐在浓郁的树荫下，世界万物都会给我以教育和启迪。实际上，那些嗡嗡作响、低声鸣叫、婉转歌唱或开花吐香的自然万物，都是我学习的对象。我常常

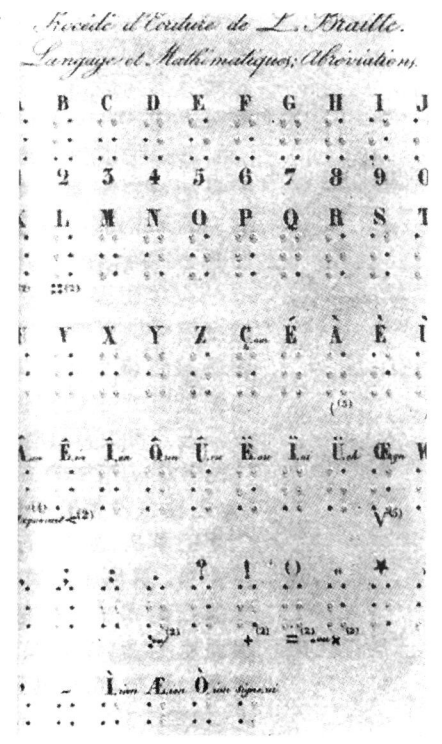

海伦学习时使用的盲文课本

将青蛙、蚂蚱和蟋蟀捂在手心里，当它们忘记了被人捉住的命运后，又会像在草丛中那样欢鸣起来。还有毛茸茸的小鸡、绽开的野花、木棉、河边的紫罗兰和刚发芽的果树。我能感觉到棉花那滑腻的纤维和毛茸茸的棉籽，感觉到微风吹过玉米秸秆发出的响声，玉米叶子互相摩擦发出来的沙沙声，以及被我们在牧场捉住并套上嚼子的小马发出来的愤怒的嘶鸣声，这些都成为我记忆中最美丽的一道风景！

有时候，在东方刚刚露出鱼肚白的时候，我就会悄悄爬起来，溜进花园里，行走在露珠覆压的花草丛中。谁能体会到把玫瑰花轻柔地握在手心里的无限乐趣?谁又能知道百合花在徐徐晨风中摇曳的美丽身姿呢?采摘鲜花的时

I was plucking, and I felt the faint noise of a pair of wings rubbed together in a sudden terror, as the little creature became aware of a pressure from without.

Another favourite haunt of mine was the orchard, where the fruit ripened early in July. The large, downy peaches would reach themselves into my hand, and as the joyous breezes flew about the trees the apples tumbled at my feet. Oh, the delight with which I gathered up the fruit in my pinafore, pressed my face against the smooth cheeks of the apples, still warm from the sun, and skipped back to the house!

Our favourite walk was to Keller's Landing, an old tumble-down lumber-wharf on the Tennessee River, used during the Civil War to land soldiers. There we spent many happy hours and played at learning geography. I built dams of pebbles, made islands and lakes, and dug river-beds, all for fun, and never dreamed that I was learning a lesson.

I listened with increasing wonder to Miss Sullivan's descriptions of the great round world with its burning mountains, buried cities, moving rivers of ice, and many other things as strange. She made raised maps in clay, so that I could feel the mountain ridges and valleys, and follow with my fingers the devious course of rivers. I liked this, too; but the division of the earth into zones and poles confused and teased my mind. The illustrative strings and the orange stick representing the poles seemed so real that even to this day the mere mention of temperate zone suggests a series of twine circles; and I believe that if any one should set about it

候，有时就会无意中抓到钻在花里面的昆虫，我能感觉到它们恐惧地想振翅飞走却又无处可逃，只好徒劳地煽动几下翅膀来反抗。

除了喜欢在花园中漫步之外，最惬意的事情莫过于流连于果园里。每年7月初便有果子成熟了。毛茸茸的大桃子几乎会垂落到手中。伴随阵阵微风，熟透了的苹果会掉在地上。这时候，我会撑开围裙，把落到脚旁的苹果捡起来，然后把脸贴在苹果上，滑滑的，暖暖的，雀跃着跑回家！

我们最喜欢去凯勒码头，那是田纳西河边一个荒芜破败的码头，是在南北战争时期为了部队登陆而修建的。我们经常在那里一待就是好几个小时，一边玩一边学习地理知识。我还经常用鹅卵石造堤建岛、筑湖开河，虽然这只是在做游戏，却不知不觉地学到了许多知识。

莎莉文老师还向我描述了我们这个又大又圆的地球，地球上的火山、被掩埋在地下的城市、不断移动的冰河以及其他许许多多的奇闻轶事，都引起了我强烈的好奇心。老师还用黏土给我做了一个立体的地图，我可以用手摸到凸出来的山脊、凹下去的山谷和蜿蜒曲折的河流。我很喜欢这些，不过我的头脑里总是分不清赤道和两极。为了更形象地描述地球，莎莉文老师用一根根线代表经纬线，用一根树枝代表贯穿南北极的地轴，这一切是如此的形象逼真，以至于只要有人提起气温带，我就会想象出许多一连串编织而成的

he could convince me that white bears actually climb the North Pole.

Arithmetic seems to have been the only study I did not like. From the first I was not interested in the science of numbers. Miss Sullivan tried to teach me to count by stringing beads in groups, and by arranging kindergarten straws I learned to add and subtract. I never had patience to arrange more than five or six groups at a time. When I had accomplished this my conscience was at rest for the day, and I went out quickly to find my playmates.

In this same leisurely manner I studied zoology and botany. Once a gentleman, whose name I have forgotten, sent me a collection of fossils-tiny mollusk shells beautifully marked, and bits of sandstone with the print of birds' claws, and a lovely fern in bas-relief. These were the keys which unlocked the treasures of the antediluvian world for me. With trembling fingers I listened to Miss Sullivan's descriptions of the terrible beasts, with uncouth, unpronounceable names, which once went tramping through the primeval forests, tearing down the branches of gigantic trees for food, and died in the dismal swamps of an unknown age. For a long time these

海伦使用的盲文课本

圆圈。我想，假如有人骗我说白熊会爬上北极的柱子，我想我会相信的。

数学好像是我唯一不喜欢的功课，我从一开始就对数字不感兴趣。莎莉文老师曾用线串上珠子来教我数数，或摆弄草棍学习加减法，但是每次总是不到五六个题，我就变得不耐烦了。每天做完几道数学题之后，我就认为自己完成任务了，然后就跑出去找伙伴们玩耍。

我也是用这种做游戏的方式学习动物和植物知识的。记得有一次，有一位我已经忘记其姓名的先生寄给我一些化石。化石中有带着美丽花纹的贝壳、有鸟爪印的砂岩以及像浮雕一样的蕨类植物。这些化石打开了我的心扉，向我展现了远古时代的珍宝。我常常惊恐地听莎莉文老师描述一些名字古怪而恐怖的野兽，它们曾在原始森林中游荡，撕断大树的枝叶当食物，最后又悄无声息地死在沼泽地里。有很长一段时间，我老是梦见这些怪兽，那阴暗可怕的地质时期同现在形成了鲜明的对照。现在的人们多么快乐啊！阳光照耀大地，百花争芳斗艳，田野中回荡着我那匹小马悦耳的蹄声。

strange creatures haunted my dreams, and this gloomy period formed a somber background to the joyous Now, filled with sunshine and roses and echoing with the gentle beat of my pony's hoof.

Another time a beautiful shell was given me, and with a child's surprise and delight I learned how a tiny mollusk had built the lustrous coil for his dwelling place, and how on still nights, when there is no breeze stirring the waves, the Nautilus sails on the blue waters of the Indian Ocean in his "ship of pearl." After I had learned a great many interesting things about the life and habits of the children of the sea-how in the midst of dashing waves the little polyps build the beautiful coral isles of the Pacific, and the foraminifera have made the chalk-hills of many a land-my teacher read me "The Chambered Nautilus, " and showed me that the shell-building process of the mollusks is symbolical of the development of the mind. Just as the wonder-working mantle of the Nautilus changes the material it absorbs from the water and makes it a part of itself, so the bits of knowledge one gathers undergo a similar change and become pearls of thought.

Again, it was the growth of a plant that furnished the text for a lesson. We bought a lily and set it in a sunny window. Very soon the green, pointed buds showed signs of opening.

拉德克利夫学院的健身房和仙女楼

还有一次，有人送给我一个美丽的贝壳。老师就给我讲小小的软体动物是如何为自己建造这么色彩斑斓的住所的，又是如何乘着它的"珍珠船"欣赏印度洋迷人夜色的。孩子般的好奇使我听得津津有味。在我知道了许多有关海洋生物生活习惯的有趣知识，知道了小巧的珊瑚虫如何在太平洋汹涌的波涛中建筑自己的家园，灵活的有孔小虫如何在岸上堆起一座座小山之后，老师为我读了《驮着房子的鹦鹉螺》，从中我知道了软体动物的造壳过程和人的大脑发展过程一样。鹦鹉螺可以用奇妙的套膜把从海水中吸收的物质转换成身体的一部分，而人类不也正是将从外界吸收到的各种知识转化为智慧，使之成为一颗颗思想的珍珠吗？

同样，植物的生长也让我学到了很多。我们买了一株百合花，放在阳光充足的窗台上。眨眼间，一个个嫩绿、尖尖的花蕾伸展出来。花蕾外边包着纤细的叶子，叶子慢慢地张开，好像极不情愿让人窥见里面的花朵。可一旦绽了头，花朵张开的速度就加快了，当然是快而不乱。不可思议的是，这些绽放的花朵中一定会有一朵最大最美丽的，它要比其他蓓蕾更显雍容华贵，

The slender, fingerlike leaves on the outside opened slowly, reluctant, I thought, to reveal the loveliness they hid; once having made a start, however, the opening process went on rapidly, but in order and systematically. There was always one bud larger and more beautiful than the rest, which pushed her outer covering back with more pomp, as if the beauty in soft, silky robes knew that she was the lily-queen by right divine, while her more timid sisters doffed their green hoods shyly, until the whole plant was one nodding bough of loveliness and fragrance.

Once there were eleven tadpoles in a glass globe set in a window full of plants. I remember the eagerness with which I made discoveries about them. It was great fun to plunge my hand into the bowl and feel the tadpoles frisk about, and to let them slip and slide between my fingers. One day a more ambitious fellow leaped beyond the edge of the bowl and fell on the floor, where I found him to all appearance more dead than alive. The only sign of life was a slight wriggling of his tail. But no sooner had he returned to his element than he darted to the bottom, swimming round and round in joyous activity. He had made his leap, he had seen the great world, and was content to stay in his pretty glass house under the big fuchsia tree until he attained the dignity of froghood. Then he went to live in the leafy pool at the end of the garden, where he made the summer nights musical with his quaint love-song.

Thus I learned from life itself. At the beginning I was only a little mass of possibilities. It was my teacher who unfolded and developed them. When she

似乎故意让躲在柔软、光滑的外衣里面的花朵知道自己是尊贵的花王。当其他的姐妹们羞答答地褪下绿色的头巾后，百合花的整个枝头挂满了怒放的花朵，芬芳袭人。

家里曾经有一个球形玻璃鱼缸，摆放在满是花盆的窗台上。鱼缸中养了11只蝌蚪。我现在还能回想起发现这些蝌蚪时的快乐来，我兴奋地把手伸进鱼缸里，享受蝌蚪在手指间游动的快慰。一天，一个胆大的家伙竟然从鱼缸中蹦出来，掉在地板上，等我发现时已经半死不活了，只有那尾巴的微弱摆动还证明它一息尚存。可当我一把它放回水里时，它马上来了精神，飞快地潜入缸底，一圈一圈地游起来。它曾经跳出鱼缸，见过了世面，现在却心甘情愿地待在这倒挂金钟花下的玻璃房子里，直到变成神气活现的青蛙。那时，它就会跳进花园那头满是绿树的池塘中，在那里用它那优雅的情歌将夏夜变成音乐的世界。

我就这样从生命本身汲取知识。起初，我只是一块有可能雕琢的顽石，正是我的老师发现并开发了我的智慧。她的到来，使我的生命充满了爱和欢乐，我的一切都充满了意义。她从不放过任何一个机会，向我指出隐藏在一切事物里面的美，她每时每刻都在动脑筋、想办法，使我的生活变得甜蜜而更有意义。

came, everything about me breathed of love and joy and was full of meaning. She has never since let pass an opportunity to point out the beauty that is in everything, nor has she ceased trying in thought and action and example to make my life sweet and useful.

It was my teacher's genius, her quick sympathy, her loving tact which made the first years of my education so beautiful. It was because she seized the right moment to impart knowledge that made it so pleasant and acceptable to me. She realized that a child's mind is like a shallow brook which ripples and dances merrily over the stony course of its education and reflects here a flower, there a bush, yonder a fleecy cloud; and she attempted to guide my mind on its way, knowing that like a brook it should be fed by mountain streams and hidden springs, until it broadened out into a deep river, capable of reflecting in its placid surface, billowy hills, the luminous shadows of trees and the blue heavens, as well as the sweet face of a little flower.

Any teacher can take a child to the classroom, but not every teacher can make him learn. He will not work joyously unless he feels that liberty is his, whether he is busy

海伦穿上了大学毕业的礼服，这一年她23岁

正是我的老师的天才、敏锐的同情心和爱的机智，使得我第一年的学习变得如此美丽。由于她抓住了适当的时机向我传授知识，所以学习成了一件愉快而易于接受的事情。她认识到孩子的心灵就像弯曲的溪水，沿着河床千回百转，一会儿在这里映出花朵，一会儿在那里映出灌木，一会儿又在另一个地方映出朵朵轻云，佳境美景连绵不绝。她用尽心思朝着这条路引导我，因为她明白，孩子的心灵和小溪一样，还需要山涧泉水来补充，直到它汇集成长江大河，在那平如镜面的河水上映出连绵起伏的山峰，映出灿烂耀眼的树影和蓝天，映出花朵的美丽面庞。

任何一个老师都可以把孩子领进教室，但并不是每个老师都能使孩子热爱学习。无论孩子是忙着还是闲着，除非让他感到知识是他自己的，否则他不会心甘情愿地学习。要让孩子体会到成功的喜悦和失败的沮丧，他才能勇敢地接受任务、迎接挑战，用自己的智慧解决问题，而不是呆板地死读书。

我的老师与我是如此的相亲相爱，我很少想到将自己和她分开来。我永

or at rest; he must feel the flush of victory and the heart-sinking of disappointment before he takes with a will the tasks distasteful to him and resolves to dance his way bravely through a dull routine of textbooks.

My teacher is so near to me that I scarcely think of myself apart from her. How much of my delight in all beautiful things is innate, and how much is due to her influence, I can never tell. I feel that her being is inseparable from my own, and that the footsteps of my life are in hers. All the best of me belongs to her-there is not a talent, or an aspiration or a joy in me that has not been awakened by her loving touch.

远也分不清，我对所有美好事物的喜爱，有多少是自己内心固有的，有多少是来自她的影响。我感到她已经成为我生活中不可分割的一部分，我沿着她的足迹向前。我生命中所有美好的东西都属于她，我的才能、抱负和欢乐，全都是由她的爱点化而成。

CHAPTER VIII

THE first Christmas after Miss Sullivan came to Tuscumbia was a great event. Every one in the family prepared surprises for me, but what pleased me most, Miss Sullivan and I prepared surprises for everybody else. The mystery that surrounded the gifts was my greatest delight and amusement. My friends did all they could to excite my curiosity by hints and half-spelled sentences which they pretended to break off in the nick of time. Miss Sullivan and I kept up a game of guessing which taught me more about the use of language than any set of lessons could have done. Every evening, seated round a glowing wood fire, we played our guessing game, which grew more and more exciting as Christmas approached.

On Christmas Eve the Tuscumbia schoolchildren had their tree, to which they invited me. In the centre of the schoolroom stood a beautiful tree ablaze and shimmering in the soft light, its branches loaded with strange, wonderful fruit. It was a moment of supreme happiness. I danced and capered around the tree in an ecstasy. When I learned that there was a gift for each child, I was delighted, and the kind people who had prepared the tree permitted me to hand the presents to the children. In the pleasure of doing this, I did not stop to look at my own gifts; but

第8章　欢乐的圣诞节

莎莉文老师来到塔斯坎比亚后的第一个圣诞节成了一个盛大活动。家中每一个人都准备给我一个惊喜，当然这些都无法与我和莎莉文老师为他们准备礼物的兴奋相比。圣诞礼物的神秘带给我最大的快乐，也成为我最好的娱乐。家人也不时逗弄我，故意给我透露一点儿暗示，或者半句不连续的话语，让我去猜测。莎莉文老师和我常常玩这种猜谜游戏，让我学会了许多语言的用法，这比上课所学到的要多得多。每天晚上，我们都围坐在燃烧的木头柴火前，玩着猜谜游戏。随着圣诞节一天天临近，我们的兴致也越来越高。

在平安夜，镇上的学生们精心准备好了圣诞树，邀请我和他们一起欢度佳节。圣诞树立在教室的中间，在柔和的灯光下发出光彩，树上挂满了新奇的果实。那是一段极其幸福的时光，我围着圣诞树，兴奋地蹦着跳着。当我得知每个孩子都有一份礼物时，高兴极了。那些准备圣诞树的好心人让我来分发礼物。我高兴地为大家分发礼物，甚至没顾得上看自己的礼物；我恨不得圣诞节马上到来，甚至无法控制自己的好奇心。我知道这些礼物还不是家

when I was ready for them, my impatience for the real Christmas to begin almost got beyond control. I knew the gifts I already had were not those of which friends had thrown out such tantalizing hints, and my teacher said the presents I was to have would be even nicer than these. I was persuaded, however, to content myself with the gifts from the tree and leave the others until morning.

That night, after I had hung my stocking, I lay awake a long time, pretending to be asleep and keeping alert to see what Santa Claus would do when he came. At last I fell asleep with a new doll and a white bear in my arms. Next morning it was I who waked the whole family with my first "Merry Christmas!" I found surprises, not in the stocking only, but on the table, on all the chairs, at the door, on the very window-sill; indeed, I could hardly walk without stumbling on a bit of Christmas wrapped up in tissue paper. But when my teacher presented me with a canary, my cup of happiness overflowed.

Little Tim was so tame that he would hop on my finger and eat candied cherries out of my hand. Miss Sullivan taught

人所暗示的东西，因为莎莉文老师说，那些礼物要比这些还要好得多。不过她叫我耐心点儿，明天一早就会知道是什么东西了。

圣诞夜的时候，我挂好长袜之后，躺在床上许久，难以入眠，就假装睡着了，想看看圣诞老人来了会做些

海伦很喜欢读书，书本是她获取知识、接触外部世界的重要媒介。图为海伦在爱犬的陪伴下读盲文书

什么。后来，我实在困得不行，抱着晚上新得到的洋娃娃和白熊睡着了。第二天早上，我起了个大早，全家人都被我的"圣诞快乐"唤醒了。我不仅在长袜里找到了令我惊喜的礼物，在桌子上、椅子上，甚至门槛以及每个窗台上，我几乎每迈出一步，都会碰到包装精美的圣诞礼物。而当莎莉文老师送给我一只金丝雀的时候，我的高兴更是难以用语言来形容。

小金丝雀蒂姆非常温顺，常常在我手指上跳来跳去，吃我手上的甜樱桃。莎莉文老师教会我如何喂养我的新宠物。每天早上吃完早饭后，我会准备给它洗澡，把笼子打扫得干干净净的，还给它的小杯子装满新鲜的草籽和

me to take all the care of my new pet. Every morning after breakfast I prepared his bath, made his cage clean and sweet, filled his cups with fresh seed and water from the well-house, and hung a spray of chickweed in his swing.

One morning I left the cage on the window-seat while I went to fetch water for his bath. When I returned I felt a big cat brush past me as I opened the door. At first I did not realize what had happened; but when I put my hand in the cage and Tim's pretty wings did not meet my touch or his small pointed claws take hold of my finger, I knew that I should never see my sweet little singer again.

海伦摸着墙上楼梯

从井房打来的水，然后再把一小捆草挂在它的跳杆上。

一天早上，我把鸟笼放在窗台上，然后去打水给它洗澡。当我回来的时候，一开门，就感到有一只大猫从我身边钻了过去。起初我并没在意，可是当我把手伸进笼子时，我意识到有些不对头了，我没有摸到蒂姆漂亮的翅膀，也没有触到它尖尖的小爪。我知道，我再也见不到我那可爱的小歌手了。

CHAPTER IX

THE next important event in my life was my visit to Boston, in May, 1888. As if it were yesterday I remember the preparations, the departure with my teacher and my mother, the journey, and finally the arrival in Boston. How different this journey was from the one I had made to Baltimore two years before! I was no longer a restless, excitable little creature, requiring the attention of everybody on the train to keep me amused. I sat quietly beside Miss Sullivan, taking in with eager interest all that she told me about what she saw out of the car window: the beautiful Tennessee River, the great cotton-fields, the hills and woods, and the crowds of laughing negroes at the stations, who waved to the people on the train and brought delicious candy and popcorn balls through the car.

On the seat opposite me sat my big rag doll, Nancy, in a new gingham dress and a beruffled sunbonnet, looking at me out of two bead eyes. Sometimes, when I was not absorbed in Miss Sullivan's descriptions, I remembered Nancy's existence and took her up in my arms, but I generally calmed my conscience by making myself believe that she was asleep.

As I shall not have occasion to refer to Nancy again, I wish to tell here a sad

第9章 波士顿之旅

接下来在我生命中重要的事情是1888年5月的波士顿之行。仿佛就像是发生在昨天一样，我依然记得整个旅途:从准备，到与老师、母亲启程，整个旅途的所见所闻以及最后抵达波士顿。这次旅行和两年前的巴尔的摩之行有着天壤之别！我已不再是那个片刻不能歇息、火车上的每个人都令我兴奋的小家伙了。我静静地坐在莎莉文老师身旁，全神贯注地听她给我讲她所看到的窗外景色:美丽的田纳西河、大片的棉花地、群山、森林和拥挤在火车站的黑人们，他们向火车上的旅客舞动着胳膊，叫卖香甜的糖果和爆米花！

与我相对而坐的是我的大布娃娃南茜，它穿着一件条纹外衣，戴着一顶皱巴巴的太阳帽，一双用玻璃球做的眼睛目不转睛地直盯着我。有时莎莉文老师的讲述引不起我的兴趣时，我便会想到南茜，把她抱在怀里——不过凭良心说，我相信她通常是熟睡了的。

既然我以后再也不会提到南茜，我愿意在此叙述我们到达波士顿后它的惨痛经历。南茜的身上沾满了脏东西——我在车上逼它吃的面包渣，尽管它对那些东西不感兴趣。帕金斯盲人学校的洗衣工偷偷地拿去给它洗个澡。这

experience she had soon after our arrival in Boston. She was covered with dirt-the remains of mud pies I had compelled her to eat, although she had never shown any special liking for them. The laundress at the Perkins Institution secretly carried her off to give her a bath. This was too much for poor Nancy. When I next saw her she was a formless heap of cotton, which I should not have recognized at all except for the two bead eyes which looked out at me reproachfully.

When the train at last pulled into the station at Boston it was as if a beautiful fairy tale had come true. The "once upon a time" was now; the "far-away country" was here.

We had scarcely arrived at the Perkins Institution for the Blind when I began to make friends with the little blind children. It delighted me inexpressibly to find that they knew the manual alphabet. What joy to talk with other children in my own language! Until then I had been like a foreigner speaking through an interpreter. In the school where Laura Bridgman was taught I was in my own country.

It took me some time to appreciate the fact that my new friends were blind. I knew I could not see; but it did not seem possible that all the eager, loving children who gathered round me and joined heartily in my frolics were also blind. I remember the surprise and the pain I felt as I noticed that they placed

海伦和莎莉文老师正在下特制的国际象棋

对它来说就有些过分了！等我第二天再见到它时，它已经成了一堆看不出形状的棉花了，除了那两个用珠子做的眼睛充满责备地瞪着我，我简直都认不出它来。

火车最终驶入了波士顿站，仿佛一个美丽的童话终于变成了现实。"从前"变成了"现在"，"天涯"变成了"咫尺"。

一到帕金斯盲人学校，我就在那里和一帮失明的孩子们交上了朋友，最使我高兴的是他们也会手语。与其他孩子一起使用我自己的语言交流，是多么快乐的一件事啊！在这以前，我就像个需要借助翻译才能同人说话的外国人。在这所劳拉·布里奇曼受到教育的学校里，我找到了自己的归属。

我用了好长时间才接受这样的事实，即我的新朋友也都是盲人。我知道自己看不见，但却从来没有想到那些围着我又蹦又跳、活泼可爱的小伙伴们也看不见。当我觉察到我与他们说话的时候他们也把手放在我的手上，读书也用手指触摸时，我现在还能想起自己的惊奇和痛苦。虽然我早就被告

their hands over mine when I talked to them and that they read books with their fingers. Although I had been told this before, and although I understood my own deprivations, yet I had thought vaguely that since they could hear, they must have a sort of "second sight", and I was not prepared to find one child and another and yet another deprived of the same precious gift. But they were so happy and contented that I lost all sense of pain in the pleasure of their companionship.

One day spent with the blind children made me feel thoroughly at home in my new environment, and I looked eagerly from one pleasant experience to another as the days flew swiftly by. I could not quite convince myself that there was much world left, for I regarded Boston as the beginning and the end of creation.

While we were in Boston we visited Bunker Hill, and there I had my first lesson in history. The story of the brave men who had fought on the spot where we stood excited me greatly. I climbed the monument, counting the steps, and wondering as I went higher and yet higher if the soldiers had climbed this great stairway and shot at the enemy on the ground below.

The next day we went to Plymouth by water. This was my first trip on the ocean and my first voyage in a steamboat. How full of life and motion it was! But the rumble of the machinery made me think it was thundering, and I began to cry, because I feared if it rained we should not be able to have our picnic out of doors. I was more interested, I think, in the great rock on which the Pilgrims landed than in anything else in Plymouth. I could touch it, and perhaps that made the coming

知过，我也能感知自己身体上的缺陷，但我一直模糊地以为既然他们可以听到，一定是有一种"第二视觉"。因此，当我发现所有的孩子都和我一样被剥夺了美好的权利时，我一时还无法适应。但他们是如此的高兴、自信，以至于我那种痛苦的感觉很快就消失在他们的友谊之中了。

与盲童待了一天之后，新环境对我来说就像在家里一样自如。我渴盼着一个又一个新奇的经历，日子也在这种渴盼中一天天地飞过。我把波士顿看成是创造的起点和终点，除了这里，我无法相信这个世界还有其他的地方。

在波士顿期间，我们还游览了邦克山。莎莉文老师在邦克山给我上了第一堂历史课。听英雄们的故事，站在勇士激战的地方，我情绪激动万分。我向山上爬，心里数着台阶，我爬得越来越高，心里想着当年英雄们是否爬到如此高的石阶向下射击敌人。

接下来的第二天，我们乘船去普利茅斯。这是我第一次海上旅行，也是第一次乘蒸汽船航行。这样的行程真是既新鲜又刺激！隆隆的机器声让我误以为是雷声，担心天要下雨，我们就不能在户外野餐了，想到这我就开始哭了。在普利茅斯所有事物中，最令我感兴趣的是当年移民们登陆时蹬踏过的那块大石头。我用手抚摸着这块石头，这使得当年那些移民和他们的艰苦创业行迹变得更加真实。我手中不时握着一位热心的先生在移民博物馆送给

of the Pilgrims and their toils and great deeds seem more real to me. I have often held in my hand a little model of the Plymouth Rock which a kind gentleman gave me at Pilgrim Hall, and I have fingered its curves, the split in the centre and the embossed figures "1620", and turned over in my mind all that I knew about the wonderful story of the Pilgrims.

How my childish imagination glowed with the splendour of their enterprise! I idealized them as the bravest and most generous men that ever sought a home in a strange land. I thought they desired the freedom of their fellow men as well as their own. I was keenly surprised and disappointed years later to learn of their acts of persecution that make us tingle with shame, even while we glory in the courage and energy that gave us our "Country Beautiful".

Among the many friends I made in Boston were Mr. William Endicott and his daughter. Their kindness to me was the seed from which many

海伦站着抚摸雕花椅背

我的那块普利茅斯岩石的模型，用手指玩石头表面的裂缝。石头上面显著位置上刻着"1620年"字样。我的脑海里也不断浮现出早期移民一桩桩、一件件可歌可泣的事迹。

在我稚嫩的心灵里，这些先驱者的事迹是那样的崇高！我把他们幻化为勇敢慷慨而又在陌生的土地寻找家园的偶像。我想他们渴望的不仅是自己的自由，也包括同胞的自由。但是多年后，在知道了他们的迫害行为之后，我不禁感到吃惊和失望，尽管我们为他们创建了我们美丽家园的勇气和能力而感到光荣。

在我所结交的波士顿朋友中，威廉·恩迪科特先生和他的女儿就是其中的两个。他们的关爱和热情就像种子一样植根于我的记忆中，伴随我一直成长。一天，我们拜访了他们位于贝弗利农场的家，我欣喜地记得我们如何穿过他们的玫瑰园，他们的两条狗——大利奥和奔拉着两个长耳朵的小弗瑞兹如何迎接我们的，还有那匹名叫尼姆罗德的跑得最快的马是如何把鼻子凑到

pleasant memories have since grown. One day we visited their beautiful home at Beverly Farms. I remember with delight how I went through their rose-garden, how their dogs, big Leo and little curly-haired Fritz with long ears, came to meet me, and how Nimrod, the swiftest of the horses, poked his nose into my hands for a pat and a lump of sugar.

  I also remember the beach, where for the first time I played in the sand. It was hard, smooth sand, very different from the loose, sharp sand, mingled with kelp and shells, at Brewster. Mr. Endicott told me about the great ships that came sailing by from Boston, bound for Europe. I saw him many times after that, and he was always a good friend to me; indeed, I was thinking of him when I called Boston "The City of Kind Hearts."

我的手边，要我拍拍它，给它一块糖吃。

  我还记得那个沙滩，我生平第一次有机会在海边的沙滩上玩耍。和布瑞斯特海滨松软而尖利、混着海草和贝壳的沙子有很大不同的是，这里的沙子坚硬而光滑。恩迪科特先生告诉我，许多从波士顿起航开往欧洲的大轮船都要经过这里。从此以后，我又多次见到他，他一直是我的好朋友。实际上，我是想到了他，才把波士顿叫作"仁爱之城"的。

CHAPTER X

JUST before the Perkins Institution closed for the summer, it was arranged that my teacher and I should spend our vacation at Brewster, on Cape Cod, with our dear friend, Mrs. Hopkins. I was delighted, for my mind was full of the prospective joys and of the wonderful stories I had heard about the sea.

My most vivid recollection of that summer is the ocean. I had always lived far inland, and had never had so much as a whiff of salt air; but I had read in a big book called "Our World" a description of the ocean which filled me with wonder and an intense longing to touch the mighty sea and feel it roar. So my little heart leaped with eager excitement when I knew that my wish was at last to be realized.

No sooner had I been helped into my bathing-suit than I sprang out upon the warm sand and without thought of fear plunged into the cool water. I felt the great billows rock and sink. The buoyant motion of the water filled me with an exquisite, quivering joy. Suddenly my ecstasy gave place to terror; for my foot struck against a rock and the next instant there was a rush of water over my head. I thrust out my hands to grab some support, I clutched at the water and at the seaweed which the waves tossed in my face. But all my frantic efforts were in vain. The waves

第10章　和大海亲密接触

就在帕金斯学校快要放暑假以前，莎莉文老师和我们的好朋友霍普金斯夫人筹划好了到科德角的布鲁斯特海滨去度假。我兴奋极了，脑海里充满了期待的喜悦，以及我所听到的有关大海的各种有趣的故事。

那个夏天，我印象最深的是大海。我一直生活在内陆，从没有机会接近海洋，当然不能尽情地呼吸咸咸的空气。不过我曾在一本很厚的书《我们的世界》中，读到过有关大海的描述，那时我就对海洋充满了好奇，渴望触摸大海，感受它的汹涌波涛。当我知道自己的夙愿就要实现时，我幼小的心因激动而狂跳不已。

在她们的帮助下，我换好了游泳衣，迫不及待地在温暖的沙滩上狂奔起来，一点恐惧都没有，就跳进了冰冷的海水中。我感受到了巨浪的起伏。海水的浮力让我体味到了极其强烈的震撼。由于我的脚撞上了一块岩石，随后一个浪头打在我头上，我的情绪突然由狂喜瞬间变成了恐惧。我伸出双手，试图抓住什么，可是抓到手的只有海水和一些缠绕在我脸旁的海草。我所有的努力都属徒劳。海浪看起来要与我开玩笑，在它们的嬉笑中，我被从这里

seemed to be playing a game with me, and tossed me from one to another in their wild frolic.

It was fearful!The good, firm earth had slipped from my feet, and everything seemed shut out from this strange, all-enveloping element-life, air, warmth, and love.

At last, however, the sea, as if weary of its new toy, threw me back on the shore, and in another instant I was clasped in my teacher's arms. Oh, the comfort of the long, tender embrace! As soon as I had recovered from my panic sufficiently to say anything, I demanded: "Who put salt in the water?"

After I had recovered from my first experience in the water, I thought it great fun to sit on a big rock in my bathing-suit and feel wave after wave dash against the rock, sending up a shower of spray which quite covered me. I felt the pebbles rattling as the waves threw their ponderous weight against the shore; the whole beach seemed racked by their terrific onset, and the air throbbed with their pulsations. The breakers would swoop back to gather themselves for a

抛到那里。

真是太可怕了！刚开始的那种好感不复存在；坚实的土地从我的脚下溜开了，生命、空气、温情、爱——在这个陌生的封闭的环境中，这些似乎全都被关在门外。

最终，大海似乎对我这个新的玩物厌倦了，把我抛上了

海伦、莎莉文、马克·吐温（坐者）和劳伦斯·赫顿于1902年的合影

岸边。随后几乎是同时，我被莎莉文老师紧紧地抱在了怀里。哦，多么永恒不变的温暖怀抱啊！我一从恐惧中恢复过来能说话的时候，就问："是谁把盐放在海水里的？"

当我从第一次下海的经历中恢复过来以后，我再也不敢下海了，只是穿着游泳衣，坐在礁石上，感受海浪一个接一个冲击岩石。海浪溅起的浪花向我袭来，我感觉小鹅卵石在浪花的猛烈拍击下不断地滚动。整个海岸似乎要被这强大的攻势摧毁了，连空气也有节奏地颤抖着。那些被阻断的海浪返回后重新聚拢来，准备更猛烈的反扑。当我感受到了海浪的冲击和呼啸声时，

mightier leap, and I clung to the rock, tense, fascinated, as I felt the dash and roar of the rushing sea!

I could never stay long enough on the shore. The tang of the untainted, fresh and free sea air was like a cool, quieting thought, and the shells and pebbles and the seaweed with tiny living creatures attached to it never lost their fascination for me.

One day, Miss Sullivan attracted my attention to a strange object which she had captured basking in the chilly water. It was a great horseshoe crab-the first one I had ever seen. I felt of him and thought it strange that he should carry his house on his back. It suddenly occurred to me that he might make a delightful pet; so I seized him by the tail with both hands and carried him home. This feat pleased me highly, as his body was very heavy, and it took all my strength to drag him half a mile. I would not leave Miss Sullivan in peace until she had put the crab in a trough near the well where I was confident he would be secure.

But the next morning I went to the trough, and lo, he had disappeared! Nobody knew where he had gone, or how he had escaped. My disappointment was bitter at the time; but little by little I came to realize that it was not kind or wise to force this poor dumb creature out of his element, and after awhile I felt happy in the thought that perhaps he had returned to the sea.

死死地扒住岩石，只感到一阵紧张和眩晕！

我从来没有在海边待过如此长的时间，那种纯净、清新而自由的空气可以令人变得更清醒和更冷静。对我来说，贝壳、鹅卵石、海草以及那些微小的生灵总是具有无限的吸引力。

一天，莎莉文老师拿着的一个东西吸引了我的注意力，当时它正在水里晒太阳，被莎莉文老师捉住了。那是我从未见过的马蹄蟹，我用手去摸它，心想马蹄蟹怎么会把房子背在背上呢？突然，在我的脑海中产生了要把它当作宠物来养的想法。于是我双手抓着它往回拖。尽管马蹄蟹很重，我还是用尽了全身力气拖着它走了大约一里半路，这才到我住的地方。我一直缠着莎莉文老师，直到她把马蹄蟹放在我确信安全的井旁的水槽里，我这才消停。

可是，第二天早上当我去水槽边的时候，马蹄蟹不见了！没有人知道它跑到哪里去了，也没有人知道它是如何溜走的。我的失望瞬间转成了痛苦。但是，渐渐地我也认识到把那可怜的、不会说话的家伙从它自己的环境中隔离开来，是既不仁义又不明智的做法。片刻之后，我想它大概又回到大海里去了吧，于是心情又好转起来。

CHAPTER XI

IN the Autumn I returned to my Southern home with a heart full of joyous memories. As I recall that visit North I am filled with wonder at the richness and variety of the experiences that cluster about it. It seems to have been the beginning of everything. The treasures of a new, beautiful world were laid at my feet, and I took in pleasure and information at every turn. I lived myself into all things. I was never still a moment; my life was as full of motion as those little insects which crowd a whole existence into one brief day.

I had met many people who talked with me by spelling into my hand, and thought in joyous symphony leaped up to meet thought, and behold, a miracle had been wrought! The barren places between my mind and the minds of others blossomed like the rose.

I spent the autumn months with my family at our summer cottage, on a mountain about fourteen miles from Tuscumbia. It was called Fern Quarry, because near it there was a limestone quarry, long since abandoned. Three frolicsome little streams ran through it from springs in the rocks above, leaping here and tumbling there in laughing cascades wherever the rocks tried to bar their way. The opening

第11章　山间秋季

秋天的时候，我带着愉快的记忆回到了南方老家。每当我回想起这次北方之旅，与此相关的丰富而又多彩的经历就会充满我的脑海。一切似乎都重新开始了，一个清新美丽的世界展现在我的脚下，我满怀喜悦和憧憬地走向人生的每一个转折。我用整个身心来感受世界万物，没有片刻的闲暇。就像那些朝生夕死的小昆虫把一生安排在一天之内一样，我的日程也被各种活动安排得满满的。

我会见了许多人，他们都把字写在我手中来与我交谈，我们的思想产生了共鸣，这真是人间奇迹！在我的心灵和他人的心灵之间的那片不毛之地开满了玫瑰花。

那年秋季，我和家人一道待在离塔斯坎比亚大约14英里的一座山上的小房子里。小房子名叫凤尾草石矿，因为它附近有一座石灰石矿而得名，不过该矿早已被废弃。从山上岩石流下来的泉水汇成三条小溪，穿越其间，溪水蜿蜒前进，遇有突起的岩石便形成一个个欢乐的小瀑布。空旷的地方满是凤尾草，石灰岩被遮得严严实实，有些地方甚至把小溪也盖住了。山上其余

was filled with ferns which completely covered the beds of limestone and in places hid the streams. The rest of the mountain was thickly wooded. Here were great oaks and splendid evergreens with trunks like mossy pillars, from the branches of which hung garlands of ivy and mistletoe, and persimmon trees, the odour of which pervaded every nook and corner of the wood-an illusive, fragrant something that made the heart glad. In places, the wild muscadine and scuppernong vines stretched from tree to tree, making arbours which were always full of butterflies and buzzing insects. It was delightful to lose ourselves in the green hollows of that tangled wood in the late afternoon, and to smell the cool, delicious odours that came up from the earth at the close of day.

Our cottage was a sort of rough camp, beautifully situated on the top of the mountain among oaks and pines. The small rooms were arranged on each side of a long open hall. Round the house was a wide piazza, where the mountain winds blew, sweet with all wood-scents. We lived on the piazza most of the time-

海伦从拉德克利夫学院毕业时身穿学位服的照片（1904年）

部分是茂密的树木，这里有高大的橡树和枝繁叶茂的常青树，树干上仿佛长满了青苔，常春藤和槲寄生从树枝上倒垂下来。树林的每一个角落都弥漫着柿子树的香气，这种芳香令人有些兴奋。有些地方，野生的圆葡萄和美卡珀农葡萄枝从这棵树上攀附到那棵树上，形成纵横交错的藤架，藤架间全是彩蝶和嗡嗡叫的昆虫。对我们来说，傍晚时分沉浸在林木缠绕的山谷之中，闻着来自泥土的清爽宜人的气味，是最惬意的时刻。

我们的小房子只是简易的房舍，但却巧妙地镶嵌在山顶上的橡树和松树丛中。中间是一个开放的大长廊，两侧盖着小房子。环绕房子四周的则是一个宽阔的广场，每当山风吹过，各种树的香味就会弥漫其间。我们的大部分时间是在广场上度过的，在那里工作、吃饭、做游戏。后门旁边有一棵又高又大的白胡桃树，树周围砌有石阶。屋前的树离我们很近，以至于我伸手就可以摸到树干，可以感觉到风在摇动树枝，或者秋风吹落树叶。

很多人来这里看望我们。晚上，篝火旁集聚着一大堆男人，他们整小时

there we worked, ate and played. At the back door there was a great butternut tree, round which the steps had been built, and in front the trees stood so close that I could touch them and feel the wind shake their branches, or the leaves twirl downward in the autumn blast.

Many visitors came to Fern Quarry. In the evening, by the campfire, the men played cards and whiled away the hours in talk and sport. They told stories of their wonderful feats with fowl, fish, and quadruped-how many wild ducks and turkeys they had shot, what "savage trout" they had caught, and how they had bagged the craftiest foxes, outwitted the most clever'possums, and overtaken the fleetest deer, until I thought that surely the lion, the tiger, the bear, and the rest of the wild tribe would not be able to stand before these wily hunters. "To-morrow to the chase!" was their good-night shout as the circle of merry friends broke up for the night. The men slept in the hall outside our door, and I could feel the deep breathing of the dogs and the hunters as they lay on their improvised beds.

At dawn I was awakened by the smell of coffee, the rattling of guns, and the heavy footsteps of the men as they strode about, promising themselves the greatest luck of the season. I could also feel the stamping of the horses, which they had ridden out from town and hitched under the trees, where they stood all night, neighing loudly, impatient to be off. At last the men mounted, and, as they say in the old songs, away went the steeds with bridles ringing and whips cracking and hounds racing ahead, and away went the champion hunters "with hark and whoop

的打牌、聊天、比赛。他们讲自己的打猎、捉鱼等引人入胜的故事，讲打了多少只野鸭和火鸡，捉住的鲑鱼如何凶猛，怎样用口袋捉狡猾透顶的狐狸，怎样用计捉住灵敏的松鼠，如何出其不意地捉住跑得飞快的鹿。这些讲述让我完全相信，在这些老谋深算的猎人面前，狮子、老虎、狗熊以及其他野生动物都无法生存。"明天猎场上见！"这是猎人们对围成圆圈的朋友晚安道别的话。这些人就睡在我们屋外走廊的大厅里，我在屋里甚至可以感觉到猎狗的叫声和临时搭建的床铺上的猎人的鼾声。

拂晓时分，我便被咖啡的香味、猎枪的撞击声以及猎人们咚咚的脚步声吵醒，猎手们互相祝福在这个季节里能够碰到好运。我甚至能感觉到马蹄踩踏的声音。这些马是猎人们从城里骑来的，拴在树上过了一整夜，到了早晨则大声嘶鸣着，不耐烦地准备出发。最后，猎人们终于纵身上马出发了，就像古老的民歌中所唱的："带着铃铛的骏马飞驰，马鞭声声，猎犬在前，猎人就要出征了！"

快到中午的时候，我们开始做准备烧烤的野餐。先在地上挖好的深坑里点上火，架上又粗又长的树枝，在上面放上肉块，并且不停地转动着。黑仆蹲在篝火旁边，用长长的枝条驱赶苍蝇。餐桌还未摆好，烤肉的香味就让我感觉饥肠辘辘。

and wild halloo!"

Later in the morning we made preparations for a barbecue. A fire was kindled at the bottom of a deep hole in the ground, big sticks were laid crosswise at the top, and meat was hung from them and turned on spits. Around the fire squatted negroes, driving away the flies with long branches. The savoury odour of the meat made me hungry long before the tables were set.

When the bustle and excitement of preparation was at its height, the hunting party made its appearance, struggling in by twos and threes, the men hot and weary, the horses covered with foam, and the jaded hounds panting and dejected-and not a single kill! Every man declared that he had seen at least one deer, and that the animal had come very close; but however hotly the dogs might pursue the game, however well the guns might be aimed, at the snap of the trigger there was not a deer in sight. They had been as fortunate as the little boy who said he came very near seeing a rabbit-he saw his tracks. The party soon forgot its disappointment, however, and we sat down, not to venison, but to a tamer feast of veal and roast pig.

One summer I had my pony at Fern Quarry. I called him Black Beauty, as I had just read the book, and he resembled his namesake in every way, from his glossy black coat to the white star on his forehead. I spent many of my happiest hours on his back. Occasionally, when it was quite safe, my teacher would let go the leading-rein, and the pony sauntered on or stopped at his sweet will to eat grass or

正当匆忙而又刺激的准备达到高潮时，打猎的人们现身了，或者两个或者三个，男人们都浑身燥热而又疲倦，马嘴里也吐着白沫儿，疲惫的猎狗喘着粗气——瞧那沮丧的样子，简直没有一点儿杀手的样子！每个人都自称说至少看见了一只鹿，而且那个家伙离得非常近，眼看猎犬就要追上，他们举枪瞄准，然而就在扣动扳机时，那头鹿却突然从视野中消失了。他们的运气简直就像童话里只看见兔子足迹而说看见了兔子的小男孩。很快，猎人们忘记了令他们不愉快的事情，我们围坐在一起，不过端上来的是烤牛肉和烤猪肉，而不是鹿肉，谁让他们打不到鹿呢！

有一年夏天，我在凤尾草石矿养了一匹小马。我叫它"黑美人"，这是我刚看完的一本书的名字。这匹马和书里的那匹马很相似，从一身黑缎子似的毛到额上的白星都很相似。我经常骑在它背上，度过了许多愉快的时光。有时马温驯时，莎莉文老师就把缰绳松开，马就可自由漫步，在小路旁吃草，或者咬狭窄的路旁小树上的叶子。

上午我不想骑马时，就和莎莉文老师吃过早餐后到树林中去散步，让自己迷失在树林和葡萄藤之间，那里除了牛马踏出的小路以外没有其他路。我们经常遇到灌木丛挡路，只好绕道而行。归来时，我们总要带回几大束桂花、秋麒麟草、凤尾草以及其他许多南方特有的花草。

nibble the leaves of the trees that grew beside the narrow trail.

On mornings when I did not care for the ride, my teacher and I would start after breakfast for a ramble in the woods, and allow ourselves to get lost amid the trees and vines, and with no road to follow except the paths made by cows and horses. Frequently we came upon impassable thickets which forced us to take a roundabout way. We always returned to the cottage with armfuls of laurel, goldenrod, ferns, and gorgeous swamp-flowers such as grow only in the South.

Sometimes I would go with Mildred and my little cousins to gather persimmons. I did not eat them; but I loved their fragrance and enjoyed hunting for them in the leaves and grass. We also went nutting, and I helped them open the chestnut burrs and break the shells of hickory-nuts and walnuts-the big, sweet walnuts!

At the foot of the mountain there was a railroad, and the children watched the trains whiz by. Sometimes a terrific whistle brought us to the steps, and Mildred told me in great excitement that a cow or a horse had strayed on the track.

About a mile distant, there was a trestle spanning a deep gorge. It was very difficult to walk over, the ties were wide apart and so narrow that one

有时，我会和妹妹米尔德里德及表姐妹们去摘柿子。我不吃柿子，但我喜欢柿子的香味，喜欢在草丛和树叶堆里找它们。我们也去采野果，我帮她们剥栗子

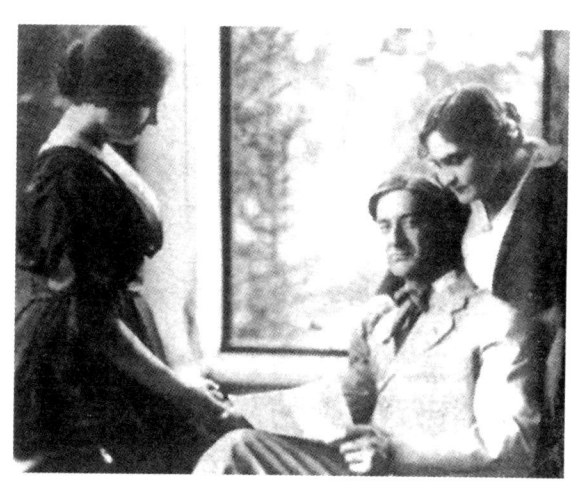

海伦和莎莉文老师及其丈夫梅西在一起，海伦正用手语和他们交谈

皮，砸山核桃和胡桃的硬壳，那胡桃真是又大又甜！

山脚下有一条铁路，孩子们常常站在旁边观看呼啸的火车疾驰而过。有时火车那令人恐怖的鸣叫声会吓得我们停住脚步。米尔德里德激动地告诉我，一头牛或马停在铁轨上了，对火车的鸣叫一点都不害怕。

大约一里远的地方，有一个很深的峡谷，上面有一座高架桥。人们很难穿越它，枕木的间隔很大，必须要小心翼翼才行，那样子就像踩着刀尖一样。我从来没有走过这座桥。直到有一天，米尔德里德、莎莉文老师带着我在树林中迷了路，我们转了好几个小时也没有找到路。突然，米尔德里德用小手指着前面，高声喊道："那就是高架桥了！"其实，我们宁愿走其他的小路，也不愿过这座桥，但由于时间很晚，天色正在变暗，高架桥是一条回家的近道。我不得不用脚尖试探那些枕木，我起初还不害怕，走得也还很

felt as if one were walking on knives. I had never crossed it until one day Mildred, Miss Sullivan and I were lost in the woods, and wandered for hours without finding a path. Suddenly Mildred pointed with her little hand and exclaimed, "There's the trestle!" We would have taken any way rather than this; but it was late and growing dark, and the trestle was a short cut home. I had to feel for the rails with my toe; but I was not afraid, and got on very well, until all at once there came a faint "puff, puff" from the distance.

"I see the train!" cried Mildred, and in another minute it would have been upon us had we not climbed down upon the crossbraces while it rushed over our heads. I felt the hot breath from the engine on my face, and the smoke and ashes almost choked us. As the train rumbled by, the trestle shook and swayed until I thought we should be dashed to the chasm below.

With the utmost difficulty we regained the track. Long after dark we reached home and found the cottage empty; the family were all out hunting for us.

稳。突然，从远处隐隐约约地传来了"噗、噗"的声音。

"火车来了！"米尔德里德喊道。要不是我们立即伏在十字交叉柱上，火车很可能从我们的脑袋顶上碾过。我感到迎面扑来的火车喷出的热气，煤烟和煤灰呛得我们几乎要窒息。火车疾驰而去，高架桥不停地震动，我们好像要被抛进下面的深谷里。

我们费了九牛二虎之力，重新爬了上来。天色已经很晚的时候，我们才回到家，屋里空无一人，他们全都出去寻找我们了。

CHAPTER XII

AFTER my first visit to Boston, I spent almost every winter in the North. Once I went on a visit to a New England village with its frozen lakes and vast snow fields. It was then that I had opportunities such as had never been mine to enter into the treasures of the snow.

I recall my surprise on discovering that a mysterious hand had stripped the trees and bushes, leaving only here and there a wrinkled leaf. The birds had flown, and their empty nests in the bare trees were filled with snow. Winter was on hill and field. The earth seemed benumbed by his icy touch and the very spirits of the trees had withdrawn to their roots, and there, curled up in the dark, lay fast asleep. All life seemed to have ebbed away, and even when the sun shone the day was shrunk and cold, as if her veins were sapless and old, and she rose up decrepitly for a last dim look at earth and sea. The withered grass and the bushes were transformed into a forest of icicles.

Then came a day when the chill air portended a snowstorm. We rushed out-of-doors to feel the first few tiny flakes descending. Hour by hour the flakes dropped silently, softly from their airy height to the earth, and the country became more

第12章 洁白的冰雪世界

自从我第一次去波士顿之后，我几乎每年的冬天都在北方度过。有一次，我拜访了新英格兰的一个小村庄，见到了封冻的湖泊和白雪皑皑的原野。直到那时，我才有机会走进洁白的冰雪世界，领略那里的无穷奥秘。

我惊讶地发现，一只神秘的怪手剥去了树木和灌木丛的外衣，只剩下零星的几片枯叶。鸟儿飞走了，光秃秃的树上留下了堆满积雪的空鸟巢。山和大地都显现出冬天的特色来，覆盖着冰碴的大地看起来有些麻木，树木的精灵也已龟缩到根部，在那里蜷缩着、熟睡着，一切生命似乎都已消失。甚至在太阳照耀的白天，天气也异常的寒冷，仿佛它的血管已经枯萎衰老，它软弱无力地爬起来，只为朦胧地最后看一眼这个冰冷的世界。枯萎的草和灌木则变成了冰柱的世界。

有一天，寒冷的空气预示着将有一场暴风雪来临。我们冲出屋子，用手去接住那最先飘落下来的小雪花，连续几个小时的雪花无声无息地从高空飘向地面。整个原野变得平而又平。白雪掊严了世界，清晨起来，人们几乎分辨不出村庄的原貌了。所有的道路都被白雪覆盖，看不到一个可以辨认道路

and more level. A snowy night closed upon the world, and in the morning one could scarcely recognize a feature of the landscape. All the roads were hidden, not a single landmark was visible, only a waste of snow with trees rising out of it.

In the evening a wind from the northeast sprang up, and the flakes rushed hither and thither in furious mêlée. Around the great fire we sat and told merry tales, and frolicked, and quite forgot that we were in the midst of a desolate solitude, shut in from all communication with the outside world. But during the night, the fury of the wind increased to such a degree that it thrilled us with a vague terror. The rafters creaked and strained, and the branches of the trees surrounding the house rattled and beat against the windows, as the winds rioted up and down the country.

On the third day after the beginning of the storm the snow ceased. The sun broke through the clouds and shone upon a vast, undulating white plain. High mounds, pyramids heaped in fantastic shapes, and impenetrable drifts lay scattered in every direction.

Narrow paths were shoveled through the drifts. I put on my cloak and hood and went out. The air stung my cheeks like fire. Half walking in the paths, half working our way though the lesser drifts, we succeeded in reaching a pine grove just outside a broad pasture. The trees stood motionless and white like figures in a marble frieze. There was no odour of pine-needles. The rays of the sun fell upon the trees, so that the twigs sparkled like diamonds and dropped in showers when we touched them. So dazzling was the light, it penetrated even the darkness that

的标志来，唯有光秃秃的树林矗立在雪地里。

傍晚，一阵狂风突然从东北方向刮过来，把积雪掀起了数米高。我们一家人围坐在熊熊的火炉旁，讲故事、做游戏，完全忘却了自己正处于与外界隔绝的孤独之中。但是到了深夜，风刮得如此大，以至于我们都感到有种莫名的恐惧。屋檐嘎嘎作响，围绕着屋子的大树树枝晃动着，拍打着窗户，发出可怕的声音。

暴风雪一直下了三天才停下来。太阳从云层中钻出来，照耀在广阔起伏的白色平原上，雪堆的形状非常怪异，有圆形的、锥形的，那些无法移动的漂移物则散乱开来。

家人在雪地里铲出一条狭窄的小路，我披上头巾和斗篷来到户外。寒风刺痛了我的脸颊。我和莎莉文老师先走一段小路，然后又穿行到小雪堆中，最后成功地到达了一处开阔的草场旁的松林里。松树在雪中静立着，白色的外表就像是大理石雕成一样，没有了松叶芬芳的气味。阳光照射在树上，树枝就好像钻石在闪光，当我们触碰的时候，积雪就像雨点一样洒落下来。光线太刺眼了，它甚至穿透了蒙在我眼睛上的那一层黑暗。

日子一天天地过去，积雪渐渐地融化，但在它还没有完全消失前，另一场暴风雪又来了，以至于我整个冬天都似乎感觉踩不着土地。树木上的冰

veils my eyes.

As the days wore on, the drifts gradually shrunk, but before they were wholly gone another storm came, so that I scarcely felt the earth under my feet once all winter. At intervals the trees lost their icy covering, and the bulrushes and underbrush were bare; but the lake lay frozen and hard beneath the sun.

Our favourite amusement during that winter was tobogganing. In places the shore of the lake rises abruptly from the water's edge. Down these steep slopes we used to coast. We would get on our toboggan, a boy would give us a shove, and off we went! Plunging through drifts, leaping hollows, swooping down upon the lake, we would shoot across its gleaming surface to the opposite bank. What joy! What exhilarating madness! For one wild, glad moment we snapped the chain that binds us to earth, and joining hands with the winds we felt ourselves divine.

凌偶尔会融化，芦苇和矮草丛都枯萎了，但是湖面即使在阳光下也始终冰冷坚硬。

  冬天，我们最喜欢的娱乐是滑雪橇。湖岸由于结冰而形成地势陡峭的坡，我们就常常从湖岸上滑下来。我们在雪橇上坐好，男孩子使劲一推，我们就可以向下俯冲！穿过积雪，跃过洼地，滑向湖面，我们可以穿过闪闪发光的湖面滑到湖的对岸。太好玩了！多么有趣的游戏啊！在那疯狂的、快乐的瞬间，我们紧紧抓住绳链，用双手与冬天连接起来。我们仿佛脱离了大地，张开双臂，乘风飞翔。

CHAPTER XIII

IT was in the spring of 1890 that I learned to speak. The impulse to utter audible sounds had always been strong within me. I used to make noises, keeping one hand on my throat while the other hand felt the movements of my lips. I was pleased with anything that made a noise, and liked to feel the cat purr and the dog bark. I also liked to keep my hand on a singer's throat, or on a piano when it was being played.

Before I lost my sight and hearing, I was fast learning to talk, but after my illness it was found that I had ceased to speak because I could not hear. I used to sit in my mother's lap all day long and keep my hands on her face because it amused me to feel the motions of her lips; and I moved my lips, too, although I had forgotten what talking was.

My friends say that I laughed and cried naturally, and for awhile I made many sounds and word-elements, not because they were a means of communication, but because the need of exercising my vocal organs was imperative. There was, however, one word the meaning of which I still remembered, water. I pronounced it "wa-wa". Even this became less and less intelligible until the time when Miss

第13章 我要说话

1890年春天，我开始学习说话。对我来说，发出能够听得到的声音，一直是我强烈的愿望。我常常把一只手放在喉咙上，用另一只手感受嘴唇的运动，这样发出一些声音来。任何能发声的东西都让我兴奋，我喜欢感受猫的咕噜、狗的吠叫，我也喜欢把手放在歌手的喉咙处，或者正在弹奏的钢琴上。

在失去听力和视力之前，我学说话很快。可是自从我得了病之后，由于耳朵听不见了，所以我就不会说话了。我整天坐在母亲的膝上，小手摸着母亲的脸颊。母亲的嘴唇一开一合，我觉得很好玩。尽管我早已忘了说话是怎么回事，但我也学着蠕动自己的嘴唇。

家里人都说，我哭和笑的声音非常自然。有一段时间，我嘴里还能够发出很多声音或者单词，但这不是在和别人交流，而是不自觉地出于练习发音器官的需要。然而，有一个词，在我发病后依然能记得，那就是"水"（water），我经常发成"wa……wa"的声音，但是这个字慢慢地变得越来越模糊了。直到莎莉文老师教我时，我不再发这个音，而改用手指拼写。

Sullivan began to teach me. I stopped using it only after I had learned to spell the word on my fingers.

I had known for a long time that the people about me used a method of communication different from mine; and even before I knew that a deaf child could be taught to speak, I was conscious of dissatisfaction with the means of communication I already possessed. One who is entirely dependent on the manual alphabet has always a sense of restraint, of narrowness. This feeling began to agitate me with a vexing, forward-reaching sense of a lack that should be filled. My thought would often rise and beat up like birds against the wind; and I persisted in using my lips and voice. Friends tried to discourage this tendency, fearing lest it would lead to disappointment. But I persisted, and an accident soon occurred which resulted in the breaking down of this great barrier-I heard the story of Ragnhild Kaata.

In 1890 Mrs. Lamson, who had been one of Laura Bridgman's teachers, and who had just returned from a visit to Norway and Sweden, came to see me, and told me of Ragnhild Kaata, a deaf and blind girl in Norway who had actually been taught to speak. Mrs. Lamson had scarcely finished

我早就知道，周围的人都用与我不同的方式交流，甚至在我知道失聪的孩子也可以学会说话之前，我就已经对自己的交流方法感到不满意了。一个人完全靠手语与别人交流，总是要受到许多约束和限制的。这使我产生了厌烦的感觉，我常常急得像小鸟逆风扑打翅膀那样，想用嘴唇和嗓子发音。家人想方设

马克·吐温正在家中打台球

法阻止我的这种努力，因为他们担心我学不好会失望。但我坚持着，一个偶然的机会，我听到了瑞格海德·卡达的故事，我更是决心突破说话的障碍。

1890年，曾教过劳拉·布里奇曼的拉姆森夫人，从挪威和瑞典访问归来后来看望我。她告诉我，挪威有一个叫瑞格海德·卡达的女孩子，她又盲又聋，但是已经学会了说话。还没等她讲完，我的热血就有些沸腾，暗下决心也要学会说话。直到莎莉文老师带着我去找贺瑞斯曼恩学校的校长莎拉·富勒小姐，求她帮我、教我，我才满意地安定下来。这位可爱而善良的女士答应亲自教我。1890年3月26日，我们开始学说话了。

富勒小姐的方法是这样的:她一边发音，一边把我的手轻轻地放在她的

telling me about this girl's success before I was on fire with eagerness. I resolved that I, too, would learn to speak. I would not rest satisfied until my teacher took me, for advice and assistance, to Miss Sarah Fuller, principal of the Horace Mann School. This lovely, sweet-natured lady offered to teach me herself, and we began the twenty-sixth of March, 1890.

Miss Fuller's method was this: she passed my hand lightly over her face, and let me feel the position of her tongue and lips when she made a sound. I was eager to imitate every motion and in an hour had learned six elements of speech: M, P, A, S, T, I. Miss Fuller gave me eleven lessons in all. I shall never forget the surprise and delight I felt when I uttered my first connected sentence, "It is warm." True, they were broken and stammering syllables; but they were human speech. My soul, conscious of new strength, came out of bondage, and was reaching through those broken symbols of speech to all knowledge and all faith.

No deaf child who has earnestly tried to speak the words which he has never heard-to come out of the prison of silence, where no tone of love, no song of bird, no strain of music ever pierces the stillness-can forget the thrill of surprise, the joy of discovery which came over him when he uttered his first word. Only such a one can appreciate the eagerness with which I talked to my toys, to stones, trees, birds and dumb animals, or the delight I felt when at my call Mildred ran to me or my dogs obeyed my commands. It is an unspeakable boon to me to be able to speak in winged words that need no interpretation. As I talked, happy thoughts fluttered up

脸上，让我感觉到她的舌头和嘴唇是怎么动的。我很用心地模仿她的每一个动作，不到一小时就学会了M、P、A、S、T、I这6个字母的发音。虽然富勒小姐总共只给我上了11堂课，但是我一辈子也不会忘记，当我第一次连贯地说出"天气很暖和"这个句子时，我是多么的惊奇和兴奋！当然，这个句子是断断续续且口吃似的发出来的几个音节，但这毕竟是人类的语言。我意识到有一种新的力量，它将我的灵魂从奴役中解放出来，并用这些断断续续的语言记号，去掌握完整的知识，获得信仰。

当失聪的孩子迫切地想用嘴说出那些他从来没有听过的字，想从寂寞的、没有爱的音调、没有鸟的声音、没有美妙的音乐的囚牢中走出来时，他不会忘记那种兴奋：当他说出第一个字时，那种狂喜的感觉就像电流一样涌遍全身。只有这样的人才知道，我是怀着多么热切的心情与玩具、石头、树木、鸟儿以及不会讲话的动物说话的；也只有这样的人才知道，我叫妹妹米尔德里德跑过来时的那份快乐，才知道我的小狗能听从我的命令时那种喜悦。对我来说，用长有翅膀的语言说话而不需要别人帮我翻译，是一种无以言说的幸福！我说话的时候，快乐的想法就从口中流露出来，不再需要用手指费劲地挣扎着表述了。

但是，千万不要以为在这样短的时间内，我真的就能说话了。我只是

out of my words that might perhaps have struggled in vain to escape my fingers.

But it must not be supposed that I could really talk in this short time. I had learned only the elements of speech. Miss Fuller and Miss Sullivan could understand me, but most people would not have understood one word in a hundred. Nor is it true that, after I had learned these elements, I did the rest of the work myself. But for Miss Sullivan's genius, untiring perseverance and devotion, I could not have progressed as far as I have toward natural speech.

In the first place, I laboured night and day before I could be understood even by my most intimate friends; in the second place, I needed Miss Sullivan's assistance constantly in my efforts to articulate each sound clearly and to combine all sounds in a thousand ways. Even now, she calls my attention every day to mispronounced words.

All teachers of the deaf know what this means, and only they can appreciate the peculiar difficulties with which I had to contend. In reading my teacher's lips, I was wholly dependent on my fingers: I had to use the sense of touch in catching the vibrations of the throat, the movements of the mouth and the expression of the face; and often this sense was at fault. In such cases I was forced to repeat the words or sentences, sometimes for hours, until I felt the proper ring in my own voice. My work was practice, practice, practice. Discouragement and weariness cast me down frequently; but the next moment the thought that I should soon be at home and show my loved ones what I had accomplished, spurred me on, and I

学会了字母的发音，富勒小姐和莎莉文老师能够明白我的意思，而其余的大多数人能听懂的还不到百分之一。也不要以为我学会了这些基本语音以后，其余的工作都是我自己完成的。如果没有莎莉文老师的天才、坚持不懈和投入，我是不会如此迅速地学会正常的语言的。

最初，我夜以继日地苦练，才使我最亲近的朋友能听懂我的意思。随后，在莎莉文老师的帮助下，我反反复复练习每一个字母的发音，练习各种发音的自由结合。一直到现在，她每天都会纠正我那些错误的发音。

只有从事聋哑儿童教育工作的人，才知道这一切意味着什么，也只有他们才能体会到我必须克服的巨大困难。在读老师的嘴唇的时候，我完全依靠自己的手指:我用触觉来把握她喉咙的颤动、嘴的运动和面部表情，而这种感觉经常是错误的。遇到这种情况，我就强迫自己反复练习这些词和句子，一练就是好几个小时，直到我感觉发出的音准确了才罢休。我的工作就是练习、练习、再练习。失败和疲劳常常将我绊倒，但第二天早晨一想到我将要回家向亲人展示我的成就时，我就有了勇气。我期待着他们为我的成功而欣喜。

"我妹妹能够理解我"是我战胜一切困难的坚强信念，我常常欣喜若狂地反复说道:"我再也不是哑巴了。"一想到同母亲说话、从她的嘴唇知

eagerly looked forward to their pleasure in my achievement.

"My little sister will understand me now, " was a thought stronger than all obstacles. I used to repeat ecstatically, "I am not dumb now." I could not be despondent while I anticipated the delight of talking to my mother and reading her responses from her lips. It astonished me to find how much easier it is to talk than to spell with the fingers, and I discarded the manual alphabet as a medium of communication on my part; but Miss Sullivan and a few friends still use it in speaking to me, for it is more convenient and more rapid than lip-reading.

Just here, perhaps, I had better explain our use of the manual alphabet, which seems to puzzle people who do not know us. I place my hand on the hand of the speaker so lightly as not to impede its movements. The position of the hand is as easy to feel as it is to see. I do not feel each letter any more than you see each letter separately when you read. Constant practice makes the fingers very flexible, and some of my friends spell rapidly-about as fast as an expert writes on a typewriter. The mere, spelling is, of course, no more a conscious act than it is in writing.

When I had made speech my own, I

海伦手持夹子，正在读盲文

道她做出的反应，我就感到非常快慰，不再沮丧了。当发现用嘴说话要比用手指说话更容易时，我简直惊呆了。我不再用手语和别人谈话，但莎莉文老师和一些朋友依然用这种方式同我交谈，因为手语比唇读更方便些，我理解得更快些。

在这里，也许我最好应说明一下我们盲人所使用的手语字母。那些不了解盲聋世界的人对手语感到不解。我轻轻地把手放在说话者的手上，不妨碍其运动，手的位置如同人们看到的那样很容易被觉察到。和人们不是一个个单词读书一样，我感觉到的也不是一个个的字母。由于持续性的练习，就会使手指变得很灵活，我的一些朋友字母拼写得非常快，就像熟练的打字员在打字机上打字一样。当然，用手拼写熟练之后，就像用笔写字一样，成了一种下意识的动作。

当我能用嘴说话以后，忍不住立刻要赶回家去。终于，这一幸福的时刻来到了，我踏上了归途，一路上和莎莉文老师说个不停，当然不是为了说话，而是为了在最后时刻有所提高。

could not wait to go home. At last the happiest of happy moments arrived. I had made my homeward journey, talking constantly to Miss Sullivan, not for the sake of talking, but determined to improve to the last minute.

Almost before I knew it, the train stopped at the Tuscumbia station, and there on the platform stood the whole family. My eyes fill with tears now as I think how my mother pressed me close to her, speechless and trembling with delight, taking in every syllable that I spoke, while little Mildred seized my free hand and kissed it and danced, and my father expressed his pride and affection in a big silence. It was as if Isaiah's prophecy had been fulfilled in me, "The mountains and the hills shall break forth before you into singing, and all the trees of the field shall clap their hands!"

在我反应过来以前，火车已经停在了塔斯坎比亚车站，全家人都在站台上迎接我们。现在只要一想到母亲是如何紧紧把我拥抱在怀里，兴奋得说不出一句话，全身颤抖着，倾听我发出的任何字音时，我的眼中都会溢满泪水。小妹妹米尔德里德抓住我那只空着的手，亲吻着，蹦跳着。父亲表现了自己的骄傲，静静地站在一旁。这一切真好像是以赛亚的预言在我身上得到了应验："群山为我齐声歌唱，大地上的林木为我拍手欢呼！"

CHAPTER XIV

THE winter of 1892 was darkened by one cloud in my childhood's bright sky. Joy deserted my heart, and for a long, long time I lived in doubt, anxiety, and fear. Books lost their charm for me, and even now the thought of those dreadful days chills my heart.

A little story called "The Frost King", which I wrote and sent to Mr. Anagnos, of the Perkins Institute for the Blind, was at the root of the trouble. In order to make the matter clear, I must set forth the facts connected with this episode, which justice to my teacher and to myself compels me to relate.

I wrote the story when I was at home, the autumn after I had learned to speak. We had stayed up at Fern Quarry later than usual. While we were there, Miss Sullivan described to me the beauties of the late foliage, and it seems that her descriptions revived the memory of a story, which must have been read to me and which I must have unconsciously retained. I thought then that I was "making up a story", as children say, and I eagerly sat down to write it before the ideas should slip from me. My thoughts flowed easily; I felt a sense of joy in the composition. Words and images came tripping to my finger ends, and as I thought out sentence

第14章 《霜王》事件

1892年的冬天，我孩提时代明亮的天空被笼罩了一块乌云。快乐远离了我的心灵，有很长一段时间，我生活在怀疑、忧虑和恐惧之中，书本也对我丧失了吸引力。即使到现在，那段阴霾依旧占据着我的心灵，使我一想到就不寒而栗。

我写了一篇题为《霜王》的短篇小说，寄给了帕金斯盲人学校的安纳格罗斯校长，没料到这竟然成为麻烦的祸根。为了澄清此事，我必须把事情的前后过程都写出来，这对我和莎莉文老师是应得的公平。

我在家中写的那篇小说，那是在我学会说话的那个秋天。那年夏天，我们在凤尾草石矿小屋住的时间比往年都长。当我们住在那里的时候，莎莉文老师经常给我描述秋叶的美丽，看起来她的描述使我头脑中的故事激活了，那个故事一定是以前别人读给我听的，我就不知不觉地记住了。当时我自以为是在"创作故事"，如同孩子们常说的，我渴望将它写出来，以免忘了。我的思绪如泉水般涌出来，写作让我体会到了一种快乐。我一句句的想，然后用流畅的语言将生动的形象落在笔尖上。我把它们写在了我的布莱叶纸板

after sentence, I wrote them on my braille slate. Now, if words and images came to me without effort, it is a pretty sure sign that they are not the offspring of my own mind, but stray waifs that I regretfully dismiss. At that time I eagerly absorbed everything I read without a thought of authorship, and even now I cannot be quite sure of the boundary line between my ideas and those I find in books. I suppose that is because so many of my impressions come to me through the medium of others' eyes and ears.

When the story was finished, I read it to my teacher, and I recall now vividly the pleasure I felt in the more beautiful passages, and my annoyance at being interrupted to have the pronunciation of a word corrected. At dinner it was read to the assembled family, who were surprised that I could write so well. Some one asked me if I had read it in a book.

The question surprised me very much; for I had not the faintest recollection of having had it read to me. I spoke up and said, "Oh, no, it is my story, and I have written it for Mr. Anagnos."

Accordingly I copied the story and sent it to him for his birthday. It was suggested that I should change the title from "Autumn Leaves" to "The Frost King", which I did. I carried the little story to the post office myself,

巡回演讲期间，莎莉文、海伦和一位朋友一起讨论提高演讲效果的办法

上。现在，如果有什么单词或者形象毫不费力地涌入我的脑海，那我敢断定它一定不是我想出来的，我就会懊悔地把它当作无主的遗失物而抛弃掉。但是在当时，我根本不会考虑作者的身份，而渴望吸收一切读到的东西。直到现在，我也常常分不清哪些是我自己的观点，哪些是别人的观点。我想，这是由于我的许多印象大都是通过别人的眼睛和耳朵而获得的缘故吧！

故事写完后，我读给莎莉文老师听。我现在还能回忆起自己是如何陶醉于那些精彩的段落，而被老师打断纠正发音时又是如何厌烦的。吃晚饭时，我又拿来念给全家人听，大家都惊讶不已，他们没想到我能写得这么好，也有人问我是不是从哪本书里看到的。

这个问题让我感到很奇怪，因为我根本想不起有谁给我读过这篇小说。我大声地回答说："没有人，这是我自己的小说，我要把它献给安纳格罗斯先生。"

feeling as if I were walking on air. I little dreamed how cruelly I should pay for that birthday gift.

Mr. Anagnos was delighted with "The Frost King" and published it in one of the Perkins Institution reports. This was the pinnacle of my happiness, from which I was in a little while dashed to earth. I had been in Boston only a short time when it was discovered that a story similar to "The Frost King" called "The Frost Fairies" by Miss Margaret T. Canby, had appeared before I was born in a book called "Birdie and His Friends." The two stories were so much alike in thought and language that it was evident Miss Canby's story had been read to me, and that mine was-a plagiarism. It was difficult to make me understand this; but when I did understand I was astonished and grieved. No child ever drank deeper of the cup of bitterness than I did. I had disgraced myself; I had brought suspicion upon those I loved best.

And yet how could it possibly have happened? I racked my brain until I was weary to recall anything about the frost that I had read before I wrote "The Frost King"; but I could remember nothing, except the common reference to Jack Frost, and a poem for children, "The Freaks of the Frost", and I knew I had not used that in my composition.

At first Mr. Anagnos, though deeply troubled, seemed to believe me. He was unusually tender and kind to me, and for a brief space the shadow lifted. To please him I tried not to be unhappy, and to make myself as pretty as possible for the celebration of Washington's birthday, which took place very soon after I received

随后，我重新抄写了这篇小说，他们建议我把标题《秋叶》改成《霜王》，我这样做了。然后，我将它作为生日礼物邮寄给了安纳格罗斯先生。我是亲自带着这本小说去邮局的，我感觉自己是在完成一件壮举。然而，我做梦也没有想到，我将为这件生日礼物付出的代价有多么的残酷！

安纳格罗斯先生对《霜王》非常感兴趣，把它刊登在了帕金斯盲人学校的校报上。我达到了得意的顶峰，不久我就从这顶峰栽到了地上。在我到波士顿不长时间，有人就发现，《霜王》与玛格丽特·T·坎贝尔小姐写的一篇名叫《霜仙子》的小说十分相似。早在我出世以前，这篇文章就已经收在一本名叫《小鸟和它的朋友》的书中。两个故事在内容和用词风格上都非常相像——很明显，一定有人给我读过坎贝尔小姐的小说。我的文章一定是剽窃来的。让我明白这些很困难，但当我知道问题的严重性以后，我感到既惊讶又伤心。没有任何孩子曾遭受过我的痛苦，深深的羞辱感笼罩着我，也使我最爱戴的人招致了猜忌。

这怎么可能发生呢？我绞尽脑汁，想自己在写《霜王》之前，到底读过多少关于霜的文章或书籍。但我什么都不记得，只是模模糊糊地记得有谁提到过杰克·弗罗斯特这个人，这是一首写给孩子的诗《霜的怪行》，可是在我的文章中并没有引用它们。

the sad news.

I was to be Ceres in a kind of masque given by the blind girls. How well I remember the graceful draperies that enfolded me, the bright autumn leaves that ringed my head, and the fruit and grain at my feet and in my hands, and beneath all the gaiety of the masque the oppressive sense of coming ill that made my heart heavy.

The night before the celebration, one of the teachers of the Institution had asked me a question connected with "The Frost King", and I was telling her that Miss Sullivan had talked to me about Jack Frost and his wonderful works. Something I said made her think she detected in my words a confession that I did remember Miss Canby's story of "The Frost Fairies", and she laid her conclusions before Mr. Anagnos, although I had told her most emphatically that she was mistaken.

Mr. Anagnos, who loved me tenderly, thinking that he had been deceived, turned a deaf ear to the pleadings of love and innocence. He believed, or at least suspected, that Miss Sullivan and I had deliberately stolen the bright thoughts of

虽然安纳格罗斯先生为其所困，但他最初还是很相信我的，甚至对我还异乎寻常地温和友善，这总算暂时驱散了我心头的乌云，但很快事情又有了变化。在学校举行庆祝华盛顿诞辰的活动时，为了使他高兴，我极力掩饰自己的不快乐，还尽力把自己打扮得漂亮些，但不久我就得到了那个不幸的消息。

海伦和莎莉文在铁路月台上的合影

在庆祝活动上，学校的孩子们演出了假面舞剧，我则带上了谷神的面具。我还记得精美的服装把我包裹得严严实实的，用秋叶编成的斑斓的花环戴在我头上，我脚上和手上也全是水果和谷物。但在欢乐的假面舞会之中，却有一种压抑的感觉深深刺痛了我。

庆祝活动的前夕，学校有一位老师问起与《霜王》相关的一个问题。我告诉她，莎莉文老师曾和我谈到过杰克·弗罗斯特和他杰出的作品。然而，我说的话竟然使她认为我承认了自己记得坎贝尔的小说《霜仙子》。虽然我一再强调她理解错了，但她还是自以为是地把她的推论告诉了安纳格罗斯先生。

another and imposed them on him to win his admiration. I was brought before a court of investigation composed of the teachers and officers of the Institution, and Miss Sullivan was asked to leave me.

Then I was questioned and cross-questioned with what seemed to me a determination on the part of my judges to force me to acknowledge that I remembered having had "The Frost Fairies" read to me. I felt in every question the doubt and suspicion that was in their minds, and I felt, too, that a loved friend was looking at me reproachfully, although I could not have put all this into words. The blood pressed about my thumping heart, and I could scarcely speak, except in monosyllables. Even the consciousness that it was only a dreadful mistake did not lessen my suffering, and when at last I was allowed to leave the room, I was dazed and did not notice my teacher's caresses, or the tender words of my friends, who said I was a brave little girl and they were proud of me.

As I lay in my bed that night, I wept as I hope few children have

海伦（中）和亚历山大·格雷厄姆·贝尔（右）与莎莉文（左下）一起交流远足的感受

对我一直都很体贴的安纳格罗斯先生认为我欺骗了他，结果无论我如何解释，他都不再相信了。他相信或至少猜疑，莎莉文老师和我故意窃取别人的名作，强塞给他，以博得他的称赞。紧接着，我被带到一个由帕金斯盲人学校的老师和行政官员组成的委员会面前，莎莉文老师也被要求离开。

然后我被迫回答他们的提问。对我来说，他们的这些问题意图就是想迫使我承认我记得有人给我读过坎贝尔的小说《霜仙子》。我感到每个问题都包含了他们头脑中的怀疑，而且我也感到那个爱我的朋友正愤恨地瞧着我，尽管我无法用语言表达出来。我的心怦怦乱跳，几乎无法说话，只能一个字一个字地说。甚至我的直觉告诉我，这纯粹是一个可怕的错误，但这丝毫不能减轻自己的痛苦。最后，当我被允许离开时，我觉得头晕目眩，根本没有留意到莎莉文老师的爱抚和朋友们的宽慰，他们说我是一个勇敢的小女孩，他们为我感到骄傲等。

当晚，我躺在自己的床上，哭得十分伤心。我感觉全身发冷，以至于心

wept. I felt so cold, I imagined I should die before morning, and the thought comforted me. I think if this sorrow had come to me when I was older, it would have broken my spirit beyond repairing. But the angel of forgetfulness has gathered up and carried away much of the misery and all of the bitterness of those sad days.

Miss Sullivan had never heard of "The Frost Fairies" or of the book in which it was published. With the assistance of Dr. Alexander Graham Bell, she investigated the matter carefully, and at last it came out that Mrs. Sophia C. Hopkins had a copy of Miss Canby's "Birdie and His Friends" in 1888, the year that we spent the summer with her at Brewster. Mrs. Hopkins was unable to find her copy; but she has told me that at that time, while Miss Sullivan was away on a vacation, she tried to amuse me by reading from various books, and although she could not remember reading "The Frost Fairies" any more than I, yet she felt sure that "Birdie and His Friends" was one of them. She explained the disappearance of the book by the fact that she had a short time before sold her house and disposed of many juvenile books, such as old schoolbooks and fairy tales, and that "Birdie and His Friends" was probably among them.

The stories had little or no meaning for me then; but the mere spelling of the strange words was sufficient to amuse a little child who could do almost nothing to amuse herself; and although I do not recall a single circumstance connected with the reading of the stories, yet I cannot help thinking that I made a great effort to

想也许天亮以前我就会死掉。这个念头倒使我安下心来。我想假如这种不幸发生在我成年以后，它一定会超出我的承受能力，而使我精神崩溃的。但是遗忘天使很快带走了我许多悲伤以及这些伤心日子里的痛苦。

莎莉文老师从未听说过《霜仙子》，也没有听过出版它的那本书。在亚历山大·格雷厄姆·贝尔博士的帮助下，莎莉文老师细心地调查了这件事情。最终结果表明，1888年，索菲亚·C·霍普金斯夫人有坎贝尔小姐的《小鸟和它的朋友》一书，而我们正是在那一年和她一起去布鲁斯特度假的。霍普金斯夫人已经无法找到那本书，但她告诉我说，当时莎莉文老师独自去度假，她就给我读各种书让我高兴。虽然她同我一样不清楚是否读过《霜仙子》，但她确信曾从《小鸟和它的朋友》中给我读过故事。她还解释了那本书消失的情况：在把布鲁斯特的那所房子卖掉之前，她处理了好多儿童读物，如小学课本、童话故事之类，《小鸟和它的朋友》或许也在那时被处理了。

当时，那个故事对我没有任何意义，但是故事中那些怪异的单词却足以引起我这个几乎没有任何其他娱乐的孩子的兴趣。尽管我不能回忆起当时讲故事的情景，但我一定费了很大气力来记住那些单词，想等老师回来后给我解释。可以肯定的是，那些单词一定深刻地印在我的脑海中，尽管很长时间

remember the words, with the intention of having my teacher explain them when she returned. One thing is certain, the language was ineffaceably stamped upon my brain, though for a long time no one knew it, least of all myself.

When Miss Sullivan came back, I did not speak to her about "The Frost Fairies" probably because she began at once to read "Little Lord Fauntleroy", which filled my mind to the exclusion of everything else. But the fact remains that Miss Canby's story was read to me once, and that long after I had forgotten it, it came back to me so naturally that I never suspected that it was the child of another mind.

In my trouble I received many messages of love and sympathy. All the friends I loved best, except one, have remained my own to the present time. Miss Canby herself wrote kindly, "Some day you will write a great story out of you own head, that will be a comfort and help to many." But this kind prophecy has never been fulfilled.

I have never played with words again for the mere pleasure of the game. Indeed, I have ever since been tortured by the fear that what I write is not my own. For a long time, when I wrote a letter, even to my mother, I was seized with a sudden feeling of terror, and I would spell the sentences over and over, to make sure that I had not read them in a book. Had it not been for the persistent encouragement of Miss Sullivan, I think I should have given up trying to write altogether.

I have read "The Frost Fairies" since, also the letters I wrote in which I used other ideas of Miss Canby's. I find in one of them, a letter to Mr. Anagnos, dated

过去了，已经没人知道这个故事，但至少我对它们还有印象。

莎莉文老师回来后，我没有跟她提起《霜仙子》，也许是因为她一回来就开始阅读《小方德诺伯爵》，我的大脑中无暇顾及其他事情。但霍普金斯夫人曾经给我读过坎贝尔小姐小说的事情我仍然记得，在我忘掉了很久以后，它很自然地浮现在我脑海里，以至于我丝毫没有怀疑它是别人的思想产物。

在那段麻烦缠身的日子里，我收到了许多对我表示同情和问候的来信。我至今都无法忘记那些最好的朋友，尤其是坎贝尔小姐。她亲自写信给我："将来总有一天，你会写出属于你自己的巨著，让许多人从中得到鼓舞和帮助。"但是，这个善意的预言却一直未能实现。

从此以后，除了做游戏之外，我再也不敢写文字了。实际上，我总是被恐惧所折磨，害怕写出来的东西不是自己的思想。很长一段时间里，当我写信时，即使是写给妈妈的，我都会被突如其来的恐惧所侵袭，我总是一遍又一遍地拼写每个句子，确保我没有在书中读到过这个句子。如果不是莎莉文老师持久的鼓励，我想我会完全放弃写作的。

后来，我再次找来《霜仙子》读了一遍，发现包括那时我写的一些信所用的字句和观点，许多都是坎贝尔小姐的观点。例如一封1891年9月29日

September 29, 1891, words and sentiments exactly like those of the book. At the time I was writing "The Frost King", and this letter, like many others, contains phrases which show that my mind was saturated with the story. I represent my teacher as saying to me of the golden autumn leaves, "Yes, they are beautiful enough to comfort us for the flight of summer"-an idea direct from Miss Canby's story.

This habit of assimilating what pleased me and giving it out again as my own appears in much of my early correspondence and my first attempts at writing. In a composition which I wrote about the old cities of Greece and Italy, I borrowed my glowing descriptions, with variations, from sources I have forgotten. I knew Mr. Anagnos's great love of antiquity and his enthusiastic appreciation of all beautiful sentiments about Italy and Greece. I therefore gathered from all the books I read every bit of poetry or of history that I thought would give him pleasure. Mr. Anagnos, in speaking of my composition on the cities, has said, "These ideas are poetic in their essence." But I do not understand how he ever thought a blind and deaf child of eleven could have invented them. Yet I cannot think that because I did not originate the ideas, my little composition is therefore quite devoid of interest. It shows me that I could express my appreciation of beautiful and poetic ideas in clear and animated language.

Those early compositions were mental gymnastics. I was learning, as all young and inexperienced persons learn, by assimilation and imitation, to put ideas into

写给安纳格罗斯先生的信，语言和情感表达与那篇小说一模一样。我写《霜王》小说、这封信以及其他许多信一样，其中的许多表述都可以看出，当时我的思想已经被这个故事渗透了。我以莎莉文老师的口吻向自己描述金黄色的秋树叶："的确，它们太美了，带给我们夏后的安逸。"而这是直接取自坎贝尔小姐小说中的句子。

在我的通信和早期尝试写作的作品中，我习惯使用那些让我感兴趣的表述，然后用我自己的表述形式写出来。在一篇描写希腊和意大利古城的文章中，我借用了一些生动而变化多端的描述，但是这些句子的出处我已经忘记了。我知道安纳格罗斯先生非常喜欢古迹，对意大利和希腊更是欣赏备至，因此我收集了我读过的所有书籍中的诗集和历史故事，摘抄了其中可以取悦他的部分内容，而安纳格罗斯先生在称赞我描写古城的作文时也说："这些观点富有诗一般的境界。"但我无法理解他竟然相信一个又盲又聋的11岁的孩子能写出这样的作品。当然，我也认为不能因为引用别人的观点，我的小文章就没有一丝价值，它表明我已经能够运用美丽而有诗意的观点以及清晰而又鲜活的文字来表达我的意境了。

早期的作品不过是我的智力体操。像所有年轻人和阅历浅的人一样，我的学习也是通过吸收、模仿而后用语言表达自己的观点。凡是在书中能引

words. Everything I found in books that pleased me I retained in my memory, consciously or unconsciously, and adapted it. The young writer, as Stevenson has said, instinctively tries to copy whatever seems most admirable, and he shifts his admiration with astonishing versatility. It is only after years of this sort of practice that even great men have learned to marshal the legion of words which come thronging through every byway of the mind.

I am afraid I have not yet completed this process. It is certain that I cannot always distinguish my own thoughts from those I read, because what I read becomes the very substance and texture of my mind. Consequently, in nearly all that I write, I produce something which very much resembles the crazy patchwork I used to make when I first learned to sew. This patchwork was made of all sorts of odds and ends-pretty bits of silk and velvet; but the coarse pieces that were not pleasant to touch always predominated.

Likewise my compositions are made up of crude notions of my own, inlaid with the brighter thoughts and riper opinions of the authors I have read. It seems to me that the great difficulty of writing is to make the language of the educated mind express our confused ideas, half feelings, half thoughts, when we are little more than bundles of instinctive tendencies. Trying to write is very much like trying to put a Chinese puzzle together. We have a pattern in mind which we wish to work out in words; but the words will not fit the spaces, or, if they do, they will not match the design. But we keep on trying because we know that others have

起我兴趣的东西，我便会自觉或不自觉地记在脑子里，转化为自己的东西。初学写作的人，正如史蒂文森说过的，本能地设法摹仿他们自己最欣赏的东西，然后潜心变化句子，以表达他的钦佩之情。这种实践需要多年的努力，即使是那些伟大的作家，也需要掌握大量的词汇，然后才能驾驭它们，自由地表达自己的思想。

恐怕直到现在我还没有完成这个过程。可以肯定的是，我常常很难严格区分哪些是我的思想，哪些又是我曾读过的别人的思想，因为我读过的东西已成为我思想的原材料，因此，从我开始学习写作以来，我所有的作品几乎都是各种思想的拼凑。这种拼凑虽然用的是旧补丁，但却饰以鲜艳的绸缎和天鹅绒；不过当摸上去时，就会发现粗布还是占了绝大部分的。

同样，我的作品包含了我自己粗浅的想法，但也夹杂着我读过的别的作者的真知灼见，这些都是我从书里得来，并记在心里的。对我来说，写作的最大难题是如何用规范的语言表达我困惑的思想，它们可能是零散的感受，也可能是断续的思想，缺乏整理与组合。呕心创作像费力猜测中国的谜语一样。我们头脑中先有一个思想的范式，这个范式需要用语言描述出来，而词语却不一定能恰如其分地表达它，或者词语能够表达出来，但是却不符合我们预先的设计。但我们一定要坚持尝试，因为我们知道其他人已经成功了，

succeeded, and we are not willing to acknowledge defeat.

"There is no way to become original, except to be born so, " says Stevenson, and although I may not be original, I hope sometime to outgrow my artificial, periwigged compositions. Then, perhaps, my own thoughts and experiences will come to the surface. Meanwhile I trust and hope and persevere, and try not to let the bitter memory of "The Frost King" trammel my efforts.

So this sad experience may have done me good and set me thinking on some of the problems of composition. My only regret is that it resulted in the loss of one of my dearest friends, Mr. Anagnos.

Since the publication of "The Story of My Life" in the Ladies' Home Journal, Mr. Anagnos has made a statement, in a letter to Mr. Macy, that at the time of " The Frost King" matter, he believed I was innocent. He says, the court of investigation before which I was brought consisted of eight people: four blind, four seeing persons. Four of them, he says, thought I knew that Miss Canby's story had been read to me, and the

既然如此，我们就不应向失败低头。

史蒂文森说："人除非有天赋，否则没有办法写出伟大的作品。"我也许不具有天赋，但我还是希望有朝一日创作出反映我个人的思想和经历的文章来。那段时间，我正是怀着这种信念和坚持不懈的努力，才抚平了《霜王》事件给我的记忆带来的痛苦。

海伦身穿白色长裙坐在椅子上读盲文书

不过，这段痛苦的经历对我也有好的一面，它让我有机会认真思考写作中的问题。当然，我唯一感到遗憾的是，这件事导致我失去了最好的朋友——安纳格罗斯先生。

自从《我的生活》一文在《家庭主妇杂志》上发表后，安纳格罗斯先生发表了一个声明。他在写给梅西先生的信中，说当初《霜王》事件发生的时候，他就相信我是无辜的。他说，当时那个调查委员会由8人组成:4个盲人，4个视力正常的人，其中4人认为我当时知道有人给我念过坎贝尔小姐的

others did not hold this view. Mr. Anagnos states that he cast his vote with those who were favourable to me.

But, however the case may have been, with whichever side he may have cast his vote, when I went into the room where Mr. Anagnos had so often held me on his knee and, forgetting his many cares, had shared in my frolics, and found there persons who seemed to doubt me, I felt that there was something hostile and menacing in the very atmosphere, and subsequent events have borne out this impression. For two years he seems to have held the belief that Miss Sullivan and I were innocent. Then he evidently retracted his favourable judgment, why I do not know. Nor did I know the details of the investigation. I never knew even the names of the members of the "court" who did not speak to me. I was too excited to notice anything, too frightened to ask questions. Indeed, I could scarcely think what I was saying, or what was being said to me.

I have given this account of "The Frost King" affair because it was important in my life and education; and, in order that there might be no misunderstanding, I have set forth all the facts as they appear to me, without a thought of defending myself or of laying blame on any one.

小说，另外4人则不同意这样的观点。安纳格罗斯先生辩白说，他投了有利于我的票。

但无论事情怎样，安纳格罗斯先生到底持何种态度，当我走进那间安纳格罗斯先生经常把我抱在膝上，不顾工作繁忙地陪我玩的屋子时，我发现那里有人看起来在怀疑我，我感到有一种敌意和险恶的气氛，后来发生的事情果然证实了我的预感。在以后的两年中，安纳格罗斯先生看起来一直支持相信我和莎莉文老师无辜的观点。但是后来我不清楚他又为什么明显地改变了他的看法。当然我也不清楚学校调查这件事的详细情况，我甚至也不知道那个委员会成员的名字，他们也不和我说话。我当时太激动而不能注意其他事情，太恐惧而不能回答问题。实际上，当时我根本就没有想我在说什么，以及人们对我说了些什么。

由于这件事情对我的早期生活和教育影响极大，所以我把《霜王》事件原原本本写出来。当然，为了不引起误解，我按照它的实际顺序记述了事情的过程，既不想为自己辩解，也不想埋怨任何人。

CHAPTER XV

THE summer and winter following " The Frost King" incident I spent with my family in Alabama. I recall with delight that home-going. Everything had budded and blossomed. I was happy. "The Frost King" was forgotten.

When the ground was strewn with the crimson and golden leaves of autumn, and the musk-scented grapes that covered the arbour at the end of the garden were turning golden brown in the sunshine, I began to write a sketch of my life-a year after I had written " The Frost King".

I was still excessively scrupulous about everything I wrote. The thought that what I wrote might not be absolutely my own tormented me. No one knew of these fears except my teacher. A strange sensitiveness prevented me from referring to " The Frost King"; and often when an idea flashed out in the course of conversation I would spell softly to her, "I am not sure it is mine." At other times, in the midst of a paragraph I was writing, I said to myself, "Suppose it should be found that all this was written by some one long ago!" An impish fear clutched my hand, so that I could not write any more that day. And even now I sometimes feel the same uneasiness and disquietude.

第15章 世界博览会

《霜王》事件发生后的那年夏天和冬天,我和家人待在亚拉巴马州的家中。回忆家庭时光让我充满了甜蜜感。一切都在开花和结果,我过着幸福的生活,《霜王》被遗忘了。

当地上堆满了深红色和金黄色的秋叶时,当花园尽头的葡萄架上的葡萄在阳光的照射下变成了酱紫色时,我开始创作《我的生活》的提纲,这时恰好是《霜王》事件一年后。

我对自己写的东西仍然心有余悸,我写的东西可能是别人的,这种想法一直在折磨着我。除了莎莉文老师,没有人能知道我的这些恐惧。过分的敏感阻止我提及《霜王》,常常是当我们聊天的过程中,突然闪现出一个念头,这时我会轻轻地在她的手心写道:"我不能确定它是否是我的。"有时候,在我写作中间,我也会自言自语地说:"要是这个跟别人很久以前写的一样,又会怎样呢!"那种孩子才有的恐惧就会向我袭来,这一天我就什么也写不了。即便是现在,我有时也感到同样的不安和焦虑。

莎莉文老师尽其可能来安慰我,但是那次恐怖的经历在我心灵上留下了

Miss Sullivan consoled and helped me in every way she could think of; but the terrible experience I had passed through left a lasting impression on my mind, the significance of which I am only just beginning to understand. It was with the hope of restoring my self-confidence that she persuaded me to write for the Youth's Companion a brief account of my life. I was then twelve years old. As I look back on my struggle to write that little story, it seems to me that I must have had a prophetic vision of the good that would come of the undertaking, or I should surely have failed.

I wrote timidly, fearfully, but resolutely, urged on by my teacher, who knew that if I persevered, I should find my mental foothold again and get a grip on my faculties. Up to the time of "The Frost King" episode, I had lived the unconscious life of a little child; now my thoughts were turned inward, and I beheld things invisible. Gradually I emerged from the penumbra of that experience with a mind made clearer by trial and with a truer knowledge of life.

The chief events of the year 1893 were my trip to Washington during the inauguration of President Cleveland, and visits to Niagara and the World's

亚历山大·格雷厄姆·贝尔（左）把手中的风筝线递给海伦，这样，在风筝飞上天的时候，海伦就能感觉到风筝的拉力

永久性的后遗症，我才开始理解其含义。莎莉文劝我给《青年之友》写一篇《我的生活介绍》的短文，目的是帮助我恢复自信。我那时只有12岁，在回想当时为写这篇文章付出的努力时，我认为那时我就已经预见到了写作给我带来的好处，否则我一定写不出来的。

在莎莉文老师的坚定鼓舞下，我小心翼翼地、谨慎地创作着。莎莉文老师知道，如果我能够坚持住，我一定能发现思想的立足之地，找到自己的生存之基。在《霜王》一事以前，我还只是一个懵懂的小孩子，过着无忧无虑的生活，但经历此事之后，我变得内向了，经常思考一些看不见的东西。渐渐地，我从那段经历的阴影中走了出来。经过磨炼，我的头脑比以前更清醒了，对生活也有了更深刻的认识和理解。

1893年的大事，是我的华盛顿之旅。我当时赶上克利夫兰总统宣誓就职，还游览了尼亚加拉瀑布，参观了世界博览会。这样的安排影响了我的学习进程，经常是几周不能学习，以至于我不能连贯地叙述这段时间的事情。

Fair. Under such circumstances my studies were constantly interrupted and often put aside for many weeks, so that it is impossible for me to give a connected account of them.

We went to Niagara in March, 1893. It is difficult to describe my emotions when I stood on the point which overhangs the American Falls and felt the air vibrate and the earth tremble.

It seems strange to many people that I should be impressed by the wonders and beauties of Niagara. They are always asking:"What does this beauty or that music mean to you? You cannot see the waves rolling up the beach or hear their roar. What do they mean to you?" In the most evident sense they mean everything. I cannot fathom or define their meaning any more than I can fathom or define love or religion or goodness.

During the summer of 1893, Miss Sullivan and I visited the World's Fair with Dr. Alexander Graham Bell. I recall with unmixed delight those days when a thousand childish fancies became beautiful realities. Every day in imagination I made a trip around the world, and I saw many wonders from the uttermost parts of the earth-marvels of invention, treasures of industry and skill and all the activities of human life actually passed under my finger tips.

I liked to visit the Midway Plaisance. It seemed like the "Arabian Nights", it was crammed so full of novelty and interest. Here was the India of my books in the curious bazaar with its Shivas and elephant-gods; there was the land of the

我们是在3月份去尼亚加拉的。我站的地方正好瀑布悬垂，空气震动，大地颤抖，因此要想描述我当时的感触很难。

许多人都会奇怪，难道我也能为尼亚加拉瀑布的壮美所陶醉吗？他们老是这样问我："你不能看到波涛汹涌，也听不到它们的怒吼，这种美景或者音乐对你来说，有什么意义呢？"其实，它们对我就意味着一切。我不能准确说出它们的意义，正如我不能准确定义"爱"、"宗教"和"善良"一样。

1893年夏天，在亚历山大·格雷厄姆·贝尔博士的陪同下，我和莎莉文老师参观了世界博览会。我小时候的许多美妙的幻想都变成了事实，这次参观给我幼小的心灵留下了珍贵的回忆！我每天都在头脑中把世界周游一番。今天，我看到了来自世界各地的、天上地下的各种发明，我用指尖去触摸每一件展品，触摸人类勤劳智慧的结晶。

我喜欢在万国馆游览，那里好像是《天方夜谭》，充满了各种新奇有趣的事物。这边是欢乐神和象神齐集在一个集市中，完全是书本上讲过的印度的再现；那边则是开罗城的缩微模型，有金字塔、清真寺、列队而行的骆驼；再远方是威尼斯的环礁湖，晚上，我们会在城市和喷泉灯光的照耀下泛舟湖中。我还登上一艘离缩微城远一些的北欧海盗船，以前在波士顿时我

Pyramids concentrated in a model Cairo with its mosques and its long processions of camels; yonder were the lagoons of Venice, where we sailed every evening when the city and the fountains were illuminated. I also went on board a Viking ship which lay a short distance from the little craft. I had been on a man-of-war before, in Boston, and it interested me to see, on this Viking ship, how the seaman was once all in all-how he sailed and took storm and calm alike with undaunted heart, and gave chase to whosoever reechoed his cry, "We are of the sea!" and fought with brains and sinews, self-reliant, self-sufficient, instead of being thrust into the background by unintelligent machinery, as Jack is to-day. So it always is- "man only is interesting to man."

At a little distance from this ship there was a model of the Santa Maria, which I also examined. The captain showed me Columbus's cabin and the desk with an hourglass on it. This small instrument impressed me most because it made me think how weary the heroic navigator must have felt as he saw the sand dropping grain by grain while desperate men were plotting

美国实业家和慈善家安德鲁·卡内基，他曾支付一笔年金给海伦，以帮助她摆脱财务困境

曾登上一艘战船，不过使我感兴趣的是这艘海盗船，因为里里外外只有一个水手，不论风平浪静还是狂风暴雨，他都大无畏地独自驾驶着船。他一面高喊"我们是海的主人"，一面用智慧、力量、自信与大海搏斗，这与完全依赖毫无智慧可言的机器船形成了鲜明的对照。"人只对人感兴趣！"这也许是大多数人的心态吧！

距离这艘船稍远处，是"圣玛利亚"船的模型，我也仔细观看了一番。船长领我参观了哥伦布的船舱，舱里的桌子上放着一个沙漏。这个小小的装置给我留下了深刻的印象，因为它使我想到，当那些绝望的人们准备反叛的时候，当哥伦布这位勇敢的航海家看着一粒粒沙子往下漏时，他是否也会感到焦躁不安呢？

海格博瑟曼先生，世界博览会的主席，爽快地允许我抚摸展品，我就像弗兰西斯科·皮萨罗掠夺秘鲁的财宝那样，贪婪地用手指去触摸那些伟大的

against his life.

Mr. Higinbotham, President of the World's Fair, kindly gave me permission to touch the exhibits, and with an eagerness as insatiable as that with which Pizarro seized the treasures of Peru, I took in the glories of the Fair with my fingers. It was a sort of tangible kaleidoscope, this white city of the West. Everything fascinated me, especially the French bronzes. They were so lifelike, I thought they were angel visions which the artist had caught and bound in earthly forms.

At the Cape of Good Hope exhibit, I learned much about the process of mining diamonds. Whenever it was possible, I touched the machinery while it was in motion, so as to get a clearer idea how the stones were weighed, cut, and polished. I searched in the washings for a diamond and found it myself-the only true diamond, they said, that was ever found in the United States.

Dr. Bell went everywhere with us and in his own delightful way described to me the objects of greatest interest. In the electrical building we examined the telephones, autophones, phonographs, and other inventions, and he made me understand how it is possible to send a message on wires that mock space and outrun time, and, like Prometheus, to draw fire from the sky.

展品，呈现在我面前的是一个美丽而奇妙的万花筒，西方白人的世界！每样东西都让我着魔，尤其是法国铜像，它们是如此逼真，以至于我疑惑他们是被艺术家们捉住的变成了人形的天使。

在好望角展览厅，我了解了许多开采钻石的过程。无论何时，只要有可能，我便用手去摸还在运转的机器，以便清楚地了解金刚石是如何被称量、切

海伦和莎莉文为未来的巡回演讲制订计划

削和磨光的。我在淘洗槽中摸钻石，并且我自己真的摸到了一块真钻石，他们说这是在美国参展的唯一的一块真钻石。

贝尔博士带我们参观了展览会的每个角落，他用他特有的热情给我描述那些展品最有趣的地方。在电器展览大厅里，我们参观了电话机、留声机、电唱机及其他一些发明。他让我懂得了电线如何可能超越时空限制传递信息的，就像普罗米修斯从天上为人类偷火一样。

我们还参观了人类学展厅，我对古代墨西哥的遗迹非常感兴趣，还有那唯一一块见证了古老历史的粗糙石器，这是在还没有文字时大自然的子孙所

We also visited the anthropological department, and I was much interested in the relics of ancient Mexico, in the rude stone implements that are so often the only record of an age-the simple monuments of nature's unlettered children (so I thought as I fingered them) that seem bound to last while the memorials of kings and sages crumble in dust away-and in the Egyptian mummies, which I shrank from touching. From these relics I learned more about the progress of man than I have heard or read since.

All these experiences added a great many new terms to my vocabulary, and in the three weeks I spent at the Fair I took a long leap from the little child's interest in fairy tales and toys to the appreciation of the real and the earnest in the workaday world.

立的丰碑。当历代帝王和圣贤都归于尘土时，它仍将永存。在参观埃及的木乃伊时，我没敢用手摸。从这些遗物上，我了解到的人类进步的知识比我听到或读书所获得的知识要多很多。

所有这些见识给我的词典里加上了很多新的条目。在这3个星期中，我的知识有了长足的进步，开始迈出童话故事和玩具时代，对这个现实世界中真实而平凡的事物充满了热爱。

CHAPTER XVI

BEFORE October, 1893, I had studied various subjects by myself in a more or less desultory manner. I read the histories of Greece, Rome and the United States. I had a French grammar in raised print, and as I already knew some French, I often amused myself by composing in my head short exercises, using the new words as I came across them, and ignoring rules and other technicalities as much as possible. I even tried, without aid, to master the French pronunciation, as I found all the letters and sounds described in the book. Of course this was tasking slender powers for great ends; but it gave me something to do on a rainy day, and I acquired a sufficient knowledge of French to read with pleasure La Fontaine's "Fables", "Le Medecin Malgrè Lui" and passages from "Athalie".

I also gave considerable time to the improvement of my speech. I read aloud to Miss Sullivan and recited passages from my favourite poets, which I had committed to memory; she corrected my pronunciation and helped me to phrase and inflect. It was not, however, until October, 1893, after I had recovered from the fatigue and excitement of my visit to the World's Fair, that I began to have lessons

第16章 学习拉丁文

1893年10月以前，我杂乱无章地自学了许多东西。我读了希腊、罗马和英国史。我有一本用凸字印刷的法语语法书。我已经知道了一些法语，常常自娱自乐地用学到的新单词在脑子里做练习，而对于语法规则或其他术语则不怎么注意。我甚至试着在没有任何人帮助的情况下，掌握法语的发音，因为我发现那本语法书给所有的字母都注了音。当然，这对我来说实在太困难了，就像是以微弱的力量去获得巨大的成功，不过这却使我在雨天有事可做，而且我也确实掌握了一些语法，使我可以带着喜悦去阅读拉·芳登的《寓言》和《被强迫的医生》以及《阿舍利》中的片段。

我还花了大量工夫来提高说话的能力。我大声读给莎莉文老师听，背诵几首我最喜欢的诗句，这些诗后来我能记住了。她不断地纠正我的发音，告诉我如何断句，怎样转调。但是直到1893年10月，我才从参观世界博览会的疲劳和兴奋中恢复过来，开始真正在固定的时间安心上课，专心致志地学习。

in special subjects at fixed hours.

Miss Sullivan and I were at that time in Hulton, Pennsylvania, visiting the family of Mr. William Wade. Mr. Irons, a neighbour of theirs, was a good Latin scholar; it was arranged that I should study under him. I remember him as man of rare, sweet nature and of wide experience. He taught me Latin grammar principally; but he often helped me in arithmetic, which I found as troublesome as it was uninteresting. Mr. Irons also read with me Tennyson's "In Memoriam". I had read many books before, but never from a critical point of view. I learned for the first time to know an author, to recognize his style as I recognize the clasp of a friend's hand.

At first I was rather unwilling to study Latin grammar. It seemed absurd to waste time analyzing every word I came across-noun, genitive, singular, feminine-when its meaning was quite plain. I thought I might just as well describe my pet in order to know it-order, vertebrate; division, quadruped; class, mammalia; genus, felinus; species, cat; individual, Tabby. But as I got deeper into the subject, I became more interested, and the beauty of the language delighted me. I often amused myself by reading Latin passages, picking up words I understood and trying to make sense. I have never ceased to enjoy this pastime.

There is nothing more beautiful, I think, than the evanescent fleeting images and sentiments presented by a language one is just becoming familiar with-ideas

那时，我和莎莉文老师正在宾夕法尼亚州的希尔顿市，我们是去拜访威廉·韦德先生一家，还认识了他们的邻居艾伦先生，他是一位出色的拉丁语专家。后来我被安排在他那里学习。我记得他是一位罕见的、温和而且博学的人，主要教我拉丁语语法，但偶尔也会教我算术，这门课我觉得既困难又乏味。艾伦先生还和我一起阅读坦尼森的《回忆》，我以前虽然读过很多书，但从来没有从评论的角度去读。这是我第一次学会如何了解一位作者，认识他的风格，我觉得这就像和老朋友握手一样。

最初，我很不情愿学拉丁语语法。因为学语法就像是在浪费时间去分析我遇到的每一个字，例如名词、所有格、单数、阴性等等，真是太乏味了。我想，也许我该用生物学的分类方法来了解我养的那只宠物猫吧。比如，目是脊椎动物；部是四足动物；纲是哺乳动物；属是猫科动物；种是猫。具体到我那只，则名叫塔比。但随着学习的深入，我兴趣越来越浓，拉丁文的优美令我陶醉不已。我常常以念拉丁文来自娱自乐，有时则用我认识的单词来造句。我一直没有中断过这种消遣方式。

我认为没有什么比得上用刚刚学会的语言来表达稍纵即逝的印象和感情更美的了。这时，思想会穿越精神的天空，各种幻想也从中形成，并多姿多彩。莎莉文老师一直在边上陪我上课，她会把艾伦先生说的一切写在我手掌

that flit across the mental sky, shaped and tinted by capricious fancy. Miss Sullivan sat beside me at my lessons, spelling into my hand whatever Mr. Irons said, and looking up new words for me. I was just beginning to read Caesar's "Gallic War" when I went to my home in Alabama.

上，为我查生词。当我回到亚拉巴马州家里的时候，我开始阅读恺撒的《高卢战记》。

CHAPTER XVII

IN the summer of 1894, I attended the meeting at Chautauqua of the American Association to Promote the Teaching of Speech to the Deaf. There it was arranged that I should go to the Wright-Humason School for the Deaf in New York City. I went there in October, 1894, accompanied by Miss Sullivan. This school was chosen especially for the purpose of obtaining the highest advantages in vocal culture and training in lip-reading. In addition to my work in these subjects, I studied, during the two years I was in the school, arithmetic, physical geography, French and German.

Miss Reamy, my German teacher, could use the manual alphabet, and after I had acquired a small vocabulary, we talked together in German whenever we had a chance, and in a few months I could understand almost everything she said. Before the end of the first year I read "Wilhelm Tell" with the greatest delight. Indeed, I think I made more progress in German than in any of my other studies. I found French much more difficult. I studied it with Madame Olivier, a French lady who did not know the manual alphabet, and who was obliged to give her instruction orally. I could not read her lips easily; so my progress was much slower than in

第17章 客居纽约的学习生活

1894年夏天，我出席了在夏达奎市举行的"美国聋人语言教学促进协会"的会议。在那里，我被安排进入纽约市的莱特—修马森聋人学校上学。1894年10月，我在莎莉文老师的陪同下前往就读。我选择这所学校的特殊原因，是为了提高口头表达和唇读的能力。除了这些内容以外，我这两年在学校还学了数学、自然地理、法语和德语。

我的德语老师瑞米小姐会使用手语。等我稍稍掌握了一些德文后，只要一有机会，我们就用德语交谈。几个月之后，我差不多能明白她说的任何事情了。第一年结束之前，我就已经能愉快地阅读《威廉·泰尔》了。事实上，我认为我在德语方面的进步比其他方面都要大。我觉得法语反而要难得多。我跟随奥利维埃夫人学习法语，她是一位法国女士，不懂手语字母，只能以口语来教我。但是我又不那么容易读得懂她的口语，结果我的法语比德语进步慢得多。不过，我还是把《被强迫的医生》又读了一遍。这本书虽然很有意思，但我还是不如对《威廉·泰尔》那样喜欢。

我在唇读和口语方面的进步并没有像老师和我期待的那样大。当然，

German. I managed, however, to read "Le Medecin Malgrè Lui" again. It was very amusing but I did not like it nearly so well as "Wilhelm Tell".

My progress in lip-reading and speech was not what my teachers and I had hoped and expected it would be. It was my ambition to speak like other people, and my teachers believed that this could be accomplished; but, although we worked hard and faithfully, yet we did not quite reach our goal. I suppose we aimed too high, and disappointment was therefore inevitable.

I still regarded arithmetic as a system of pitfalls. I hung about the dangerous frontier of "guess", avoiding with infinite trouble to myself and others the broad valley of reason. When I was not guessing, I was jumping at conclusions, and this fault, in addition to my dullness, aggravated my difficulties more than was right or necessary.

But although these disappointments caused me great depression at times, I pursued my other studies with unflagging interest, especially physical geography. It was a joy to learn the secrets of nature: how-in the picturesque language of the Old Testament-the winds are made to blow from the four corners of the

我强烈地渴望能和其他人讲得一样好，我的老师也相信这一目标一定能实现。然而，尽管我们训练得十分努力而且满怀信心，但依然没有完全达到预期的目标。我猜想也许是我们将目标定得太高了，所以失望也是不可避免的。

我仍旧将数学看作是可怕的陷阱。我遇到问题时喜欢推测，而不是推理，总是尽量逃避困难，这个

海伦在船甲板上，海鸥在她的头顶上飞翔

毛病加上我的愚钝，给我和老师带来了无穷无尽的麻烦。我不仅时常胡乱推测，而且还随意做出结论。这种愚笨再加上学习不得法，更加大了我学数学的困难。

虽然这些失望使我的情绪不时地沮丧颓废，但我对于其他功课，尤其是自然地理却有着极大的兴趣。探索自然奥秘充满无穷的乐趣:那些形象而生动的文字向我描述风是如何从天空的四周吹来的，水蒸气是如何从大地的尽头升起的，河流是如何穿越岩石奔流向前的，山峰是如何形成的，人类又是

heavens, how the vapours ascend from the ends of the earth, how rivers are cut out among the rocks, and mountains overturned by the roots, and in what ways man may overcome many forces mightier than himself. The two years in New York were happy ones, and I look back to them with genuine pleasure.

I remember especially the walks we all took together every day in Central Park, the only part of the city that was congenial to me. I never lost a jot of my delight in this great park. I loved to have it described every time I entered it; for it was beautiful in all its aspects, and these aspects were so many that it was beautiful in a different way each day of the nine months I spent in New York.

In the spring we made excursions to various places of interest. We sailed on the Hudson River and wandered about on its green banks, of which Bryant loved to sing. I liked the simple, wild grandeur of the palisades. Among the places I visited were West Point, Tarrytown, the home of Washington Irving, where I walked through "Sleepy Hollow".

The teachers at the Wright-Humason School were always

梅尔文·马斯少将向海伦颁发奖牌

如何战胜比自己强大得多的自然力量的。在纽约的两年非常快乐，我总是极其愉快地回忆起这段岁月。

我记忆特别深刻的是，每天莎莉文老师和我都要去中央公园。这是纽约城中我唯一喜欢的地方。我从未忘却在这座宏伟的公园里我所拥有的欢乐。每次进入公园时，我都渴望有人为我描述它的美景，因为它每个地方都景致怡人，以至于我停留在纽约的9个月中的每一天，都那样多姿多彩，变化多端。

春天，我们去各个感兴趣的地方漫游，尽情享受纽约的殊地胜景。我们在哈德逊河上泛舟，在绿草如茵的河岸散步，这里曾是布赖恩特喜欢吟咏的地方。我尤其喜欢那纯朴而又宏伟的峭壁。我们到过的地方有西点、塔里敦、华盛顿·欧文的故乡，有那里我们还穿行过"睡谷"。

莱特—修马森学校的老师们总是尽他们一切能力，让聋哑儿童享受到普通孩子所能享有的各种学习机会，即使是我们当中的小同学，也充分发挥他

planning how they might give the pupils every advantage that those who hear enjoy-how they might make much of few tendencies and passive memories in the cases of the little ones-and lead them out of the cramping circumstances in which their lives were set.

Before I left New York, these bright days were darkened by the greatest sorrow that I have ever borne, except the death of my father. Mr. John P. Spaulding, of Boston, died in February, 1896. Only those who knew and loved him best can understand what his friendship meant to me. He, who made every one happy in a beautiful, unobtrusive way, was most kind and tender to Miss Sullivan and me. So long as we felt his loving presence and knew that he took a watchful interest in our work, fraught with so many difficulties, we could not be discouraged. His going away left a vacancy in our lives that has never been filled.

们被动记忆能力强等特点，帮助他们克服先天性缺陷所导致的限制。

在我离开纽约之前，这些快活的日子突然被波士顿的约翰·P·斯波尔丁先生不幸去世的阴霾所打乱，这种阴霾仅次于当年我父亲的逝世。他于1896年2月去世。只有那些最了解和敬爱他的人，才了解他对我的友谊是何等重要。他是那种帮助别人过上快乐生活，而又不使你感到过意不去的人，他对莎莉文老师和我尤其如此。只要一想起他对我们的慈爱和对我们的学习所给予的关注，我们就不会泄气失落。他的离去给我们的生活造成的真空，是永远也无法填补的。

CHAPTER XVIII

IN October, 1896, I entered the Cambridge School for Young Ladies, to be prepared for Radcliffe.

When I was a little girl, I visited Wellesley and surprised my friends by the announcement, "Some day I shall go to college-but I shall go to Harvard!"

When asked why I would not go to Wellesley, I replied that there were only girls there. The thought of going to college took root in my heart and became an earnest desire, which impelled me to enter into competition for a degree with seeing and hearing girls, in the face of the strong opposition of many true and wise friends. When I left New York the idea had become a fixed purpose; and it was decided that I should go to Cambridge. This was the nearest approach I could get to Harvard and to the fulfillment of my childish declaration.

At the Cambridge School the plan was to have Miss Sullivan attend the classes with me and interpret to me the instruction given.

Of course my instructors had had no experience in teaching any but normal pupils, and my only means of conversing with them was reading their lips. My studies for the first year were English history, English literature, German, Latin,

第18章　剑桥女子中学

1896年10月，我进入剑桥女子中学，为考拉德克利夫学院做准备。

当我还是一个孩子的时候，我曾参观过卫斯理女子学院，并令朋友们惊讶地宣称："总有一天，我要上大学，而且我要上哈佛大学。"

他们问我为什么不愿进卫斯理女子学院，我回答说那里只有女学生。上大学的想法已经在我心中深深地扎根了，而且成为一个最热切的愿望。这使得我不顾许多真诚而聪明的朋友的强烈反对，逼迫自己和具有正常视力和听力的女孩子们直接竞争。当我离开纽约时，这个想法已经牢牢地在我心中扎根了，这也成为我上剑桥女子中学读书的动力，因为这是我能够通往哈佛、实现童年梦想的最便捷途径。

在剑桥中学求学的办法，就是让莎莉文老师和我一同上课，把老师讲的所有东西翻译给我听。

当然，我的老师们在教育聋哑孩子方面没有任何经验，我和他们接触的唯一途径就是读他们的嘴唇。我第一年的课程有英国史、英国文学、德文、

arithmetic, Latin composition and occasional themes. Until then I had never taken a course of study with the idea of preparing for college; but I had been well drilled in English by Miss Sullivan, and it soon became evident to my teachers that I needed no special instruction in this subject beyond a critical study of the books prescribed by the college. I had had, moreover, a good start in French, and received six months' instruction in Latin; but German was the subject with which I was most familiar.

In spite, however, of these advantages, there were serious drawbacks to my progress. Miss Sullivan could not spell out in my hand all that the books required, and it was very difficult to have textbooks embossed in time to be of use to me, although my friends in London and Philadelphia were willing to hasten the work. For a while, indeed, I had to copy my Latin in braille, so that I could recite with the other girls. My instructors soon became sufficiently familiar with my imperfect speech to answer my questions readily and correct mistakes. I could not make notes in class or write exercises; but I wrote all my compositions and translations

海伦与肯尼迪总统于1961年的合影

拉丁文、数学、拉丁文作文和其他科目。在此之前，我从来都没有为上大学而专门学习过某种课程，但在莎莉文老师的训练下，我的英语很不错。不久老师们就认为，除了大学专门指定的几本书外，我不用再在这门课上特意学习了。更重要的是，我的法语已经有了很好的基础，而且还有6个月的拉丁文学习也是如此，而德语我是最得心应手的。

不过，尽管有这些有利条件，我前进的道路上还是有一些无法克服的困难。莎莉文老师不可能在我手上把所有书本要求的内容都写出来，虽然我在伦敦和费城的朋友们努力地把书本刻成盲文，但还是无法满足我的需求。事实上，有一段时间，我必须把拉丁文用盲文抄下来，这样我才能像别的女孩子一样朗读。老师们很快就习惯了我不完整的语言，能充分地解答我提出的问题，纠正我的错误。我在课堂上无法记笔记和做练习，但是我课后能在家中用打字机写作文和做翻译。

莎莉文老师每天和我一起去上课，用她极大的耐心把老师们讲的东西都写在我手上。在自习时间，她必须帮我从字典中查新单词，帮我反反复复阅

at home on my typewriter.

Each day Miss Sullivan went to the classes with me and spelled into my hand with infinite patience all that the teachers said. In study hours she had to look up new words for me and read and reread notes and books I did not have in raised print. The tedium of that work is hard to conceive. Frau Grote, my German teacher, and Mr. Gilman, the principal, were the only teachers in the school who learned the finger alphabet to give me instruction. No one realized more fully than dear Frau Grote how slow and inadequate her spelling was. Nevertheless, the goodness of her heart she laboriously spelled out her instructions to me in special lessons twice a week, to give Miss Sullivan a little rest. But, though everybody was kind and ready to help us, there was only one hand that could turn drudgery into pleasure.

That year I finished arithmetic, reviewed my Latin grammar, and read three chapters of Caesar's "Gallic War". In German I read, partly with my fingers and partly with Miss Sullivan's assistance, Schiller's "Lied von der Glocke" and "Taucher", Heine's "Harzreise", Freytag's "Aus dem Staat Friedrichs des Grossen", Rieh's "Fluch Der Schonheit", Lessing's "Minna von Barnhelm", and Goethe's "Aus meinem Leben". I took the greatest delight in these German books, especially Schiller's wonderful lyrics, the history of Frederick the Great's magnificent achievements and the account of Goethe's life. I was sorry to finish "Die Harzreise", so full of happy witticisms and charming descriptions of vine-clad hills, streams that sing and ripple in the sunshine, and wild regions, sacred

读没有凸字的笔记和课本。这些事情的单调乏味简直令人难以忍受。我的德语老师弗洛·葛洛和校长吉尔曼先生，是学校唯一学过手语的老师，他们都不遗余力地给我进行指导。虽然葛洛小姐拼字时极慢，然而她却从不厌倦，心地善良的她每星期都要为我上两节特别的课，把她的教学内容在我手上拼写出来，这样也好让莎莉文老师有一点时间休息一下。虽然每个人都这么仁慈地帮助我，可惜的是，只有我一个人能将这种辛苦的工作变成快乐。

这一年，我修完了数学、复习了拉丁语语法，读完了恺撒的《高卢战记》前三章。在半靠手指、半靠莎莉文老师的帮助下，我读完了德文版席勒的《钟之歌》和《潜水者》、海涅的《哈尔茨山游记》、佛雷格的《腓特烈大帝统治时代散记》、里尔的《美的诅咒》、莱辛的《米娜·冯彭尔姆》以及歌德的《我的一生》。我带着极大的愉悦读的这些德文书，特别是席勒那些精美绝伦的抒情诗、菲特烈大帝丰功伟绩的历史以及歌德生平的记述，都给我留下了深刻的印象，《哈尔茨山游记》更让人回味无穷，使我久久不能忘怀。它充满了诙谐的语言，引人入胜，书中描述了爬满蔓藤的山冈、阳光下汩汩奔流的小溪、富有传奇色彩的荒蛮地区，还有神话中的灰姑娘。这些如此生动的篇章，只有那些完全将自己的嗜好和情趣融入大自然的人才能写得出来。

to tradition and legend, the gray sisters of a long-vanished, imaginative age-descriptions such as can be given only by those to whom nature is "a feeling, a love and an appetite."

Mr. Gilman instructed me part of the year in English literature. We read together, "As You Like It", Burke's "Speech on Conciliation with America", and Macaulay's "Life of Samuel Johnson". Mr. Gilman's broad views of history and literature and his cleaver explanations made my work easier and pleasanter than it could have been had I only read notes mechanically with the necessarily brief explanations given in the classes.

Burke's speech was more instructive than any other book on a political subject that I had ever read. My mind stirred with the stirring times, and the characters round which the life of two contending nations centered seemed to move right before me. I wondered more and more, while Burke's masterly speech rolled on in mighty surges of eloquence, how it was that King George and his ministers could have turned a deaf ear to his warning prophecy of our victory and their humiliation. Then I entered into the melancholy details of the relation in which the great statesman stood to his party and to the representatives of the

吉尔曼先生教了我半学期的英国文学。我们一起阅读了《随你所愿》、贝克的《调停美洲的演讲词》、麦考利的《塞缪尔·约翰逊传》。吉尔曼先生宽广的历史视野和文学功底以及他那传神的讲解，使我的学习变得更容易而且更有趣，这是机械背诵和记笔记所无法比拟的。

年轻时期的海伦，虽然盲聋哑，但对生活充满了热爱

贝克的演说是我所读过的政治著作中最启发人的。在读他的演说稿的时候，我心潮澎湃，许多重要的历史人物都纷纷出现在我眼前。但是令我感到非常困惑不解的是，贝克滔滔不绝的雄辩，预言如果坚持敌对，得益的将是美国，英国将蒙受屈辱，可是英王和大臣们为什么对他的预言充耳不闻呢？然后，我又忧虑如此伟大的、代表政党和人民利益的陈述不能被采纳。我觉得思想的火花和智慧的种子竟然播种在无知与腐朽的草堆里，实在是太奇怪了！

麦考利的《塞缪尔·约翰逊传》读起来却另有一种趣味。我的心走近了这个孤独者，他在克鲁勃大街上乞讨，却能够对那些卑微的劳苦大众给

people. I thought how strange it was that such precious seeds of truth and wisdom should have fallen among the tares of ignorance and corruption.

In a different way Macaulay's "Life of Samuel Johnson" was interesting. My heart went out to the lonely man who ate the bread of affliction in Grub Street, and yet, in the midst of toil and cruel suffering of body and soul, always had a kind word, and lent a helping hand to the poor and despised. I rejoiced over all his successes, I shut my eyes to his faults, and wondered, not that he had them, but that they had not crushed or dwarfed his soul. But in spite of Macaulay's brilliancy and his admirable faculty of making the commonplace seem fresh and picturesque, his positiveness wearied me at times, and his frequent sacrifices of truth to effect kept me in a questioning attitude very unlike the attitude of reverence in which I had listened to the Demosthenes of Great Britain.

At the Cambridge school, for the first time in my life, I enjoyed the companionship of seeing and hearing girls of my own age. I lived with several others in one of the pleasant house connected with the school, the house where Mr. Howells used to live, and we all had the advantage of home life. I joined them in many of their games, even blind man's buff and frolics in the snow; I took long walks with them; we discussed our studies and read aloud the things that interested us. Some of the girls learned to speak to me, so that Miss Sullivan did not have to repeat their conversation.

At Christmas, my mother and little sister spent the holidays with me, and Mr.

予慰藉，伸出援助的手臂。他的一切成功都使我欢欣鼓舞，而对他的受冷遇却闭眼不看。我惊异的不是他的这些冷遇，而是这些冷遇竟然没有击垮他的精神。尽管麦考利才华出众，犀利的笔锋能够化腐朽为神奇，实在是令人钦佩，但是他的自负有时却令我厌烦。还有他经常迁就实用而牺牲真理的做法，也使我对他抱怀疑的态度，我不认同有人说他是英国伟大的德摩斯梯尼。

在剑桥中学，我平生第一次享受到和视听正常的同龄女孩子们生活在一起的乐趣。我和几个同学住在临近校舍的一间房子里，豪威尔斯先生（译注：美国小说家，批评家，1837～1920）曾经在那所房子住过，我们把这里当成了自己的家。我参加了她们的大部分活动，我们一起做游戏、捉迷藏、打雪仗。我们常常外出漫步，讨论功课，高声朗读我们感兴趣的作品。有些女孩也学会了手语，以至于莎莉文老师不必重复她们的谈话。

圣诞节到了，母亲和小妹来和我共度节日。善良的吉尔曼先生提出，让我妹妹米尔德里德在剑桥中学学习。因此，米尔德里德就和我一起留在剑桥，几乎形影不离地度过了6个月，它使我快乐地回忆起我们在一起学习时相互帮助而度过的快乐时光。

1897年6月29日到7月3日，我参加了拉德克利夫学院的入学考试。考试

Gilman kindly offered to let Mildred study in his school. So Mildred stayed with me in Cambridge, and for six happy months we were hardly ever apart. It makes me most happy to remember the hours we spent helping each other in study and sharing our recreation together.

I took my preliminary examinations for Radcliffe from the 29th of June to the 3rd of July in 1897. The subjects I offered were Elementary and Advanced German, French, Latin, English, and Greek and Roman history, making nine hours in all. I passed in everything, and received "honours" in German and English.

Perhaps an explanation of the method that was in use when I took my examinations will not be amiss here. The student was required to pass in sixteen hours-twelve hours being called elementary and four advanced. He had to pass five hours at a time to have them counted. The examination papers were given out at nine o'clock at Harvard and brought to Radcliffe by a special messenger. Each candidate was known, not by his name, but by a number. I was No. 233, but, as I had to use a typewriter, my identity could not be concealed.

It was thought advisable for me to have my examinations in a room by myself, because the noise of the typewriter might disturb the other girls. Mr. Gilman read all the papers to me by means of the manual alphabet. A man was placed on guard at the door to prevent interruption.

The first day I had German. Mr. Gilman sat beside me and read the paper through first, then sentence by sentence, while I repeated the words aloud, to

的科目有初级和高级德语、法语、拉丁语、英语、希腊文和罗马史，考试共9个小时。我每科都通过了，而且德语和英语得了"优"。

在这里，我想解释一下我当时考试的情形也许不会显得繁琐。每个学生要求过16个学分——初级考试12分，高级考试4分。每次至少要得到5分才能有效。试卷于早晨9点钟由专人从哈佛送到拉德克利夫学院。考生在试卷上不写名字，只写号码，我的号码是233号。但是因为我必须用打字机答试卷，所以我的身份不是保密的。

为了不让打字机的声音影响其他考生，学校为我安排了一个房间考试。吉尔曼先生把试题用手语字母读给我听，门口还派了一个专人监考，以免受到干扰。

第一天我考德语，吉尔曼先生坐在我身边，先通读了一遍试卷，然后逐句地写在我的手上，我再大声逐句复述，确保我准确无误地理解了他。考题很难，我每在打字机上做完一道题时，都感觉非常紧张。吉尔曼先生把我写出来的读给我听，我会告诉他我认为需要修改的地方，他再改过来。我在这里想说，在我以后的考试中，这样便利的条件再也没有了。进了拉德克利夫学院以后，我答完试卷之后就没有人读给我听了。除非时间允许，否则我就没有机会加以改正。即使有时间，也只是根据我的记忆，在几分钟之内把要

make sure that I understood him perfectly. The papers were difficult, and I felt very anxious as I wrote out my answers on the typewriter. Mr. Gilman spelled to me what I had written, and I made such changes as I thought necessary, and he inserted them. I wish to say here, that I have not had this advantage since in any of my examinations. At Radcliffe no one reads the papers to me after they are written, and I have no opportunity to correct errors unless I finish before the time is up. In that, case I correct only such mistakes as I can recall in the few minutes allowed, and make notes of these corrections at the end of my paper. If I passed with higher credit in the preliminaries than in the finals, there are two reasons. In the finals, no one read my work over to me, and in the preliminaries I offered subjects with some of which I was in a measure familiar before my work in the Cambridge school; for at the beginning of the year I had passed examinations in English, History, French and German, which Mr. Gilman gave me from previous Harvard papers.

Mr. Gilman sent my written work to the examiners with a certificate that I, candidate No. 233, had written the papers.

All the other preliminary examinations were conducted in the same manner. None of them was so difficult as the first. I remember that the day the Latin paper was brought to us, Professor Schilling came in and informed me I had passed satisfactorily in German. This encouraged me greatly, and I sped on to the end of the ordeal with a light heart and a steady hand.

海伦参加电影拍摄，与演员们一起翩翩起舞

改正的统统写在卷子的末尾。如果我初试的成绩比复试好的话，可能有两个原因：一是复试时没有人把我打出的答案读给我听；二是初试的科目有些是在进剑桥中学以前就有了一些基础的，因为在年初我就已经通过了英语、历史、法语和德语的考试，试题是吉尔曼先生从哈佛大学以前的考题中拿来的。

吉尔曼先生把我的答卷交给监考人并写了一个证明，说明是我（233号考生）写的答卷。

其他几科考试也大致如此，但都没有德语难。我记得那天拉丁文试卷发给我们时，希林教授走来对我说，我已经令人满意地通过了德语考试。这极大地鼓舞了我，我轻松愉快而且得心应手地完成了剩余的考试。

CHAPTER XIX

WHEN I began my second year at the Gilman school, I was full of hope and determination to succeed. But during the first few weeks I was confronted with unforeseen difficulties. Mr. Gilman had agreed that that year I should study mathematics principally. I had physics, algebra, geometry, astronomy, Greek and Latin. Unfortunately, many of the books I needed had not been embossed in time for me to begin with the classes, and I lacked important apparatus for some of my studies. The classes I was in were very large, and it was impossible for the teachers to give me special instruction. Miss Sullivan was obliged to read all the books to me, and interpret for the instructors, and for the first time in eleven years it seemed as if her dear hand would not be equal to the task.

It was necessary for me to write algebra and geometry in class and solve problems in physics, and this I could not do until we bought a braille writer, by means of which I could put down the steps and processes of my work. I could not follow with my eyes the geometrical figures drawn on the blackboard, and my only means of getting a clear idea of them was to make them on a cushion with straight and curved wires, which had bent and pointed ends. I had to carry in my mind,

第19章　冲出困境

当我在剑桥中学开始第二年的学习时，充满了希望，并决心获得成功。但是在最初的几个星期，我遇上了没有预料到的麻烦。吉尔曼先生同意我这一年主修数学，而我还要修物理、代数、几何、天文学、希腊文和拉丁文等课程。非常不幸的是，课程开始的时候我手上还没有盲文版的教材，又缺少帮助我理解课程所必需的学习器具。我所在的班级学生很多，老师不可能单独给我辅导。莎莉文老师不得不为我读所有的书，并翻译老师的讲解。11年来她那双灵巧的手似乎已经难以胜任那么多的工作了。

我必须在课堂上完成代数、几何题，并解决物理课的问题。后来我们买了一架盲文打字机，才解决了这个难题。借助这架机器我可以"写"下作业的每一个步骤。我看不见黑板上的几何图形，我弄懂几何图形概念的唯一方法，就是用直的和弯曲的金属丝在坐垫上做成几何图形。至于图中的字母符号，以及假设、结论和证明的各个步骤，正如基思在他的报告中所说的那样，我必须完全靠脑子去记忆。一句话，学习中处处都存在障碍。有时候，

as Mr. Keith says in his report, the lettering of the figures, the hypothesis and conclusion, the construction and the process of the proof. In a word, every study had its obstacles. Sometimes I lost all courage and betrayed my feelings in a way I am ashamed to remember, especially as the signs of my trouble were afterward used against Miss Sullivan, the only person of all the kind friends I had there, who could make the crooked straight and the rough places smooth.

Little by little, however, my difficulties began to disappear. The embossed books and other apparatus arrived, and I threw myself into the work with renewed confidence. Algebra and geometry were the only studies that continued to defy my efforts to comprehend them. As I have said before, I had no aptitude for mathematics; the different points were not explained to me as fully as I wished. The geometrical diagrams were particularly vexing because I could not see the relation of the different parts to one another, even on the cushion. It was not until Mr. Keith taught me that I had a clear idea of mathematics.

I was beginning to overcome these difficulties when an event occurred which changed everything.

Just before the books came, Mr. Gilman had begun to remonstrate with Miss Sullivan on the ground that I was working too hard, and in spite of my

汤玛森（左坐者）、海伦（中）和安妮·莎莉文（右）在加利福尼亚州的好莱坞观看电影，影片的情节由喜剧杂耍演员查理·卓别林做现场解说

我心灰意冷之极，而且还把这种情绪流露出来，特别是我还因为这些而向莎莉文老师发脾气，她不但是我在那里的唯一一位好朋友，而且是为我披荆斩棘的人。所以，至今想起来我就惭愧不已。

渐渐地，这些困难都开始消失了，凸字书和其他学习用具也都陆续到达了，我又恢复了信心，全身心投入到学习中去。代数和几何是我仅有的两门需要努力学习的课程。如前所述，我对数学没有悟性，加之许多观点不能如我所愿地做出满意的解释。我对几何图形更是头疼，即使在椅垫上拼了许多图形，我也看不清各部分之间的相互关系。一直到基思先生来教我数学，我才对数学有了清晰的概念。

我刚刚克服了这些困难，这时又发生了一件意外的事情，它改变了一切事情。

在我拿到盲文课本之前，吉尔曼先生已开始私下建议莎莉文老师，说

earnest protestations, he reduced the number of my recitations. At the beginning we had agreed that I should, if necessary, take five years to prepare for college, but at the end of the first year the success of my examinations showed Miss Sullivan, Miss Harbaugh (Mr. Gilman's head teacher), and one other, that I could without too much effort complete my preparation in two years more. Mr. Gilman at first agreed to this; but when my tasks had become somewhat perplexing, he insisted that I was overworked, and that I should remain at his school three years longer. I did not like his plan, for I wished to enter college with my class.

On the seventeenth of November I was not very well, and did not go to school. Although Miss Sullivan knew that my indisposition was not serious, yet Mr. Gilman, on hearing of it, declared that I was breaking down and made changes in my studies which would have rendered it impossible for me to take my final examinations with my class. In the end the difference of opinion between Mr. Gilman and Miss Sullivan resulted in my mother's withdrawing my sister Mildred and me from the Cambridge school.

After some delay it was arranged that I should continue my studies under a tutor, Mr. Merton S. Keith, of Cambridge. Miss Sullivan and I spent the rest of the winter with our friends, the Chamberlins in Wrentham, twenty-five miles from Boston.

From February to July, 1898, Mr. Keith came out to Wrentham twice a week, and taught me algebra, geometry, Greek and Latin. Miss Sullivan interpreted his

我的课程太重了，并且他还不顾我的强烈抗议，减少了我的课时。起初，我们同意在必要的情况下，用5年时间来为考大学做准备，但在第一学年结束时，我的考试成绩使莎莉文老师、哈伯女士（吉尔曼先生的上司）以及另一位老师相信，我再学两年就可以毫无困难地完成考试的准备了，吉尔曼先生最初也赞同。但后来我的功课进展不太顺利，他坚持认为我超负荷学习了，认为我必须在学校再读3年。我不喜欢这个计划，因为我希望能和其他同学一起进入大学。

11月17日，我有点不舒服，没有去上课。尽管莎莉文老师知道我病情不严重，但吉尔曼先生听说之后，认定我的身体被拖垮了，就改变了我的学习计划，这使得我不能跟班上的同学一起参加期末考试。最终由于吉尔曼先生与莎莉文老师出现了意见分歧，导致我母亲决定让我妹妹米尔德里德和我从剑桥中学退学。

经过短暂的耽搁，决定让我在家庭教师、剑桥中学的米尔顿·基思先生的指导下继续完成学业。就这样，莎莉文老师和我以及我们的朋友一起在距离波士顿25公里外伦萨姆的凯姆柏林度过了那个退学的冬天。

1898年2月至7月期间，基思先生每星期去伦萨姆两次，教我代数、几何、希腊文和拉丁文，莎莉文老师为我翻译他的课程。

instruction.

In October, 1898, we returned to Boston. For eight months Mr. Keith gave me lessons five times a week, in periods of about an hour. He explained each time what I did not understand in the previous lesson, assigned new work, and took home with him the Greek exercises which I had written during the week on my typewriter, corrected them fully, and returned them to me.

In this way my preparation for college went on without interruption. I found it much easier and pleasanter to be taught by myself than to receive instruction in class. There was no hurry, no confusion. My tutor had plenty of time to explain what I did not understand, so I got on faster and did better work than I ever did in school. I still found more difficulty in mastering problems in mathematics than I did in any other of my studies. I wish algebra and geometry had been half as easy as the languages and literature. But even mathematics Mr. Keith made interesting; he succeeded in whittling problems small enough to get through my brain. He kept my mind alert and eager, and trained it to reason clearly, and to seek conclusions calmly and logically, instead of jumping wildly into space and arriving nowhere. He was always gentle and forbearing,

海伦骑在马背上拍摄电影

1898年10月，我们回到波士顿。其后的8个月，基思先生每周教我5次，每次1个小时。他每次先讲解我上次课中不明白的地方，然后再留新的作业，并把我一周中用打字机做的希腊文作业带回去，仔细修改，然后再发回给我。

通过这种方式，我为大学入学考试所进行的准备一直没有中断。我发现单独接受教育比在班上听课不但要好懂，而且更加轻松愉快，不存在忙乱，也不存在疑惑。我的辅导老师有充裕的时间讲解我不明白之处，因此我比以前在学校学得更快更好。我还发现，我的数学和其他功课相比，仍然是最困难的弱项。我真希望代数和几何有语言和文学课一半容易！不过，即使数学如此难学，基思先生却能教得趣味横生，他能够成功地把问题和困难降到最低限度，使我能够完全理解。他使我的大脑思路敏捷，训练得推理严密，能冷静而合乎逻辑地寻找答案，而不是不着边际地随意猜测。无

no matter how dull I might be, and, believe me, my stupidity would often have exhausted the patience of Job.

On the 29th and 30th of June, 1899, I took my final examinations for Radcliffe College. The first day I had Elementary Greek and Advanced Latin, and the second day Geometry, Algebra and Advanced Greek.

The college authorities did not allow Miss Sullivan to read the examination papers to me; so Mr. Eugene C. Vining, one of the instructors at the Perkins Institution for the Blind, was employed to copy the papers for me in American braille. Mr. Vining was a stranger to me, and could not communicate with me, except by writing braille. The proctor was also a stranger, and did not at tempt to communicate with me in any way.

The braille worked well enough in the languages, but when it came to geometry and algebra, difficulties arose. I was sorely perplexed, and felt discouraged wasting much precious time, especially in algebra. It is true that I was familiar with all literary braille in common use in this country-English, American, and New York Point; but the various signs and symbols in geometry and algebra in the three systems are very different, and I had used only the English braille in my algebra.

Two days before the examinations, Mr. Vining sent me a braille copy of one of the old Harvard papers in algebra. To my dismay I found that it was in the American notation. I sat down immediately and wrote to Mr. Vining, asking him to explain the signs. I received another paper and a table of signs by return mail, and

论我多么笨，要知道，我甚至笨得连上帝都不能容忍，可是他却总是那样温和而充满耐心。

1899年6月29日和30日，我参加了拉德克利夫女子学院入学考试的复试。第一天我考了初级希腊文和高级拉丁文，第二天考了几何、代数和高级希腊文。

校方不允许莎莉文老师为我读试卷，而是专门从帕金斯盲人学校请来了教盲人的尤金·C·文尼先生，由他为我把试卷译成美国盲文。文尼先生和我还很陌生，除了使用盲文外，我们不能交谈。帮我誊写试卷的人也是如此，无论如何也不能同我交谈。

盲文可以适用于各种语言，但是当它用于几何和代数时，就立刻显示出局限性来。我被数学搞得一塌糊涂，觉得浪费了大量的宝贵时间而泄气不已，尤其是在代数上花的时间最多。事实上，我对于英国式、美国式或者纽约式这三种美国人常用的盲文都非常熟悉，但三种盲文在几何和代数里的各种符号却大不相同，而我在代数中使用的只是英国式盲文。

考试前两天，文尼先生给了我一套盲文本的哈佛大学的旧代数试题，令我感到沮丧的是，试卷用的是美式盲文。我立即坐下来给文尼先生写信，请他解释上面的符号。我很快就从回信中收到了另一份试卷和一张符号表。我

I set to work to learn the notation. But on the night before the algebra examination, while I was struggling over some very complicated examples, I could not tell the combinations of bracket, brace and radical. Both Mr. Keith and I were distressed and full of forebodings for the morrow; but we went over to the college a little before the examination began, and had Mr. Vining explain more fully the American symbols.

In geometry my chief difficulty was that I had always been accustomed to read the propositions in line print, or to have them spelled into my hand; and somehow, although the propositions were right before me, I found the braille confusing, and could not fix clearly in my mind what I was reading. But when I took up algebra I had a harder time still. The signs, which I had so lately learned, and which I thought I knew, perplexed me. Besides, I could not see what I wrote on my typewriter. I had always done my work in braille or in my head. Mr. Keith had relied too much on my ability to solve problems mentally, and had not trained me to write examination papers. Consequently my work was painfully slow, and I had to read the examples over and over before I could form

海伦和她的爱犬

开始熟悉这些符号。在考代数的前一天夜里，我算了一晚上的复杂例题，却老是分不清楚那些括号、大括号和方根的交叉使用。基思先生和我都有些泄气，为第二天的考试担心。考试开始之前我们提早到了学校，请文尼先生将美式盲文符号做了充分讲解。

由于我习惯逐行读题，或让人把题目写在手上，这成了我考几何的最大困难。不知为什么，尽管题目是正确的，但用盲文看却很乱，在脑子里总是记不住我读过的东西。考代数时，困难更大了，刚刚学过的符号我自以为懂了，但是到考试时又糊涂了。此外，我看不见自己用打字机打出来的文字。我原来一直都是用盲文演算，或是用心算。基思先生过于着重训练我的心算能力，而没有训练我如何答考卷，结果我的答题速度非常慢，而且我必须反复读试题，才能弄清楚应该如何去做。事实上，我现在也不能确保我读过了所有的符号。我发现要把一切都弄对，确实太困难了。

但是我不责备任何人。拉德克利夫学院的执事先生不会意识到他们将我

any idea of what I was required to do. Indeed, I am not sure now that I read all the signs correctly. I found it very hard to keep my wits about me.

But I do not blame any one. The administrative board of Radcliffe did not realize how difficult they were making my examinations, nor did they understand the peculiar difficulties I had to surmount. But if they unintentionally placed obstacles in my way, I have the consolation of knowing that I overcame them all.

的考题搞得多么难，他们也无法了解我要克服的种种特殊困难。不过，如果他们是无意识地在我前进的道路上设置了许多障碍的话，我将感到欣慰和自豪的是，我把它们全都克服了。

CHAPTER XX

THE struggle for admission to college was ended, and I could now enter Radcliffe whenever I pleased. Before I entered college, however, it was thought best that I should study another year under Mr. Keith. It was not, therefore, until the fall of 1900 that my dream of going to college was realized.

I remember my first day at Radcliffe. It was a day full of interest for me. I had looked forward to it for years. A potent force within me, stronger than the persuasion of my friends, stronger even than the pleadings of my heart, had impelled me to try my strength by the standards of those who see and hear.

I knew that there were obstacles in the way; but I was eager to overcome them. I had taken to heart the words of the wise Roman who said, "To be banished from Rome is but to live outside of Rome." Debarred from the great highways of knowledge, I was compelled to make the journey across country by unfrequented roads-that was all; and I knew that in college there were many bypaths where I could touch hands with girls who were thinking, loving and struggling like me.

I began my studies with eagerness. Before me I saw a new world opening in beauty and light, and I felt within me the capacity to know all things. In the

第20章　实现大学的梦想

考大学的艰苦奋斗虽然结束了，现在我可以随时进入拉德克利夫学院。然而，人们都建议在入学之前，我最好在基思先生的指导下再学习一年。因此，直到1900年秋天，我上大学的梦想才得以实现。

我至今还记得第一天在拉德克利夫学院的情景，那天对我来说充满了乐趣。我期待这一天已经多年了，在我体内有一股潜在的力量，比我的朋友们的规劝还要强烈，甚至比我内心的祈求还要强烈，这促使我以那些视听正常的人的标准来要求自己，推动我努力向前迈进。

我知道，我的道路上还会有许多障碍，但我有决心克服它。我牢记着一句罗马人的名言："被驱逐出罗马，只不过是生活于罗马之外而已。"我也正是被挤出了知识的高速公路，而被迫去走那条偏僻的羊肠小道。我也知道，在大学里我将有充分的机会，和那些像我一样思考、爱憎和奋斗的女孩子们携手前进。

我的大学生活就这样热切地开始了。在我面前，我看到了一个壮美而又

wonderland of Mind I should be as free as another. Its people, scenery, manners, joys, tragedies should be living, tangible interpreters of the real world. The lecture-halls seemed filled with the spirit of the great and the wise, and I thought the professors were the embodiment of wisdom. If I have since learned differently, I am not going to tell anybody.

But I soon discovered that college was not quite the romantic lyceum I had imagined. Many of the dreams that had delighted my young inexperience became beautifully less and "faded into the light of common day". Gradually I began to find that there were disadvantages in going to college.

The one I felt and still feel most is lack of time. I used to have time to think, to reflect, my mind and I. We would sit together of an evening and listen to the inner melodies of the

光明的新世界正在向我打开，我感到自己有能力掌握自己的命运，在思想的王国中和别人一样自由自在。我的思想王国里的人物、背景，其喜怒哀乐应该是真实世界生动具体的反映。我认为，大学的讲堂应该洋溢着贤哲圣人的精神和思

海伦为了生存，和莎莉文老师一起在马戏团客串演出，向观众讲述海伦受教育的详细情况

想，教授们则是智慧的化身。如果我和别人之间有见解的不同，我也不会告诉任何人。

然而，我很快就发现大学并不像我所想象的那么浪漫。年幼时的许多无知梦想渐渐变得不那么美丽了，我又回复到平常的日子中来了。渐渐地，我开始发现上大学也有许多不利之处。

我感觉最深的一件事，就是没有时间。以前，我有大量的时间来思考、反省。我们可以整晚静坐，聆听自己心灵深处美妙的音乐，她只有在安静闲暇之中才能听得到。这时候，我心爱的诗人吟诵出的诗句就会打动我的心弦，直到归于空灵安逸的境界。而在大学，却没有时间与自己的思想沟通，

spirit, which one hears only in leisure moments when the words of some loved poet touch a deep, sweet chord in the soul that until then had been silent. But in college, there is no time to commune with one's thoughts. One goes to college to learn, it seems, not to think. When one enters the portals of learning, one leaves the dearest pleasures- solitude, books and imagination-outside with the whispering pines. I suppose I ought to find some comfort in the thought that I am laying up treasures for future enjoyment, but I am improvident enough to prefer present joy to hoarding riches against a rainy day.

My studies the first year were French, German, history, English composition and English literature. In the French course I read some of the work of Corneille, Molière, Racine, Alfred de Musset and Sainte-Beuve, and in the German those of Goethe and Schiller. I reviewed rapidly the whole period of history from the fall of the Roman Empire to the eighteenth century, and in English literature studied critically Milton's poems and "Aeropagitica".

I am frequently asked how I overcome the peculiar conditions under which I work in college. In the classroom, I am of course practically alone. The professor is as remote as if he were speaking through a telephone. The lectures are spelled into my hand as rapidly as possible, and much of the individuality of the lecturer is lost to me in the effort to keep in the race. The words rush through my hand like hounds in pursuit of a hare which they often miss. But in this respect I do not think I am much worse off than the girl who takes notes. If the mind is occupied with

似乎人们进大学仅仅是为了学习，而不是为了思考。进入大学校门后，就将许多最可宝贵的乐趣——独处、书本和想象——连同那窃窃私语的松树一起弃之门外了。我猜想我也许应该在想象中找到自我安慰的方法：现在放弃愉悦是为了将来的享受，然而，我毕竟是一个现实的人，我情愿要眼前的快乐，而不愿未雨绸缪，为将来做准备。

我大学第一年的课程有法语、德语、历史、英语写作和英国文学。在法语方面，我读了高乃依、莫里哀、拉辛、阿尔弗雷德·德米塞和圣·贝夫等大师的作品；在德语方面读了歌德和席勒的作品。我很快就把从罗马帝国的覆灭到18世纪的整个历史复习了一遍；在英国文学方面，我用批判的眼光研究了弥尔顿的诗歌和他的《阿罗帕第卡》。

我也常常问自己是如何克服在大学中遇到的各种特殊困难的。在教室里，我当然是孤单寂寞，教授上课也好像是在电话那头一样遥不可及，莎莉文老师则尽可能快地将教授讲课的内容拼写在我手上。然而，为了赶速度，许多授课者的个性没有了。我就好像追逐野兔的猎犬，对于那些急速地拼写到我手上的字，常常顾此失彼，无法全面掌握。不过在这方面，我认为我并不比那些记笔记的正常女生差多少。如果一个人的大脑一边机械地忙着听讲，一边急匆匆地记笔记，我觉得他是不可能有多少心思去思考讲课的内容

the mechanical process of hearing and putting words on paper at pellmell speed, I should not think one could pay much attention to the subject under consideration or the manner in which it is presented. I cannot make notes during the lectures, because my hands are busy listening. Usually I jot down what I can remember of them when I get home. I write the exercises, daily themes, criticisms and hour-tests, the mid-year and final examinations, on my typewriter, so that the professors have no difficulty in finding out how little I know. When I began the study of Latin prosody, I devised and explained to my professor a system of signs indicating the different meters and quantities.

I use the Hammond typewriter. I have tried many machines, and I find the Hammond is the best adapted to the peculiar needs of my work. With this machine movable type shuttles can be used, and one can have several shuttles, each with a different set of characters-Greek, French, or mathematical, according to the kind of writing one wishes to do on the typewriter. Without it, I doubt if I could go to college.

Very few of the books required in the various courses are printed for the blind, and I am obliged to have them spelled into my hand. Consequently I need more time to prepare my lessons than other girls. The manual part takes longer, and I have perplexities which they have not. There are days when the close attention I must give to details chafes my spirit, and the thought that I must spend hours reading a few chapters, while in the world without other girls are laughing and

或解决问题的方式方法的。我上课时无法做笔记，因为我的手正忙着听课。通常是我回家后，赶紧将脑子里记住的东西记下来。我做练习和每天的短篇作文、评论、小测验、期中考试和期末考试等，都是用我的打字机完成的。所以老师很容易就知道我学到了多少。当我开始学拉丁文韵律时，我自己设计了一套能说明诗的格律和音韵的符号，并详细解释给我的老师听。

我使用的是哈蒙德牌打字机，我使用过许多种打字机，我发现哈蒙德打字机最适合我学习上的特殊需要。它可以使用活动字板，一台打字机有好几种活字板，如希腊文、法文或数学符号的，可以根据每个人的需要来使用。如果没有它，我怀疑我是否能上大学。

我所学习的各种教材很少是盲文本的，因此，我必须让人将这些内容拼写在我的手上，所以我要比别的同学花更多的时间预习功课。大量的手工劳动让我遇到了许多难题，但是我的同学们则不会遇到这些麻烦。有时，一些小事情我就要付出很大的心血，就会让我心烦意乱；一想到我要花好几个小时才能读几章，而别的同学都在外面嬉笑、唱歌、跳舞，更让我觉得难以忍受。不过，我很快又能调整自己的心态，对这些愤懑不平一笑置之。毕竟任何一个人要想得到真才实学，就必须靠自己攀越困难的险峰；既然人生的道路上没有任何捷径可以到达顶峰，我就得在自己的小路上迂回曲折地前进。

singing and dancing, makes me rebellious; but I soon recover my buoyancy and laugh the discontent out of my heart. For, after all, every one who wishes to gain true knowledge must climb the Hill Difficulty alone, and since there is no royal road to the summit, I must zigzag it in my own way. I slip back many times, I fall, I stand still, I run against the edge of hidden obstacles, I lose my temper and find it again and keep it better, I trudge on, I gain a little, I feel encouraged, I get more eager and climb higher and begin to see the widening horizon. Every struggle is a victory. One more effort and I reach the luminous cloud, the blue depths of the sky, the uplands of my desire. I am not always alone, however, in these struggles. Mr. William Wade and Mr. E. E. Allen, Principal of the Pennsylvania Institution for the Instruction of the Blind, get for me many of the books I need in raised print. Their thoughtfulness has been more of a help and encouragement to me than they can ever know.

Last year, my second year at Radcliffe, I studied English composition, the Bible as English literature, the governments of America and Europe, the Odes of Horace, and Latin comedy. The class in composition was the pleasantest. It was very lively. The lectures were always interesting, vivacious, witty; for

海伦坐在小船上给天鹅喂食

我失败后退过好几次，跌倒了又站起来，遇到过意想不到的障碍，发过脾气，接着又克服自己的脾气，然后又向上攀爬。我一步步前进，感觉到了自己的勇气。我获得的越多，攀爬得越高，就开始看到了广阔的地平线。每一次抗争都是一次胜利，再加点儿油我就能到达璀璨的云端、蓝天的深处——我希望的顶峰。在奋斗的路途中，我并不总是孤家寡人，威廉·韦德先生和宾夕法尼亚盲人学院的院长艾伦先生就是我的知音和密友，他们尽量为我提供我所需要的凸版印刷书籍。他们无私的关怀和帮助，给了我莫大的激励，这种激励是他们也不曾想象得到的。

去年，我在拉德克利夫学院的第二年，我学习了英文写作，还有将《圣经》作为英国文学来研习，以及美洲和欧洲的行政制度、古罗马诗人霍勒斯的抒情诗和拉丁喜剧。写作课最有趣、最生动。查尔斯·唐森德·科普兰是我至今仍然最钦佩的讲师，他把文学作品的原汁原味完全表述出来，而没有

the instructor, Mr. Charles Townsend Copeland, more than any one else I have had until this year, brings before you literature in all its original freshness and power. For one short hour you are permitted to drink in the eternal beauty of the old masters without needless interpretation or exposition. You revel in their fine thoughts. You enjoy with all your soul the sweet thunder of the Old Testament, forgetting the existence of Jahweh and Elohim; and you go home feeling that you have had "a glimpse of that perfection in which spirit and form dwell in immortal harmony; truth and beauty bearing a new growth on the ancient stem of time."

This year is the happiest because I am studying subjects that especially interest me, economics, Elizabethan literature, Shakespeare under Professor George L. Kittredge, and the History of Philosophy under Professor Josiah Royce. Through philosophy one enters with sympathy of comprehension into the traditions of remote ages and other modes of thought, which erewhile seemed alien and without reason.

But college is not the universal Athens I thought it was. There one does not meet the great and the wise face to face; one does not even feel their living touch. They are there, it is true; but they seem mummified. We must extract them from the crannied wall of learning and dissect and analyze them before we can be sure that we have a Milton or an Isaiah, and not merely a clever imitation.

Many scholars forget, it seems to me, that our enjoyment of the great works of literature depends more upon the depth of our sympathy than upon our

添加一点点多余的解释。他能在短短的一小时之内，就让你体味到文学大师们所创造的意境，令你全身心地陶醉在永恒的美之中，沉迷于大师的人格魅力之中。他能让你忘记耶和华的存在，全身心地领略《旧约圣经》的庄严胜美。当你走出教室回家时，常常会有"窥见灵魂和肉体的合和、真与美的新生"之感。

这一年是我最快乐的一年，因为我所学的功课都特别有趣:《经济学》、《伊丽莎白时代文学》、乔治·L·基特里奇教授开的《莎士比亚》、乔赛亚·罗伊斯教授主讲的《哲学史》。通过哲学，一个人可以与那些远古时代朴素的思想家产生共鸣，理解他们曾被认为是无理性的异己思想。

但是，拉德克利夫学院也并不是我想象中的万能的古都雅典。在这儿，一个人并不能和那些伟人及智者面对面，甚至不能感觉到他们的真实存在。是的，他们曾经存在过，但现在只是抽象的存在。我们只能从学问的缝隙之中一点一滴地汲取，然后对他们进行解剖和分析，才能肯定他们是弥尔顿或者是以赛亚，而不仅仅是一个纯粹的模仿。

在我看来，许多大师都被遗忘了，因为我们对文学巨著的态度往往取决于我们对它的领悟深度，而不是靠理解；而问题恰恰在于，许多学者似乎忘了应该如何领略那些伟大的文学作品，他们往往费了很大工夫进行讲解，

understanding. The trouble is that very few of their laborious explanations stick in the memory. The mind drops them as a branch drops its overripe fruit. It is possible to know a flower, root and stem and all, and all the processes of growth, and yet to have no appreciation of the flower fresh bathed in heaven's dew.

Again and again I ask impatiently, "Why concern myself with these explanations and hypotheses?" They fly hither and thither in my thought like blind birds beating the air with ineffectual wings. I do not mean to object to a thorough knowledge of the famous works we read. I object only to the interminable comments and bewildering criticisms that teach but one thing: there are as many opinions as there are men. But when a great scholar like Professor Kittredge interprets what the master said, it is "as if new sight were given the blind." He brings back Shakespeare, the poet.

There are, however, times when I long to sweep away half the things I am expected to learn; for the overtaxed mind cannot enjoy the treasure it has secured at the greatest cost. It is impossible, I think, to read in one day four or five different books in different languages and treating of widely different subjects, and not lose sight of the very ends for which one reads. When one reads hurriedly and nervously, having in mind written tests and examinations, one's brain becomes encumbered with a lot of choice bric-à-brac for which there seems to be little use. At the present time my mind is so full of heterogeneous matter that I almost despair of ever being able to put it in order. Whenever I enter the region that

而未能在学生的头脑中留下多少印象。这就好比成熟了的果实从枝头坠落一般，这种分析讲解往往很快从我们心上掉落了。了解花朵、枝叶和根茎以及其生长过程是可能的，但是，我们也许仍然不懂得如何欣赏一朵带着露水的鲜花。

我常常一遍又一遍地问自己："为什么要为这些说明和假设而费尽心思呢？"这些问题在我的脑海里翻来覆去，好像一群看不见方向的盲鸟，无助地拍打着它们的双翅。我并不是否定对名著做透彻的理解，我反对的只是那些迷惑人的无休止的评论和批评，因为它们只能给人一种印象：千人千面，世界上有多少人，就会有多少观点。但是像基特里奇教授这样的大师在讲解伟大诗人莎士比亚的作品时，则犹如给盲人安上了一双慧眼一样，能够让人拨云见雾。

然而，在那段时间，我有好多次冲动想将学习的知识去掉一半，因为那些让人心灵超载的内容只会让人白费力气，而不能容纳那些真正有价值的知识珍宝。我认为，要想在一天之内读四五种不同文字和内容的书，而且不失重点，根本是不可能的。当一个人匆忙而紧张地读书，又在脑子里堆满了各种杂乱无章、毫无用处的小玩意儿时，对学习是一点儿帮助都没有的。当时，我脑子里就塞满了这些杂七杂八的东西，我甚至难以理出头绪。每当

was the kingdom of my mind I feel like the proverbial bull in the china shop. A thousand odds and ends of knowledge come crashing about my head like hailstones, and when I try to escape them, theme-goblins and college nixies of all sorts pursue me, until I wish-oh, may I be forgiven the wicked wish!-that I might smash the idols I came to worship.

But the examinations are the chief bugbears of my college life. Although I have faced them many times and cast them down and made them bite the dust, yet they rise again and menace me with pale looks, until like Bob Acres I feel my courage oozing out at my finger ends. The days before these ordeals take place are spent in cramming your mind with mystic formula and indigestible dates-unpalatable diets, until you wish that books and science and you were buried in the depths of the sea.

At last the dreaded hour arrives, and you are a favoured being indeed if you feel prepared, and are able at the right time to call to your standard thoughts that will aid you in that supreme effort. It happens too often that your trumpet call is unheeded. It is most perplexing and exasperating that just at the moment when you need your

我进入自己的心灵王国时，我感觉自己好像是闯进了瓷器店的公牛，成千上万种知识的碎片犹如冰雹一样朝我头上打来。当我想努力躲过它们时，各种论文和大学的精灵就会紧追上来。对这些我曾经崇拜的偶像——啊，请宽恕我这邪恶的愿望吧——现在真想把它们全都摔成碎片。

海伦和爱犬在一起，海伦在用手触摸圣诞树

不过，考试算是大学生活中最恐怖的事情了，虽然我已顺利通过了许多次，全都把它们打翻在地，但它们总是无法击垮，而是从地上爬起来张牙舞爪地扑向我，吓得我一点力气也没有了。考试的前几天，我拼命地往脑子里填充各种神秘的公式和无法消化的年代资料——犹如强行咽下那些无法入口的饭菜，那感觉真令人希望同书本和科学一起同归于尽。

最后，可怕的时刻终于来临了。如果你看了试卷以后，觉得早有准备，并能把你需要的东西呼之即出，那你就是个幸运儿了。但事情常常是无论你的军号吹得多么响，也无人听见，当你最需要记忆和精确的分辨能力的时候，它们却偏偏张开翅膀，飞得不知去向。你千辛万苦地塞进脑子里的东

memory and a nice sense of discrimination, these faculties take to themselves wings and fly away. The facts you have garnered with such infinite trouble invariably fail you at a pinch.

"Give a brief account of Huss and his work." Huss? Who was he and what did he do? The name looks strangely familiar. You ransack your budget of historic facts much as you would hunt for a bit of silk in a rag bag. You are sure it is somewhere in your mind near the top-you saw it there the other day when you were looking up the beginnings of the Reformation. But where is it now? You fish out all manner of odds and ends of knowledge-revolutions, schisms, massacres, systems of government; but Huss-where is he? You are amazed at all the things you know which are not on the examination paper. In desperation you seize the budget and dump everything out, and there in a corner is your man, serenely brooding on his own private thought, unconscious of the catastrophe which he has brought upon you.

Just then the proctor informs you that the time is up. With a feeling of intense disgust you kick the mass of rubbish into a corner and go home, your head full of revolutionary schemes to abolish the divine right of professors to ask questions without the consent of the questioned.

It comes over me that in the last two or three pages of this chapter I have used figures which will turn the laugh against me. Ah, here they are-the mixed metaphors mocking and strutting about before me, pointing to the bull in the

西，在此紧要关头却无论如何也想不起来了。

"简述赫斯及其作品。"赫斯?谁是赫斯?他做过什么?这名字听起来出奇地熟悉，你搜肠刮肚地搜索自己历史材料的口袋，就像要在一个碎布包里找出一小块绸子来。你可以肯定这个问题曾经背过，似乎就近在眼前——而且那天当你回想宗教改革的起源时，还曾碰到过它，可是现在它又到哪里去了呢?你把脑子里记忆的东西全都翻了出来——历次革命、教会的分裂、大屠杀、各种政治制度，等等。但是赫斯呢，他又到哪里去了?使你奇怪的是，你记得的东西考卷上一个也没有。绝望之余，你把脑子里的东西都倒了出来。啊! 在那角落正好有一个是你千寻万找的，而他却在那里独自思索，一点儿也没有意识到给你带来了多大的灾难。

可就在这时，监考人过来说时间到了。你厌恶之极地把一堆垃圾一脚踢到角落里，然后回到家里，脑子里不禁蹦出一个革命的想法——废除教授们不征求同意就提问题的神圣权利。

在本章的最后两三页，我运用了一些形象的比喻，可能会引起人们的笑话。那闯进瓷器店里受到冰雹般袭击的公牛，还有那面目狰狞的鬼怪，似乎都显得不伦不类，可是现在它们都在嘲笑我。我觉得自己所使用的言词确切地刻画了我读大学的心境，因此对这些嘲笑也就不屑一顾。我必须郑重声明

china shop assailed by hailstones and the bugbears with pale looks, an unanalyzed species! Let them mock on. The words describe so exactly the atmosphere of jostling, tumbling ideas I live in that I will wink at them for once, and put on a deliberate air to say that my ideas of college have changed.

While my days at Radcliffe were still in the future, they were encircled with a halo of romance, which they have lost; but in the transition from romantic to actual I have learned many things I should never have known had I not tried the experiment. One of them is the precious science of patience, which teaches us that we should take our education as we would take a walk in the country, leisurely, our minds hospitably open to impressions of every sort. Such knowledge floods the soul unseen with a soundless tidal wave of deepening thought.

"Knowledge is power." Rather, knowledge is happiness, because to have knowledge-broad, deep knowledge-is to know true ends from false, and lofty things from low. To know the thoughts and deeds that have marked man's progress is to feel the great heart-throbs of humanity through the centuries; and if one does not feel in these pulsations a heavenward striving, one must indeed be deaf to the harmonies of life.

的是，我对大学的看法已经改变了。

当进入拉德克利夫学院还是我美丽的梦想时，我把大学生活想得非常浪漫迷人，但是进入大学之后，这层浪漫的光环已经消失。在从浪漫向现实的转变过程中，我学到了许多东西。如果没有这段经历，我根本不会懂得这些经验。我所学到的宝贵经验之一就是耐心，它教会我们要接受教育，就像我们在乡村散步一样，从容而恬静、胸襟宽广、兼收并蓄。这样得来的知识就好像无声的潮水，把各种深刻的思想毫无形迹地冲进我们的心田。

"知识就是力量。"当然，知识也是幸福，因为有了知识——广博而精深的知识——就可以分辨真伪、区别高低。掌握了标志着人类进步的各种思想和业绩，也就摸到了有史以来人类思想活动的脉搏。如果一个人不能从这种脉搏中体会到人类积极向上的崇高的愿望，那他就根本不懂得人类生命的和音。

CHAPTER XXI

I HAVE thus far sketched the events of my life, but I have not shown how much I have depended on books not only for pleasure and for the wisdom they bring to all who read, but also for that knowledge which comes to others through their eyes and their ears. Indeed, books have meant so much more in my education than in that of others, that I shall go back to the time when I began to read.

I read my first connected story in May, 1887, when I was seven years old, and from that day to this I have devoured everything in the shape of a printed page that has come within the reach of my hungry finger tips. As I have said, I did not study regularly during the early years of my education; nor did I read according to rule.

At first I had only a few books in raised print-"readers" for beginners, a collection of stories for children, and a book about the earth called "Our World". I think that was all; but I read them over and over, until the words were so worn and pressed I could scarcely make them out. Sometimes Miss Sullivan read to me, spelling into my hand little stories and poems that she knew I should understand; but I preferred reading myself to being read to, because I liked to read again and again the things that pleased me.

第21章 爱书如命

至此，我已经简略地叙述了我自己的生平。但我还没有告诉大家，我是多么的爱书如命。我对书的依赖，不仅是因为书能给我带来快乐和智慧，而且给了我知识。其他人可以通过视听来获得这些知识，而我则全靠书。实际上，在我的教育中，书比其他任何东西都更重要，书对我来说就是我教育的全部。因此，我将回过头来从我开始读书时说起。

1887年5月，我第一次读一篇完整的短篇小说，当时我还只有7岁。从那以后直到现在，我如饥似渴地吞食我的手指所接触到的一切印刷品。正如我前面所说的，我早期所接受的教育并不是正规系统的，我的读书同样也毫无规矩和章法可循。

起初，我只有少数几本盲文书：一套启蒙读本，一套儿童故事集和一本介绍地球的书，名叫《我们的世界》，我想这就是我所有的书了。我将它们读了一遍又一遍，直到上面的字被磨损得无法辨认。有时候，莎莉文老师会读书给我"听"，把她认为我能懂的故事和诗歌写在我的手上。但我宁愿自己读，也不愿人家读给我"听"，因为我喜欢一遍又一遍地读我自己觉得

It was during my first visit to Boston that I really began to read in good earnest. I was permitted to spend a part of each day in the Institution library, and to wander from bookcase to bookcase, and take down whatever book my fingers lighted upon. And read I did, whether I understood one word in ten or two words on a page.

The words themselves fascinated me; but I took no conscious account of what I read. My mind must, however, have been very impressionable at that period, for it retained many words and whole sentences, to the meaning of which I had not the faintest clue; and afterward, when I began to talk and write, these words and sentences would flash out quite naturally, so that my friends wondered at the richness of my vocabulary. I must have read parts of many books (in those early days I think I never read any one book through) and a great deal of poetry in this uncomprehending way, until I discovered "Little Lord Fauntleroy", which was the first book of any consequence I read understandingly.

One day my teacher found me in a corner of the library poring over the pages of "The Scarlet Letter". I was then about eight years old. I remember she asked me if I liked little Pearl, and

有趣的作品。

　　但事实上，我是第一次去波士顿时，才真正开始系统读书的。在学校里，我被允许每天花一些时间到图书馆看书。我在书架前摸索着走来走去，随便挑自己喜欢的图书阅读。不管书中的文字我能认识多少，也不管是否能看明白，我都照读不误。

　　文字本身使我深深地着迷，尽管我对自己所读内容并不明白多少。那时我的记忆力一定很好，因为许多我一点儿也不明白其涵义的字句都能记在脑子里。后来，当我开始学会说和写的时候，这些字句很自然地闪现在我眼前，朋友们都很惊奇我的词汇如此丰富。我当时一定是不求甚解地读过很多书的片断（在那段时期，我从未从头到尾读完一本书）以及大量的诗歌，直到我发现《小方德诺伯爵》这本书，我才第一次完整地读懂了一本有价值的书。

　　一天，莎莉文老师发现我在图书馆的一个角落里翻阅小说《红字》，那时我大约只有8岁。我记得她还问我是否喜欢书中的皮尔，并为我讲解了

洛克菲勒，美国著名财阀、"石油大王"，他创建了标准石油公司，并创造了无数财富，是世界上第一位亿万富翁

explained some of the words that had puzzled me. Then she told me that she had a beautiful story about a little boy which she was sure I should like better than "The Scarlet Letter". The name of the story was "Little Lord Fauntleroy", and she promised to read it to me the following summer. But we did not begin the story until August; the first few weeks of my stay at the seashore were so full of discoveries and excitement that I forgot the very existence of books. Then my teacher went to visit some friends in Boston, leaving me for a short time.

When she returned almost the first thing we did was to begin the story of "Little Lord Fauntleroy". I recall distinctly the time and place when we read the first chapters of the fascinating child's story. It was a warm afternoon in August. We were sitting together in a hammock which swung from two solemn pines at a short distance from the house. We had hurried through the dish-washing after luncheon, in order that we might have as long an afternoon as possible for the story.

As we hastened through the long grass toward the hammock, the grasshoppers swarmed about us and fastened themselves on our clothes, and I remember that my teacher

海伦1926年拜会柯立芝总统时的合影

几个我不明白的单词，然后她又说她有一本有趣的书，是描写一个小男孩的小说，这本书比《红字》更有意思，书的名字就叫《小方德诺伯爵》。她答应到夏天给我读这个故事，但我们直到8月才开始读这本书。因为我们刚到海边时的几个星期，总是被不断发现的许多新奇有趣的事情所吸引，结果把这件事给忘了，而老师又要去波士顿看朋友，也耽搁了几天时间。

莎莉文老师回来后，我们所做的第一件事就是读《小方德诺伯爵》。我现在还能清楚地回忆起当时第一次读《小方德诺伯爵》这个引人入胜的故事的情景。那是8月一个炎热的下午，我们一同坐在屋外不远处两棵墨绿色松树之间的吊床上。我们吃过午饭后，匆匆忙忙地洗干净餐具，以便下午能有更多的时间读那本小说。

当我们穿过草地时，许多蚱蜢跳到了我们的衣角上，我还记得老师坚

insisted on picking them all off before we sat down, which seemed to me an unnecessary waste of time. The hammock was covered with pine needles, for it had not been used while my teacher was away. The warm sun shone on the pine trees and drew out all their fragrance. The air was balmy, with a tang of the sea in it.

Before we began the story Miss Sullivan explained to me the things that she knew I should not understand, and as we read on she explained the unfamiliar words. At first there were many words I did not know, and the reading was constantly interrupted; but as soon as I thoroughly comprehended the situation, I became too eagerly absorbed in the story to notice mere words, and I am afraid I listened impatiently to the explanations that Miss Sullivan felt to be necessary. When her fingers were too tired to spell another word, I had for the first time a keen sense of my deprivations. I took the book in my hands and tried to feel the letters with an intensity of longing that I can never forget.

Afterward, at my eager request, Mr. Anagnos had this story embossed, and I read it again and again, until I almost knew it by heart; and all through my childhood "Little Lord Fauntleroy" was my sweet and gentle companion. I have given these details at the risk of being tedious, because they are in such vivid contrast with my vague, mutable and confused memories of earlier reading.

From "Little Lord Fauntleroy" I date the beginning of my true interest in books. During the next two years I read many books at my home and on my visits to Boston. I cannot remember what they all were, or in what order I read them; but I

持要把这些小虫子从衣服上弄干净才愿意坐下来，而我认为这是一种不必要的时间浪费。由于莎莉文老师不在时，吊床就无人使用，所以上面落满了松针。松树在灼热的太阳照射下，散发出阵阵松香，空气中弥漫着沁人心脾的植物清香，还夹杂着海水的味道。

故事开始前，莎莉文老师先给我介绍了一些我不了解的基本情况，在阅读过程中还不断地为我讲解生字。起初，我有很多生字不认识，读一会儿就得停下来，因此很不顺畅。可是一旦我了解了故事情节后，就被深深地吸引了，迫不及待地想跟上故事的发展，根本顾不上那些生字了，就连莎莉文老师认为很有必要的解释，我也听得有些不耐烦了。当她的手指拼写得太累而不得不停下来时，我就急得不得了，表现出了强烈的占有欲，一把将书抢过来，用手去摸上面的字。那种急切的心情，我永远都无法忘记。

后来，在我的强烈要求下，安纳格罗斯先生把这部小说印成了凸字版。我读了一遍又一遍，几乎能背下来。在我的整个童年时代，《小方德诺伯爵》成了我最亲密、最忠实的伙伴。我之所以如此不厌其烦地讲述这些细节，是因为和我以前随意性的阅读相比，这还是我第一次专注地读一本书。

《小方德诺伯爵》是我真正对书产生兴趣的开始。在接下来的两年时间，我在家里以及波士顿读了很多书。那些书的书名和作者我已经忘了，也

know that among them were "Greek Heroes", La Fontaine's "Fables", Hawthorne's "Wonder Book", "Bible Stories", Lamb's "Tales from Shakespeare"; "A Child's History of England" by Dickens, "The Arabian Nights", " The Swiss Family Robinson", "The Pilgrim's Progress", "Robinson Crusoe", "Little Women", and "Heidi", a beautiful little story which I afterward read in German.

I read them in the intervals between study and play with an ever-deepening sense of pleasure. I did not study nor analyze them-I did not know whether they were well written or not; I never thought about style or authorship. They laid their treasures at my feet, and I accepted them as we accept the sunshine and the love of our friends.

I loved "Little Women" because it gave me a sense of kinship with girls and boys who could see and hear. Circumscribed as my life was in so many ways, I had to look between the covers of books for news of the world that lay outside my own. I did not care especially for "The Pilgrim's Progress", which I think I did not finish, or for the "Fables".

I read La Fontaine's "Fables" first in an English translation, and enjoyed them only after a half-hearted fashion. Later I read the book again in French, and I found that, in spite of the vivid word-pictures, and the wonderful mastery of language, I liked it no better. I do not know why it is, but stories in which animals are made to talk and act like human beings have never appealed to me very strongly. The ludicrous caricatures of the animals occupy my mind to the exclusion of the moral.

记不起来先读的是哪一本，后读的是哪一本。我还记得的有《希腊英雄》、拉·芳登的《寓言》、霍索恩的《神奇的书》和《圣经故事》、拉姆的《莎士比亚故事》、狄更斯的《儿童版英国史》，还有《天方夜谭》、《瑞士家庭鲁滨逊》、《天路历程》、《鲁滨逊漂流记》、《小妇人》和《海蒂》。《海蒂》是一篇美丽的小故事，我后来又读过它的德文版。

我读这些书是在学习和游戏之余进行的。对这些书，我几乎从不做什么研究分析，既不管它们写得是好是坏，也不管它们的文体和作者情况如何。作家们用文字的方式将自己的思想珍宝呈现在我面前，我像领受阳光和友爱般地接受了这些珍宝。

我喜欢《小妇人》，因为它让我感受到了和视听正常的孩子同样的思想感情。既然我的生命有缺陷，我就只好从一本本书中去探索外部世界的信息。我尤其不喜欢《天路历程》和《寓言》，当然也没有读完它们。

我最早读拉·芳登的《寓言》是英文版的，我当初只是简略地读了一遍，后来我读了法文原版书，虽然故事生动有趣，语言也很精练，但依然不能引起我的兴趣。具体原因我也说不出来，可能是用拟人化的写作手法来阐释动物，所以永远无法让我特别感兴趣，而我也无心领会其中的寓意吧！

而且拉·芳登的作品激发不了人类高尚的道德情操。他认为，自爱和理

Then, again, La Fontaine seldom, if ever, appeals to our higher moral sense. The highest chords he strikes are those of reason and self-love. Through all the fables runs the thought that man's morality springs wholly from self-love, and that if that self-love is directed and restrained by reason, happiness must follow. Now, so far as I can judge, self-love is the root of all evil; but, of course, I may be wrong, for La Fontaine had greater opportunities of observing men than I am likely ever to have. I do not object so much to the cynical and satirical fables as to those in which momentous truths are taught by monkeys and foxes.

But I love "The Jungle Book" and "Wild Animals I Have Known". I feel a genuine interest in the animals themselves, because they are real animals and not caricatures of men. One sympathizes with their loves and hatreds, laughs over their comedies, and weeps over their tragedies. And if they point a moral, it is so subtle that we are not conscious of it.

My mind opened naturally and joyously to a conception of antiquity. Greece, ancient Greece, exercised a mysterious

泰戈尔，印度作家、诗人、社会活动家，一生创作丰富。作品多揭露英国殖民统治下印度人民的悲惨生活，对印度文学的发展影响很大，于1913年获诺贝尔文学奖

性是人性最重要的东西，因此他的作品中自始至终贯穿着这样一种思想：个人的道德感完全来源于自爱，自爱又需要用理性来驾驭和控制，这样人们就会产生真正的幸福。但是我认为，自私之爱乃邪恶之源头——当然，也许我是错的，因为拉·芳登对人类的了解和观察比我要深入得多。不过，我这样讲并不表明我反对讽刺寓言，而是觉得没有必要通过猴子和狼来宣扬伟大的真理。

不过，我很喜欢《丛林之书》和《我所了解的野生动物》，因为它们不是人类创造出来的拟人化的生灵，而是真正意义上的动物。我和它们同爱同恨，它们的滑稽和趣事会逗得我放声大笑，它们的悲惨遭遇有时也会让我流下同情的泪水，其中也包含了许多深刻的寓意，但都非常含蓄，使你难以意识到。

fascination over me. In my fancy the pagan gods and goddesses still walked on earth and talked face to face with men, and in my heart I secretly built shrines to those I loved best. I knew and loved the whole tribe of nymphs and heroes and demigods-no, not quite all, for the cruelty and greed of Medea and Jason were too monstrous to be forgiven, and I used to wonder why the gods permitted them to do wrong and then punished them for their wickedness. And the mystery is still unsolved. I often wonder how

God can dumbness keep
While Sin creeps grinning through His house of Time.

It was the Iliad that made Greece my paradise. I was familiar with the story of Troy before I read it in the original, and consequently I had little difficulty in making the Greek words surrender their treasures after I had passed the borderland of grammar. Great poetry, whether written in Greek or in English, needs no other interpreter than a responsive heart. Would that the host of those who make the great works of the poets odious by their analysis, impositions and laborious comments might learn this simple truth! It is not necessary that one should be able to define every word and give it its principal parts and its grammatical position in the sentence in order to understand and appreciate a fine poem. I know my learned professors have found greater riches in the Iliad than I shall ever find; but I am not avaricious. I am content that others should be wiser than I. But with all their wide and comprehensive knowledge, they cannot measure their enjoyment

我喜欢远古的知识。希腊（尤其是古希腊）历史对我有一种神秘的吸引力。在我的想象中，希腊天神依然在地上行走，和人类进行面对面的交流。在我内心深处的神殿中，依然为这些神灵留着敬仰的圣地。希腊神话中的仙女、英雄和半神半人，我不但熟悉，而且喜爱——不，不完全如此，美狄亚和伊阿松的残忍和贪婪，真让人无法忍受。我一直搞不明白的是，为什么上帝一定要等他们做了那么多坏事之后，再去惩罚他们。我经常奇怪的是——

"妖魔嬉笑着爬出殿堂，上帝却视而不见。"

正是史诗《伊利亚特》让我把古希腊看成了天堂。在阅读原文以前，我就已经对特洛伊的故事非常熟悉了。在掌握古希腊语法以后，我对探索古希腊文化宝藏更是毫无困难了。伟大的诗篇——不论是英文还是古希腊文，只要用心领悟就足够了，而不需要借助别人的翻译。相反，那些反客为主的人却常常喜欢用分析和评论的方法来理解古希腊文，结果歪曲了伟大作品的意义。如果他们能懂得这个简单的道理，就太好了！欣赏一首好诗，根本不需要弄清楚其中的每一个字，也不必弄清楚它们的词法和句法。那些满是学问的教授们从史诗《伊利亚特》中挖掘出来的东西，比我的要多得多，但我从不会妒忌。我也知道别人可能比我更聪明，但是我并不在意，因为他们即使有着广博的知识，却体现不出对这首光辉史诗究竟能欣赏到何种程度——当

of that splendid epic, nor can I. When I read the finest passages of the Iliad, I am conscious of a soul-sense that lifts me above the narrow, cramping circumstances of my life. My physical limitations are forgotten-my world lies upward, the length and the breadth and the sweep of the heavens are mine!

My admiration for the Ineid is not so great, but it is none the less real. I read it as much as possible without the help of notes or dictionary, and I always like to translate the episodes that please me especially. The word-painting of Virgil is wonderful sometimes; but his gods and men move through the scenes of passion and strife and pity and love like the graceful figures in an Elizabethan mask, whereas in the Iliad they give three leaps and go on singing. Virgil is serene and lovely like a marble Apollo in the moonlight; Homer is a beautiful, animated youth in the full sunlight with the wind in his hair.

How easy it is to fly on paper wings! From "Greek Heroes" to the Iliad was no day's journey, nor was it altogether pleasant. One could have traveled round the world many times while I trudged my weary way through the labyrinthine mazes of

海伦站在钢琴旁边，用手摸着钢琴，通过感觉琴键与琴弦的振动来欣赏钢琴演奏

然，我自己也无法表达出来。每当我读到《伊利亚特》最精彩的部分时，就感到自己的灵魂在升华，使我从狭窄的生活圈子里解脱出来，灵魂开始神游于肉体之外，广阔无垠的天堂中只有我一人存在。

我对《伊尼阿特》的喜爱仅次于《伊利亚特》。我读这本书的时候，尽可能不借助注释和词典，我还经常试图把自己最喜欢的那些篇章翻译过来。维吉尔描绘人物的本领出神入化，他笔下充满了喜怒哀乐的天神和凡人好像蒙上了一层伊丽莎白时代的面纱。而《伊利亚特》中的天神和凡人则是又跳又唱的，活灵活现，惟妙惟肖。维吉尔笔下的人物则宁静和谐，好似月光下的阿波罗大理石像，而荷马则是阳光下秀发飘逸的英俊活泼的少年。

在书中自由自在地畅游，真是一件轻松愉快的事！从《希腊英雄》到《伊利亚特》用不了一天的时间。不过，旅途中也并非总是心情愉快的。对别人来说花费相同的时间可能已经周游世界多次，但对我来说，可能还得在语法和词典的迷宫中费力地寻找出路，或者掉进了更恐怖的陷阱，这陷阱就是考试，是学校专门为那些猎取知识的人而设定的。我知道阅读《天路历

grammars and dictionaries, or fell into those dreadful pitfalls called examinations, set by schools and colleges for the confusion of those who seek after knowledge. I suppose this sort of Pilgrim's Progress was justified by the end; but it seemed interminable to me, in spite of the pleasant surprises that met me now and then at a turn in the road.

I began to read the Bible long before I could understand it. Now it seems strange to me that there should have been a time when my spirit was deaf to its wondrous harmonies; but I remember well a rainy Sunday morning when, having nothing else to do, I begged my cousin to read me a story out of the Bible. Although she did not think I should understand, she began to spell into my hand the story of Joseph and his brothers. Somehow it failed to interest me. The unusual language and repetition made the story seem unreal and far away in the land of Canaan, and I fell asleep and

海伦坐在椅子上，左手放在收录机上感受音乐

程》可能会逐渐地引人入胜，但对我来说终究太漫长了，尽管途中也偶尔出人意料地出现几处佳境美景。

我很早就开始接触《圣经》，但直到很久之后才充分理解其内容。现在想起来觉得有些奇怪，为什么这么美妙的和音我却很长一段时间无法接受。我清晰地记得那是一个下雨的星期天早上，我闲得无聊，就让表姐为我读一段《圣经》里的故事。虽然她认为我无法听懂，但还是在我手上拼写约瑟兄弟的故事。我听了确实一点儿兴趣都没有，因为那奇怪的语言和不断的重复，使人觉得故事很不真实，认为那不过是天国里的事情。还没有讲到约瑟兄弟穿着五颜六色的衣服进入雅各的帐篷里去说谎，我就呼呼地睡着了。我至今也弄不明白，为什么希腊故事比《圣经》里的故事更能吸引我。难道是因为我在波士顿时，被我认识的几个希腊人所讲述的故事感染了，而我又从来没有遇到过一个希伯来人或埃及人，并由此推断他们是一群野蛮人，他们的故事也都是由后人编造出来的？因此，我觉得《圣经》故事中的名字和重复的叙述方式十分古怪，相反我却从未觉得希腊人的姓名古怪。

wandered off to the land of Nod, before the brothers came with the coat of many colours unto the tent of Jacob and told their wicked lie! I cannot understand why the stories of the Greeks should have been so full of charm for me, and those of the Bible so devoid of interest, unless it was that I had made the acquaintance of several Greeks in Boston and been inspired by their enthusiasm for the stories of their country; whereas I had not met a single Hebrew or Egyptian, and therefore concluded that they were nothing more than barbarians, and the stories about them were probably all made up, which hypothesis explained the repetitions and the queer names. Curiously enough, it never occurred to me to call Greek patronymics "queer".

But how shall I speak of the glories I have since discovered in the Bible? For years I have read it with an ever-broadening sense of joy and inspiration; and I love it as I love no other book. Still there is much in the Bible against which every instinct of my being rebels, so much that I regret the necessity which has compelled me to read it through from beginning to end. I do not think that the knowledge which I have gained of its history and sources compensates me for the unpleasant details it has forced upon my attention. For my part, I wish, with Mr. Howells, that the literature of the past might be purged of all that is ugly and barbarous in it, although I should object as much as any one to having these great works weakened or falsified.

There is something impressive, awful, in the simplicity and terrible directness

那么，我该如何描述我后来从《圣经》中发现其光辉的呢？这么多年以来，随着我眼界的加宽，我再读《圣经》时，获得的喜悦和灵感与日俱增，我也渐渐地把它当作自己最珍爱的书。不过，我对于《圣经》中的许多地方还不能全盘接受，因此也从未能把它从头到尾读完，这一点也令我感到惭愧。后来，尽管我明白了《圣经》产生的历史背景及其渊源，但这种情绪依然没有丝毫的减弱。我和豪威斯先生都希望从《圣经》中剔除掉一切丑恶和野蛮的东西，但我们也坚决反对把这部不朽的作品改得面目全非，失去了它原有的思想性和文学性。

《旧约圣经》中《以斯书》简洁明快，描写准确，气势强大，给人的印象深刻。还有比以斯面对自己邪恶的丈夫时那么强烈而富有戏剧性的场景吗？尽管她清楚地知道自己的生命系于对方手中，也没有人能够拯救她，但是她克服了女性的懦弱，勇敢地走向她的丈夫。高尚的责任感鼓舞着她，她的心中只有一个念头："如果我死，我就死吧！如果我生，我的人民都将获救。"

还有路德的故事，是多么富有神奇的东方色彩啊！朴实的乡村生活，同繁华的首都波斯之间的对比是多么强烈啊！路德忠贞而热情，当她与那些正在收割庄稼的农民们一起站在翻滚的麦浪之中时，使人们自然而然地爱上了

of the book of Esther. Could there be anything more dramatic than the scene in which Esther stands before her wicked lord? She knows her life is in his hands; there is no one to protect her from his wrath. Yet, conquering her woman's fear, she approaches him, animated by the noblest patriotism, having but one thought: "If I perish, I perish; but if I live, my people shall live."

The story of Ruth, too-how Oriental it is! Yet how different is the life of these simple country folks from that of the Persian capital! Ruth is so loyal and gentle-hearted, we cannot help loving her, as she stands with the reapers amid the waving corn. Her beautiful, unselfish spirit shines out like a bright star in the night of a dark and cruel age. Love like Ruth's, love which can rise above conflicting creeds and deep-seated racial prejudices, is hard to find in all the world.

The Bible gives me a deep, comforting sense that "things seen are temporal, and things unseen are eternal."

I do not remember a time since I have been capable of loving books that I have

爱迪生，美国著名实业家、发明大王，一生有上千项发明专利。他的许多发明给人类生活带来了巨大的变化

她。在那黑暗残暴的年代，她的美丽无私和高尚情操，犹如黑暗残暴年代中高悬在夜空的闪耀星辰。路德广博的爱超越了冲突与斗争的宗教信仰和根深蒂固的种族偏见，成为世上罕见的珍宝。

《圣经》给了我深远的慰藉："有形的东西是短暂的，无形的东西才能够永垂不朽。"

自从我喜欢读书以来，莎士比亚的作品就让我再也不忍释手了。我记不清楚自己是从何时开始读兰姆的《莎士比亚故事》的，但我却记得第一次读它的时候，就对它有很深的理解和感叹。我印象最深刻的似乎是《麦克白》，虽然我只读过一遍，但其中的人物和故事情节却永远铭刻在我的记忆中。在很长一段时间里，书中的鬼魂和女巫总是缠着我，甚至跑到梦中来追我。我仿佛看到了那把剑和麦克白夫人那纤细的手——可怕的血迹在我眼前出现，就像那忧伤的王后亲眼看到的一样。

我读完《麦克白》之后，接着读了《李尔王》。当我读到格洛赛斯特的

not loved Shakespeare. I cannot tell exactly when I began Lamb's "Tales from Shakespeare"; but I know that I read them at first with a child's understanding and a child's wonder. "Macbeth" seems to have impressed me most. One reading was sufficient to stamp every detail of the story upon my memory forever. For a long time the ghosts and witches pursued me even into Dreamland. I could see, absolutely see, the dagger and Lady Macbeth's little white hand-the dreadful stain was as real to me as to the grief-stricken queen.

I read "King Lear" soon after "Macbeth", and I shall never forget the feeling of horror when I came to the scene in which Gloucester's eyes are put out. Anger seized me, my fingers refused to move, I sat rigid for one long moment, the blood throbbing in my temples, and all the hatred that a child can feel concentrated in my heart.

I must have made the acquaintance of Shylock and Satan about the same time, for the two characters were long associated in my mind. I remember that I was sorry for them. I felt vaguely that they could not be good even if they wished to, because no one seemed willing to help them or to give them a fair chance. Even now I cannot find it in my heart to condemn them utterly. There are moments when I feel that the Shylocks, the Judases, and even the Devil, are broken spokes in the great wheel of good which shall in due time be made whole.

It seems strange that my first reading of Shakespeare should have left me so many unpleasant memories. The bright, gentle, fanciful plays-the ones I like best

眼睛被挖出来时，我浑身紧张，不由自主地哆嗦起来，心里充满了恐惧。同时，我又是如此的愤怒，以至于根本就读不下去了，一颗心在咚咚直跳，好长时间都呆呆地坐在那里。

我大概是在同一时间接触到的夏洛克和撒旦，使得这两个人物在我脑海中紧密相连。记得当时我心里对他们充满了同情和怜悯，我模模糊糊地觉得，即使他们希望自己变好，但还是成不了好人，因为似乎没有人愿意帮助他们，或给他们一个机会来改过自新。即使直至今天，我也依然很难将他们描写得十恶不赦，我甚至还有这样一种感觉:像夏洛克、犹大这样一类人，甚至魔鬼，也都只是那完好的车轮上一根断了的车轴，他们总有一天会被修好的。

奇怪的是，我最初读莎士比亚的作品时，留下的大都是一些不怎么愉快的记忆。相反，那些欢快温和而又富于想象的作品一开始却并不如何吸引我，而现在它们却是我最喜欢的。这或许因为是它们反映了儿童生活的快乐，而我当初对此还没有多少理解的缘故吧。然而"世上最变幻莫测的就是儿童的想象了。保持什么，丢掉什么，都很难预料。"

莎士比亚的剧本我读过很多遍，对其中某些片段甚至能脱口而出，但若要说我自己最喜欢的，恐怕我现在也无法弄清楚。我对它们的喜爱，就像

now-appear not to have impressed me at first, perhaps because they reflected the habitual sunshine and gaiety of a child's life. But "there is nothing more capricious than the memory of a child: what it will hold, and what it will lose."

I have since read Shakespeare's plays many times and know parts of them by heart, but I cannot tell which of them I like best. My delight in them is as varied as my moods. The little songs and the sonnets have a meaning for me as fresh and wonderful as the dramas. But, with all my love for Shakespeare, it is often weary work to read all the meanings into his lines which critics and commentators have given them. I used to try to remember their interpretations, but they discouraged and vexed me; so I made a secret compact with myself not to try any more. This compact I have only just broken in my study of Shakespeare under Professor Kittredge. I know there are many things in Shakespeare, and in the world, that I do not understand; and I am glad to see veil after veil lift gradually, revealing new realms of thought

亨利·福特,美国著名企业家、汽车大王,一生致力于汽车设计和制造,改写了美国交通的历史,被誉为"20世纪最伟大的企业家",他热心慈善事业,经常捐赠孤残者

我的心情一样变化不定。对我来说,莎士比亚的短诗和十四行诗以及他的戏剧同样新奇而精彩,尽管我喜欢莎士比亚,但我却讨厌按评论家们的观点来读莎翁的作品。我曾试图结合评论家们的解释来理解莎翁的作品,但总是灰心和失望,于是发誓再也不这样做了。自从我跟随基特里奇教授学习莎士比亚以后,我的这个看法才逐渐改变。今天,我终于明白,不但在莎翁的著作里,而且在这个世界上有许多东西是我所不能理解的,而我则很高兴地看到一层又一层帷幕逐渐升起,显露出思想和美的新境界。

除了诗歌以外,我还非常喜欢历史。我几乎阅读了我能接触到的所有的历史著作,从各种单调而枯燥的大事记,甚至更乏味的年表,一直到格林撰写的独特而公正的《英国民族史》,从弗里曼的《欧洲史》到埃默顿的《中世纪》。在这些书中,我第一次真正体会历史价值的书是斯温顿的《世界史》。那是我12岁生日时别人送给我的礼物。现在这本书可能没什么了不起

and beauty.

Next to poetry I love history. I have read every historical work that I have been able to lay my hands on, from a catalogue of dry facts and dryer dates to Green's impartial, picturesque "History of the English People"; from Freeman's "History of Europe" to Emerton's "Middle Ages". The first book that gave me any real sense of the value of history was Swinton's "World History", which I received on my thirteenth birthday. Though I believe it is no longer considered valid, yet I have kept it ever since as one of my treasures. From it I learned how the races of men spread from land to land and built great cities, how a few great rulers, earthly Titans, put everything under their feet, and with a decisive word opened the gates of happiness for millions and closed them upon millions more: how different nations pioneered in art and knowledge and broke ground for the mightier growths of coming ages; how civilization underwent, as it were, the holocaust of a degenerate age, and rose again, like the Phoenix, among the nobler sons of the North; and how by liberty, tolerance and education the great and the wise have opened the way for the salvation of the whole world.

In my college reading I have become somewhat familiar with French and German literature. The German puts strength before beauty, and truth before convention, both in life and in literature. There is a vehement, sledgehammer vigour about everything that he does. When he speaks, it is not to impress others, but because his heart would burst if he did not find an outlet for the thoughts that

的，但我一直像珍宝一样珍藏着。我从书中了解到了世界各地的人们是如何在地球上逐步发展的，是如何建立城市的，少数伟大的统治者（他们是人世间的巨人）又是如何把人踩于脚下，把千百万人掌控在自己一人手中的；我了解到了人类文明是如何用文化艺术推动历史发展、开辟道路的；我了解到了人类文明如何在经历了腐朽堕落的浩劫之后，又像凤凰涅一样死而复生，以及伟大的圣贤先知为了拯救全世界而如何以自由、宽容和教育来披荆斩棘的。

由于在大学时代读过一些书，所以我对德国和法国的文学作品也比较熟悉。德国人在生活和文学上，喜欢用力量来显示美，他们追求真理，打破常规。德国人做任何事都精力充沛，他们说话不是为了影响别人，而是如鲠在喉不吐不快。

德国文学的一大特点就是含蓄，这也是我非常喜爱的。我还发现，德国文学中最光辉的地方，就是对妇女自我牺牲的爱情的伟大力量的承认，这种思想渗透到了几乎所有的德国文学作品中，尤其是在歌德的《浮士德》中表现得最为显著：

那昙花一现，

不过是象征而已。

burn in his soul.

Then, too, there is in German literature a fine reserve which I like; but its chief glory is the recognition I find in it of the redeeming potency of woman's self-sacrificing love. This thought pervades all German literature and is mystically expressed in Goethe's "Faust":

All things transitory
But as symbols are sent.
Earth's insufficiency
Here grows to event.
The indescribable
Here it is done.
The Woman Soul leads us upward and on!

Of all the French writers that I have read, I like Molière and Racine best. There are fine things in Balzac and passages in Mérimée which strike one like a keen blast of sea air. Alfred de Musset is impossible! I admire Victor Hugo-I appreciate his genius, his brilliancy, his romanticism; though he is not one of my literary passions.

But Hugo and Goethe and Schiller and all great poets of all great nations are interpreters of eternal things, and my spirit reverently follows them into the regions where Beauty and Truth and Goodness are one.

I am afraid I have written too much about my book-friends, and yet I have

人间缺憾，

也会成为圆满。

那无法形容的，

已经在此完成。

女性的灵魂，

引导我们永远向上。

我读过的所有法国作家中，莫里哀和拉辛是我最喜欢的。巴尔扎克和梅里美的作品犹如阵阵袭人的海风，带给人清新的感受。阿尔弗雷德·缪塞更是如有神笔，妙不可言！我很敬仰维克多·雨果，我欣赏他的才华、他的卓尔不凡、他的浪漫主义情怀，尽管在文学上我并不是非常喜欢他。

雨果、歌德、席勒以及所有伟大国家的伟大诗人，都是人类永恒主题的探索者，是他们用自己伟大的作品引领我的灵魂，虔诚地追随他们，进入真善美的殿堂。

也许我介绍我的书友太多了些，但我实际上只说了我自己最喜欢的一部分而已。也许读者会因此而误以为我的阅读面很窄，其实很多作者都有其独特的风格值得我欣赏，比如卡莱尔的粗犷以及对虚伪的憎厌，伍兹华斯的天人一体观，以及胡德的神怪之笔、赫里克的典雅及其作品中所蕴含的百合

mentioned only the authors I love most; and from this fact one might easily suppose that my circle of friends was very limited and undemocratic, which would be a very wrong impression. I like many writers for many reasons-Carlyle for his ruggedness and scorn of shams; Wordsworth, who teaches the oneness of man and nature; I find an exquisite pleasure in the oddities and surprises of Hood, in Herrick's quaintness and the palpable scent of lily and rose in his verses; I like Whittier for his enthusiasms and moral rectitude. I knew him, and the gentle remembrance of our friendship doubles the pleasure I have in reading his poems. I love Mark Twain-who does not? The gods, too, loved him and put into his heart all manner of wisdom; then, fearing lest he should become a pessimist, they spanned his mind with a rainbow of love and faith. I like Scott for his freshness, dash and large honesty. I love all writers whose minds, like Lowell's, bubble up in the sunshine of optimism-fountains of joy and good will, with occasionally a splash of anger and here and there a healing spray of sympathy and pity.

In a word, literature is my Utopia. Here I am not disfranchised. No barrier of the senses shuts me out from the sweet, gracious discourse of my book-friends. They talk to me without embarrassment or awkwardness. The things I have learned and the things I have been taught seem of ridiculously little importance compared with their "large loves and heavenly charities."

和玫瑰的花香味儿，这一切都对我有深远的影响。我还喜欢惠蒂尔的热情正直，我认识他，对于我们之间友谊的美好回忆，使我在读他的诗歌时倍感亲切。我喜欢马克·吐温——谁能不喜欢他呢?就连天神也喜欢他，并赋予他无所不能的智慧，而且为了不使他成为悲观主义者，又在他的心中织起了一道关爱和信仰的彩虹。我还爱司各特的清新不凡、泼辣和诚实。我爱所有像洛厄那样的作家，他们的内心充满了乐观主义精神，犹如阳光下泛起涟漪的池水，带给世人无穷的欢乐和友善，还不时地带点愤怒，有时又因为同情和怜悯而扬起轻雾。

　　总而言之，文学是我的乌托邦。在这块乐土里，我享有一切权利。任何生理上的障碍都不能阻止我和作者以及作品中的人物交流。我们侃侃而谈，没有困窘，没有尴尬，也没有嘲笑。和我学到的东西本身所具有的"广博的爱和高尚的仁慈"相比，我的知识是那么微小，是那么幼稚可笑。

CHAPTER XXII

I TRUST that my readers have not concluded from the preceding chapter on books that reading is my only pleasure; my pleasures and amusements are many and varied.

More than once in the course of my story I have referred to my love of the country and out-of-door sports. When I was quite a little girl, I learned to row and swim, and during the summer, when I am at Wrentham, Massachusetts, I almost live in my boat. Nothing gives me greater pleasure than to take my friends out rowing when they visit me. Of course, I cannot guide the boat very well. Some one usually sits in the stern and manages the rudder while I row. Sometimes, however, I go rowing without the rudder. It is fun to try to steer by the scent of watergrasses and lilies, and of bushes that grow on the shore. I use oars with leather bands, which keep them in position in the oarlocks, and I know by the resistance of the water when the oars are evenly poised. In the same manner I can also tell when I am pulling against the current. I like to contend with wind and wave. What is more exhilarating than to make your staunch little boat, obedient to your will and muscle, go skimming lightly over glistening, tilting waves, and to feel the steady,

第22章 享受多彩的生活

我相信读者不会从我前面的叙述中得出结论，认为读书是我唯一的乐趣。事实上，我的乐趣是广泛而又富有情趣的。

我在自述中多次提到了我非常喜爱乡村和户外活动。当我还是一个小孩子的时候，我就学会了划船和游泳。夏天，在马萨诸塞州伦萨姆时，一到夏天，我几乎就住在了船上。没有什么比朋友来访时出去划船更有趣的了。当然，我总是掌握不好船的方向，因此我驾船时，通常要有人坐在船尾掌舵。有时，我也在没有舵手的情况下划船。我通过辨别水草和睡莲以及岸上灌木的气味来掌握方向，我会用皮绳把船桨固定在桨环上，我还能够通过水的阻力大小来判断双桨用力是否平衡。同样，我还知道什么时候是逆水而上。我喜欢和风浪搏斗，驾着一叶轻舟，按照自己的意志和力量，穿越波光粼粼、微波荡漾的湖面，感受水波不停地流淌，没有什么比这更令人愉悦的了！

我还喜欢划独木小船。我说我特别喜欢在月夜泛舟时，你们听了也许会哑然失笑。不错，我确实看不见月亮从松树后面爬上枝头，高挂苍穹，给大

imperious surge of the water!

 I also enjoy canoeing, and I suppose you will smile when I say that I especially like it on moonlight nights. I cannot, it is true, see the moon climb up the sky behind the pines and steal softly across the heavens, making a shining path for us to follow; but I know she is there, and as I lie back among the pillows and put my hand in the water, I fancy that I feel the shimmer of her garments as she passes. Sometimes a daring little fish slips between my fingers, and often a pond-lily presses shyly against my hand.

 Frequently, as we emerge from the shelter of a cove or inlet, I am suddenly conscious of the spaciousness of the air about me. A luminous warmth seems to enfold me. Whether it comes from the trees which have been heated by the sun, or from the water, I can never discover. I have had the same strange sensation even in the heart of the city. I have felt it on cold, stormy days and at night.

地罩上银白色的月光，但我能感觉到月亮的存在。当我累了之后，享受般地躺到垫子上，把手放进水中时，我好像看见了明如白昼的月光正在经过，而我则触到了她的衣裳。一条大胆的小鱼间

海伦在公园散步，坐在长椅上休息

或从我的手指间匆匆游过，睡莲则含羞地亲吻我的手指。

  当小船从避风的小港湾隐蔽处驶出时，我会感觉到迎面吹来的风，会有豁然开朗之感，一股热气把我包围住，我不知道这热气是从树林中来的，还是从水汽里蒸发出来的。在内心深处，我也常常有这种奇异的感觉：在风雪交加的日子里，在漫漫长夜中，这种感觉悄然袭来，仿佛温暖的嘴唇在我脸上亲吻。

  我最喜欢乘船远航。1901年夏天，我去斯科迪亚半岛旅行时，第一次有机会领略大海的风貌。莎莉文老师和我在伊万杰琳的故乡盘桓数日。朗费罗有几首赞美此地的名诗，无形中也增添了它的魅力。我们还去了哈利发克斯，并在那里消磨了大半个夏天。哈利发克斯海港成了我们的快乐港湾，我

It is like the kiss of warm lips on my face.

My favourite amusement is sailing. In the summer of 1901 I visited Nova Scotia, and had opportunities such as I had not enjoyed before to make the acquaintance of the ocean. After spending a few days in Evangeline's country, about which Longfellow's beautiful poem has woven a spell of enchantment, Miss Sullivan and I went to Halifax, where we remained the greater part of the summer. The harbour was our joy, our paradise. What glorious sails we had to Bedford Basin, to McNabb's Island, to York Redoubt, and to the Northwest Arm! And at night what soothing, wondrous hours we spent in the shadow of the great, silent men-of-war. Oh, it was all so interesting, so beautiful! The memory of it is a joy forever.

One day we had a thrilling experience.

There was a regatta in the Northwest Arm, in which the boats from the different warships were engaged. We went in a sail-boat along with many others to watch the races. Hundreds of little sail-boats swung to and fro close by, and the sea was calm. When the races were over, and we turned our faces homeward, one of the party noticed a black cloud drifting in from the sea, which grew and spread and thickened until it covered the whole sky. The wind rose, and the waves chopped angrily at unseen barriers. Our little boat confronted the gale fearlessly; with sails spread and ropes taut, she seemed to sit upon the wind. Now she swirled in the billows, now she sprang upward on a gigantic wave, only to be driven down with

们就像进了天堂。我们还乘船去了贝德福拜森、麦克纳勃岛、约克锐道特以及西北湾，那次经历简直太难忘了！一些庞大的船舰静静地停泊在海港里，夜晚我们悠闲地在舰侧荡桨划行，真是有趣极了！这些令人愉快的情景，我始终难以忘怀。

有一天，我们在这里还有过惊心动魄的经历呢。

当时，西北湾正在举行赛艇比赛，许多军舰都放出了小船参赛。人们从四面八方乘帆船来看比赛，我们也加入其中，数百艘小帆船在海面上穿梭往来。比赛的时候，海面一片风平浪静，比赛结束后，大家都掉转船头准备回家。这时，我的一个同伴发现从海面上漂来一块乌云，而且乌云越来越多，越来越厚，很快整个天空都被遮盖住了，顷刻间海风骤起，波浪滔天。我们的船虽然很小，但面对大风大浪没有丝毫的畏惧，我们挂满风帆，拉紧船绳，犹如迎风飞翔一般，在波涛中随着巨浪翻滚，一会儿被推上浪头，一会儿又跌落下来。风在怒吼，帆在嘶鸣，我们的心也随着风浪中飘动的小船而起伏直跳，手臂也因为精神紧张而在颤抖，这可不是因为畏惧！因为我们崇尚维京人的冒险精神，我们也相信我们的船长完全能驾驭风浪。他凭着坚实的双手和熟悉海浪的眼睛，已经闯过了无数次大风大浪。港湾中所有船只驶近我们的船时，都鸣号向我们致敬，水手们欢呼，向我们这唯一一艘在暴

angry howl and hiss. Down came the mainsail. Tacking and jibbing, we wrestled with opposing winds that drove us from side to side with impetuous fury. Our hearts beat fast, and our hands trembled with excitement, not fear; for we had the hearts of vikings, and we knew that our skipper was master of the situation. He had steered through many a storm with firm hand and sea-wise eye. As they passed us, the large craft and the gunboats in the harbour saluted and the seamen shouted applause for the master of the only little sail-boat that ventured out into the storm. At last, cold, hungry and weary, we reached our pier.

Last summer I spent in one of the loveliest nooks of one of the most charming villages in New England. Wrentham, Massachusetts, is associated with nearly all of my joys and sorrows. For many years Red Farm, by King Philip's Pond, the home of Mr. J. E. Chamberlin and his family, was my home. I remember with deepest gratitude the kindness of these dear friends and the happy days I spent with them. The sweet companionship of their children meant much to me. I joined in all their sports and rambles through the woods and frolics in the water. The prattle of the little ones and their pleasure in the stories I told them of elf and gnome, of hero and wily bear, are pleasant things to remember. Mr. Chamberlin initiated me into the mysteries of tree and wild-flower, until with the little ear of love I heard the flow of sap in the oak, and saw the sun glint from leaf to leaf.

Even as the roots, shut in the darksome earth,
Share in the tree-top's joyance, and conceive

风雨中搏斗的小帆船的船长致敬。最后,我们拖着又饿又冷、疲惫不堪的身体,终于驶抵码头。

去年夏天,我是在新英格兰一个风景迷人的幽静乡村里度过的。马萨诸塞州的伦萨姆仿佛包含了我生命中几乎所有欢乐和忧愁的地方,我的快乐和忧愁似乎都与这个地方连在一起。多年来,靠近菲利浦王池的钱布林先生的红色农庄成了我自己的家。每每想起和这里的亲朋好友共同度过的快乐时光,以及他们对我的恩惠,我心里就充满了感激之情。他们的孩子和我结成了亲密伙伴,对我帮助很大。我们一起做游戏,携手在林中散步,在水中嬉戏。我给孩子们讲小精灵、小妖怪、英雄和狡猾的狗熊的故事,他们则围着我说这讲那的,这一切想起来都令我心里甜滋滋的。钱布林先生还教我去探究树木和野花的秘密,后来我仿佛能听见橡树中树液的奔腾流动,能看见阳光挥洒在树叶上的光辉。

树根即使深埋于地下,
也能分享到枝头上的
愉悦和想象。
灿烂的阳光、宽广的天空和自由的飞翔,
因为与自然有着共鸣

Of sunshine and wide air and wingéd things,
By sympathy of nature, so do I
gave evidence of things unseen.

It seems to me that there is in each of us a capacity to comprehend the impressions and emotions which have been experienced by mankind from the beginning. Each individual has a subconscious memory of the green earth and murmuring waters, and blindness and deafness cannot rob him of this gift from past generations. This inherited capacity is a sort of sixth sense-a soul-sense which sees, hears, feels, all in one.

I have many tree friends in Wrentham. One of them, a splendid oak, is the special pride of my heart. I take all my other friends to see this king-tree. It stands on a bluff overlooking King Philip's Pond, and those who are wise in tree lore say it must have stood there eight hundred or a thousand years. There is a tradition that under this tree King Philip, the heroic Indian chief, gazed his last on earth and sky.

I had another tree friend, gentle and more approachable than the great oak-a linden that grew in the dooryard at Red Farm. One afternoon, during a terrible thunderstorm, I felt a tremendous crash against the side of the house and knew, even before they told me, that the linden had fallen. We went out to see the hero that had withstood so many tempests, and it wrung my heart to see him prostrate who had mightily striven and was now mightily fallen.

But I must not forget that I was going to write about last summer in particular.

所以我

能理解那看不见的世界

我认为，每个人都有一种潜能，都可以理解人类有史以来所经历的印象和情感。每个人的潜意识里还残留着对绿色大地、淙淙流水的记忆。即使是盲聋人，也不能剥夺他们这种从先祖那里遗传下来的本能天性。这种遗传的本能是第六感——一种融合了视觉、听觉、触觉的灵性。

在伦萨姆我有许多树木朋友，其中有一棵硕大的橡树，它是我心中的骄傲。每当有朋友来访时，我总会带着他们去欣赏这棵"百树之王"。它矗立在菲利浦王池陡峭的岸上，据那些对树木比较了解的人说，它已有800年到1000年的树龄。传说中印第安人的英雄领袖菲利浦王，就是在这棵树下去世的。

另外一个树友是一棵长在红色庄园里的椴树，它比这棵大橡树还要温和可亲。一天下午，电闪雷鸣，我感觉从后墙传来了一声巨大的碰撞声，不用别人告诉我，我就知道是椴树倒下了。我们走出去看这棵经历了无数狂风暴雨的英雄树，虽然它曾奋力拼搏，但最终还是倒下了，这让我感到非常心痛。

无论如何我一定要特别提及去年夏天的生活。考试结束后，我就和莎莉

As soon as my examinations were over, Miss Sullivan and I hastened to this green nook, where we have a little cottage on one of the three lakes for which Wrentham is famous. Here the long, sunny days were mine, and all thoughts of work and college and the noisy city were thrust into the background. In Wrentham we caught echoes of what was happening in the world-war, alliance, social conflict. We heard of the cruel, unnecessary fighting in the far-away Pacific, and learned of the struggles going on between capital and labour. We knew that beyond the border of our Eden men were making history by the sweat of their brows when they might better make a holiday. But we little heeded these things. These things would pass away; here were lakes and woods and broad daisy-starred fields and sweet-breathed meadows, and they shall endure forever.

People who think that all sensations reach us through the eye and the ear have expressed surprise that I should notice any difference, except possibly the absence of pavements, between walking in city streets and in country roads. They forget that my whole body is alive to the conditions about

海伦和莎莉文坐在起居室的长椅上，正用手语进行交谈

文老师立刻前往伦萨姆幽静的乡村。我们在那里有一栋小别墅，伦萨姆有三个著名的湖，它就坐落在其中一个湖的边上。在这里，我可以尽情地享受充满阳光的日子，将所有的工作、学习和喧嚣的城市全都弃置脑后。在这里我们听到了来自世界各地的消息：战争、结盟、社会冲突。我们得知了遥远的太平洋彼岸正在发生的残酷的战争以及资本家和劳工之间的斗争。就在我们这个人间乐园之外，人们却顾不上休闲娱乐，整日纷纷攘攘，忙碌奔波，丝毫不懂得悠闲自得之乐。我们也顾不得这一切，尽情地享受湖光山色之美。这里静静的湖水、茂密的树木、漫山遍野长满雏菊的宽广的田野、沁人心扉的草原，它们都是永恒存在的。

人们都认为，人类的知觉都是通过眼睛和耳朵传达的，所以他们觉得很奇怪，我除了能分辨出城市街道和乡间小道外，还能分辨其他的东西。可是他们忘了，我的整个身体对于外界事物是保持警醒的，乡间小道除了没有砌造的路面以外，同城市街道并没有什么区别，但是城市的喧闹刺激着我的

me. The rumble and roar of the city smite the nerves of my face, and I feel the ceaseless tramp of an unseen multitude, and the dissonant tumult frets my spirit. The grinding of heavy wagons on hard pavements and the monotonous clangour of machinery are all the more torturing to the nerves if one's attention is not diverted by the panorama that is always present in the noisy streets to people who can see.

In the country one sees only Nature's fair works, and one's soul is not saddened by the cruel struggle for mere existence that goes on in the crowded city. Several times I have visited the narrow, dirty streets where the poor live, and I grow hot and indignant to think that good people should be content to live in fine houses and become strong and beautiful, while others are condemned to live in hideous, sunless tenements and grow ugly, withered and cringing. The children who crowd these grimy alleys, half-clad and underfed, shrink away from your outstretched hand as if from a blow. Dear little creatures, they crouch in my heart and haunt me with a constant sense of pain. There are men

海伦手持一本书，坐在书架前的椅子上

面部神经，我还能感觉到路上看不见的行人急匆匆地步履。各种各样的不和谐的吵嚷声扰乱着我的精神。载重车轧过坚硬的路面所发出来的隆隆巨响声，还有机器单调的轰鸣声，这一切对于一个需要集中注意力来辨别事物的盲人来说，常常是难以忍受的。

而在乡间，到处都可以看到大自然的鬼斧神工，人们可以尽情放松自我，不必担心城市的那种残酷的生存斗争。我曾多次访问过那些住在又窄又脏的街道里的穷人，一想到那些居住在高楼大厦里的有钱有势的人过着精制而幽雅的生活，而穷人们却住在暗无天日的贫民窟里，我就觉得愤恨不平。孩子们挤在肮脏狭窄的小巷子里，衣不蔽体、食不果腹。当你向他们伸出友好的手时，他们也避之唯恐不及，好像你要打他们似的。可怜的孩子，你们不仅蜷缩在街头巷尾，也蜷缩在我的心灵深处，无时无刻不在折磨着我的情感。更令我感到痛苦的是，还有一些男人和女人已经如行尸走肉一样，蜷曲得不成人形。我抚摸过他们那粗糙的手，使我联想到他们的生存实在是一场无休止的斗争——不断的奋战、失败

and women, too, all gnarled and bent out of shape. I have felt their hard, rough hands and realized what an endless struggle their existence must be-no more than a series of scrimmages, thwarted attempts to do something. Their life seems an immense disparity between effort and opportunity.

The sun and the air are God's free gifts to all, we say; but are they so? In yonder city's dingy alleys the sun shines not, and the air is foul. Oh, man, how dost thou forget and obstruct thy brother man, and say, "Give us this day our daily bread, " when he has none! Oh, would that men would leave the city, its splendour and its tumult and its gold, and return to wood and field and simple, honest living! Then would their children grow stately as noble trees, and their thoughts sweet and pure as wayside flowers. It is impossible not to think of all this when I return to the country after a year of work in town.

What a joy it is to feel the soft, springy earth under my feet once more, to follow grassy roads that lead to ferny brooks where I can bathe my fingers in a cataract of rippling notes, or to clamber over a stone wall into green fields that tumble and roll and climb in riotous gladness!

Next to a leisurely walk I enjoy a "spin" on my tandem bicycle. It is splendid to feel the wind blowing in my face and the springy motion of my iron steed. The rapid rush through the air gives me a delicious sense of strength and buoyancy, and the exercise makes my pulses dance and my heart sing.

Whenever it is possible, my dog accompanies me on a walk or ride or sail. I

和失望，他们是那么的努力，可是机遇却不垂青于他们，他们的成功和失败形成了巨大的反差。

我们常说上帝把阳光和空气赐给众生，但真的是这样吗？在城市边缘肮脏的小巷里，阳光难以普照，空气污浊不堪。啊，世人啊！难道你们忘记了他们吗？他们是你的骨肉同胞啊，为什么你们不珍爱他们，反而要摧残他们呢？当你们每顿饭祷告"上帝赐给我面包"时，你们的同胞却无衣无食。我真希望人们离开城市，舍弃城里富丽堂皇、纸醉金迷的生活，回到森林和田野，过着简朴而纯真的生活啊！那么他们的孩子就能像挺拔的松树一样健康茁壮地成长，他们的思想也会像路边的花朵一样清新纯洁。每当我在城市忙碌地生活一年回到乡村之后，我就会产生这样的感想。

现在，我再次踏上了柔软而富有弹性的土地，又沿着绿草茵茵的小路走向蕨草丛生的小溪旁边，把手伸进潺潺溪水中，或者是翻过一道石墙，跑进那狂欢似的高低起伏的绿色田野。这一切是多么令我高兴啊！

除了从容悠闲地散步之外，我还喜欢骑着双人自行车到处去转悠。吹着那习习凉风，胯下铁马跳跃前进，实在是舒服惬意之极。迎着风儿快速骑车，使我感到轻快有力，怡然自得，这种锻炼也增强了我的肌肉灵活性和心脏的跳动。

have had many dog friends- huge mastiffs, soft- eyed spaniels, wood-wise setters and honest, homely bull terriers. At present the lord of my affections is one of these bull terriers. He has a long pedigree, a crooked tail and the drollest "phiz" in dogdom. My dog friends seem to understand my limitations, and always keep close beside me when I am alone. I love their affectionate ways and the eloquent wag of their tails.

When a rainy day keeps me indoors, I amuse myself after the manner of other girls. I like to knit and crochet; I read in the happy-go-lucky ways I love, here and there a line; or perhaps I play a game or two of checkers or chess with a friend. I have a special board on which I play these games. The squares are cut out, so that the men stand in them firmly. The black checkers are flat and the white ones curved on top. Each checker has a hole in the middle in which a brass knob can be placed to distinguish the king from the commons. The chessmen are of two sizes, the white larger than the black, so that I have no trouble in following my opponent's maneuvers

海伦接受金色生日蛋糕，葆丽·汤玛森引导着她的手抚摸蛋糕

只要有可能，我散步、骑马和划船时都会带着我的狗。我有过很多爱犬，如身高体大的玛斯第夫犬、目光温顺的斯派尼尔犬、善于在丛林中追逐的萨脱猎犬，还有外表平常却忠实的第锐尔狼狗。目前，我最喜欢的是一条纯种狼狗，尾巴卷曲、长相滑稽、很惹人喜爱。这些狗似乎都很了解我的生理缺陷，因此每当我单独一人时，它们总是寸步不离地在我身边陪伴着我。我喜欢它们的温柔和那似乎会说话的尾巴。

每当下雨天我不能出门时，我会和其他女孩子一样待在屋里，用各种办法来自娱自乐。我喜欢编织，或者随便看看书，或者和朋友下一两盘棋。我有一个特制的棋盘，棋子可以稳稳当当地插在凹陷的格子里面。黑棋是平的，白棋顶部则是弯曲的，每个棋子中间都有一个孔，主将上面装了一个铜钮，这样就和其他棋子区分开来了。棋子也大小不同，白棋比黑棋要大些，这样我就可以通过用手触摸棋盘，来了解对方棋的情况。当棋子从一个格子移到另一个格子时，会出现震动，这样我就知道什么时候轮到我走棋了。

by moving my hands lightly over the board after a play. The jar made by shifting the men from one hole to another tells me when it is my turn.

If I happen to be all alone and in an idle mood, I play a game of solitaire, of which I am very fond. I use playing cards marked in the upper right-hand corner with braille symbols which indicate the value of the card.

If there are children around, nothing pleases me so much as to frolic with them. I find even the smallest child excellent company, and I am glad to say that children usually like me. They lead me about and show me the things they are interested in. Of course the little ones cannot spell on their fingers; but I manage to read their lips. If I do not succeed they resort to dumb show. Sometimes I make a mistake and do the wrong thing. A burst of childish laughter greets my blunder, and the pantomime begins all over again. I often tell them stories or teach them a game, and the winged hours depart and leave us good and happy.

Museums and art stores are also sources of pleasure and inspiration. Doubtless it will seem strange to many that the hand unaided by sight can feel action, sentiment, beauty in the cold marble; and yet it is true that I derive genuine pleasure from touching great works of art. As my finger tips trace line and curve, they discover the thought and emotion which the artist has portrayed. I can feel in the faces of gods and heroes hate, courage and love, just as I can detect them in living faces I am permitted to touch. I feel in Diana's posture the grace and freedom of the forest and the spirit that tames the mountain lion and subdues the

当我独自一人寂寞无聊时，我还会玩我非常喜爱的单人纸牌游戏。我玩的纸牌，右上角有一个盲文符号，所以我很容易就能辨别是什么牌。

如果身边有孩子们，没有比和他们一起做各种游戏更快乐的了。我发现即使是再小的孩子，也都是非常好的玩伴，我很高兴他们能喜欢我。他们领着我到处走动，把他们感兴趣的事情告诉我。年龄太小的孩子不会用手指拼字，我就设法通过唇读来明白他们的意思；有时唇读也弄不明白他们的话，他们就笨拙可爱地试着用肢体语言来表达。每当我误解了他们的意思，或者做错了事时，他们就会哄然大笑，示意我做错了，然后哑剧就得再次重演一遍。我也经常给他们讲故事，教他们做游戏。和他们在一起时间过得很快，而留给我们的是快乐幸福的回忆。

博物馆和艺术馆是我乐趣和灵感的来源。许多人都怀疑，我不用眼睛，仅仅用手就能感觉出一块冰凉的大理石所表现出来的动作、感情和艺术美吗？但千真万确的是，我的确能从触摸这些典雅的艺术品中获得真正的乐趣。当我的手指触摸到艺术品的曲线时，我就能感受到艺术家们所要表达的思想感情。我能通过触摸神像、英雄人物雕像的脸，感觉到他们的爱恨、勇敢和情感，就像我通过触摸真人的脸来了解人的情感和品格一样。从狄安娜雕像的神态上，我体会到了森林中的壮美和自由，领悟到了一种足以驯服猛

fiercest passions. My soul delights in the repose and gracious curves of the Venus; and in Barré's bronzes the secrets of the jungle are revealed to me.

A medallion of Homer hangs on the wall of my study, conveniently low, so that I can easily reach it and touch the beautiful, sad face with loving reverence. How well I know each line in that majestic brow-tracks of life and bitter evidences of struggle and sorrow; those sightless eyes seeking, even in the cold plaster, for the light and the blue skies of his beloved Hellas, but seeking in vain; that beautiful mouth, firm and true and tender. It is the face of a poet, and of a man acquainted with sorrow. Ah, how well I understand his deprivation-the perpetual night in which he dwelt-

O dark, dark, amid the blaze of noon,
Irrecoverably dark, total eclipse
Without all hope of day!

In imagination I can hear Homer singing, as with unsteady, hesitating steps he gropes his way from camp to camp-singing of life, of love, of war, of the splendid achievements of a noble race. It was a wonderful, glorious song, and it won the blind poet an immortal crown, the admiration of all ages.

I sometimes wonder if the hand is not more sensitive to the beauties of sculpture than the eye. I should think the rhythmical flow of lines and curves could be more subtly felt than seen. Be this as it may, I know that I can feel the heart-throbs of the ancient Greeks in their marble gods and goddesses.

狮、克服最强烈情感的精神；维纳斯雕像的安详和优美的曲线，使我的心灵充满了喜悦；而巴雷的铜像则向我揭示了丛林的秘密。

在我书房的墙上，挂了一幅荷马的圆雕，由于挂得很低，我伸手就能摸到那张美丽慈祥而又略带忧郁的脸。我对这张脸上的每一道皱纹都非常熟悉：那线条是高贵气宇和求索的证明。即使是冰冷的石膏像，也可以看出他在用自己那双盲眼为他心爱的祖国希腊寻求光明与蓝天，然而结果总是归于失望。那美丽的嘴角显得坚毅、真实而柔和。这是一张饱经忧患的诗人的脸。啊！我能真的体会他一生的遗憾，在那个犹如漫漫长夜的时代：

漫漫长夜，永无尽头。

啊，黑暗、黑暗，

即使正午的阳光，也无法摆脱的黑暗，

夜色茫茫，看不到一丝光明的希望！

我仿佛听见荷马在歌唱，试探着蹒跚的步伐，从一个营帐摸索着走到另一个营帐。他歌唱生活、爱情和战争，歌唱一个伟大民族的光辉业绩。这是一首瑰丽雄壮的歌，为诗人赢得了不朽的桂冠，让他获得了后世的景仰。

有时我会想，手对雕塑的美不比眼睛更敏锐，但它比视觉更能体会到精细线条的节奏感。不管事实是否如此，我认为我可以从希腊的大理石神像上

Another pleasure, which comes more rarely than the others, is going to the theatre. I enjoy having a play described to me while it is being acted on the stage far more than reading it, because then it seems as if I were living in the midst of stirring events. It has been my privilege to meet a few great actors and actresses who have the power of so bewitching you that you forget time and place and live again in the romantic past. I have been permitted to touch the face and costume of Miss Ellen Terry as she impersonated our ideal of a queen; and there was about her that divinity that hedges sublimest woe. Beside her stood Sir Henry Irving, wearing the symbols of kingship; and there was majesty of intellect in his every gesture and attitude and the royalty that subdues and overcomes in every line of his sensitive face. In the king's face, which he wore as a mask, there was a remoteness and inaccessibility of grief which I shall never forget.

I also know Mr. Jefferson. I am proud to count him among my friends. I go to see him whenever I happen to be where he is acting. The first time I saw him act was while at school in New York. He

海伦·凯勒获天普大学荣誉文学博士学位，莎莉文获"Honoris Causa"学位

觉察出古希腊人情绪的起伏波动。

去剧院欣赏歌剧对我来说是一种奢侈的享受。我喜欢有人给我讲述舞台上正在上演的剧情，这比读剧本要有意思得多，因为这样我常常可以产生身临其境之感。我曾有幸见过几位优秀的演员，他们的魅力能使你忘却尘世的羁绊，被他们带进那充满浪漫色彩的古代。埃伦·特里小姐具有非凡的艺术天赋，有一次她正扮演一名我们心目中理想的王后，我曾被允许抚摸她的脸和服饰。她身上好像有一种可以化解哀愁的神奇力量。在她的身旁站着亨利·欧文先生，他穿着国王戏装，他的行为举止无不显露出超群不凡的睿智，脸上流露出一种压倒一切的王者的威严表情。在他扮演的国王的脸上，有一种冷漠、难以捉摸的悲愤神情，我永远都不会忘记。

我还认识杰斐逊先生，我很骄傲他是我的朋友。无论在哪里，如果我碰巧到了他演出的地方，我一定会去看他。我第一次看他的演出是在纽约读书的时候。他正主演《瑞普·冯·温克尔》。我以前常常读这篇故事，但我从

played "Rip Van Winkle". I had often read the story, but I had never felt the charm of Rip's slow, quaint, kind ways as I did in the play. Mr. Jefferson's beautiful, pathetic representation quite carried me away with delight. I have a picture of old Rip in my fingers which they will never lose. After the play Miss Sullivan took me to see him behind the scenes, and I felt of his curious garb and his flowing hair and beard. Mr. Jefferson let me touch his face so that I could imagine how he looked on waking from that strange sleep of twenty years, and he showed me how poor old Rip staggered to his feet.

I have also seen him in " The Rivals". Once while I was calling on him in Boston he acted the most striking parts of "The Rivals" for me. The reception-room where we sat served for a stage. He and his son seated themselves at the big table, and Bob Acres wrote his challenge. I followed all his movements with my hands, and caught the drollery of his blunders and gestures in a way that would have been impossible had it all been spelled to me. Then they rose to fight the duel, and I followed the swift thrusts and parries of the swords and the wavering of poor Bob as his courage oozed out at his finger ends. Then the great actor gave his coat a hitch and his mouth a twitch, and in an instant I was in the village of Falling Water and felt Schneider's shaggy head against my knee. Mr. Jefferson recited the best dialogues of "Rip Van Winkle", in which the tear came close upon the smile. He asked me to indicate as far as I could the gestures and action that should go with the lines. Of course, I have no sense whatever of dramatic action, and could

来都没想到老瑞普的性子会如此缓慢、古怪和善良，直到看了杰斐逊先生的演出时，我才体会到这些。杰斐逊先生完美的演技给了我极大的艺术享受，老瑞普的形象我永远都不会忘记。看完戏之后，莎莉文老师带我去了舞台后面的化妆间去看他，我摸了摸他奇怪的服饰、卷卷的头发和胡须。杰斐逊先生还让我摸他的脸，以便我能理解当他从那离奇的20年沉睡中苏醒过来时是什么样子的；他还给我表演了可怜的老瑞普是如何颤颤巍巍地站起来的。

我曾看过他演的《竞争者》。那是有一次在波士顿，我去看他时，他给我表演了剧中几个最吸引人的角色。我们坐的会客室被当成了舞台，他和儿子坐在一张大桌子边上，鲍勃·阿克记下了他的对话。我用手摸他的动作，感觉到了他犯错误时的滑稽可笑，还有那些难以用文字表达出来的肢体动作。他们开始决斗，我察觉到一方正在出击，而另一方则在躲闪。老鲍勃在发抖，他的情感从他的指尖上流露了出来。突然，这位演技超群的演员将衣服一把扯掉，嘴角一阵抽搐，我立刻就转到了瀑布村的场景里，感觉到施耐德乱糟糟的头放在了我的膝盖上。杰斐逊开始背《瑞普·冯·温克尔》中的精彩对白，笑脸渐渐消失，泪花涌出双眼。他还让我用手势来表演一些剧情，但我对此一窍不通，只能根据想象随便做几下，而他凭着扎实的艺术功底，为我这些动作配了台词。瑞普自言自语道："啊，人一旦离开，就这么

make only random guesses; but with masterful art he suited the action to the word. The sigh of Rip as he murmurs, "Is a man so soon forgotten when he is gone?" the dismay with which he searches for dog and gun after his long sleep, and his comical irresolution over signing the contract with Derrick-all these seem to be right out of life itself; that is, the ideal life, where things happen as we think they should.

I remember well the first time I went to the theatre. It was twelve years ago. Elsie Leslie, the little actress, was in Boston, and Miss Sullivan took me to see her in "The Prince and the Pauper". I shall never forget the ripple of alternating joy and woe that ran through that beautiful little play, or the wonderful child who acted it. After the play I was permitted to go behind the scenes and meet her in her royal costume. It would have been hard to find a lovelier or more lovable child than Elsie, as she stood with a cloud of golden hair floating over her shoulders, smiling brightly, showing no signs of shyness or fatigue, though she had been playing

快被遗忘了吗？"瑞普长眠之后找狗和枪时的那种惊慌失措、和里德签约时的那种令人发笑的犹豫不决的表情，都好像出自生活，出自我们想象的生活，而我们认为生活就应该这样进行。

莎莉文在把一篇课文的词句写到海伦手上

我至今还清楚地记得12年前第一次看戏的情景。那天，小演员伊利斯·莱斯莉在波士顿演出，莎莉文老师带我去看她演的《王子与穷小子》。我永远都忘不了贯穿整个剧情的喜怒哀乐，随着剧情的发展，观众一会儿喜，一会儿悲，这位小演员也演得惟妙惟肖。演出结束之后，我被允许到后台和这位穿着华丽戏装的伊利斯见面。没有比她更可爱的孩子了：她站在那里向我微笑，一头金发披散在肩上。尽管演出刚刚结束，但她一点儿也没有疲惫不堪和不愿见人的样子。当时我才刚刚学会说话，为了说出她的名字，在与她见面之前，我曾反复练习，直到可以清楚地说出来。当她听懂了我说的话时，她毫不犹豫地伸出手来欢迎我，我的高兴也可想而知了！

不错，虽然我的生命中有很多缺憾，但我不是有这么多的方式触摸到这个多姿多彩的世界吗？世界上到处都有美好的东西，甚至黑暗和寂寞的世界

to an immense audience. I was only just learning to speak, and had previously repeated her name until I say it perfectly. Imagine my delight when she understood the few words I spoke to her and without hesitation stretched her hand to greet me.

Is it not true, then, that my life with all its limitations touches at many points the life of the World Beautiful? Everything has its wonders, even darkness and silence, and I learn, whatever state I may be in, therein to be content.

Sometimes, it is true, a sense of isolation enfolds me like a cold mist as I sit alone and wait at life's shut gate. Beyond there is light, and music, and sweet companionship; but I may not enter. Fate, silent, pitiless, bars the way. Fain would I question his imperious decree; for my heart is still undisciplined and passionate; but my tongue will not utter the bitter, futile words that rise to my lips, and they fall back into my heart like unshed tears.

Silence sits immense upon my soul. Then comes hope with a smile and whispers, "There is joy in self-forgetfulness." So I try to make the light in others' eyes my sun, the music in others' ears my symphony, the smile on others' lips my happiness.

也是如此。无论处于什么样的环境，都要不断努力学会满足。

有时候，孤独感就像冷雾一样笼罩着我，我好像独自坐在一扇紧闭的大门前等着。在这附近有光明、音乐和友谊，但我却进不去，命运之神无情地挡住了大门。我真想义正词严地抗议，因为我的内心仍然充满了热情。然而，那些酸楚无益的话语一到嘴边却欲言又止，和着泪水往肚里流。

我的世界一片寂静，但是希望又在我心中升起。这时，一个声音在我耳边悄然响起："忘我就是快乐。"因此，我要把别人眼睛所看见的光明当作我的太阳，别人耳朵所听见的音乐当作我的乐曲，别人嘴边的微笑当作我的幸福。

CHAPTER XXIII

WOULD that I could enrich this sketch with the names of all those who have ministered to my happiness! Some of them would be found written in our literature and dear to the hearts of many, while others would be wholly unknown to most of my readers. But their influence, though it escapes fame, shall live immortal in the lives that have been sweetened and ennobled by it.

Those are red-letter days in our lives when we meet people who thrill us like a fine poem, people whose handshake is brimful of unspoken sympathy, and whose sweet, rich natures impart to our eager, impatient spirits a wonderful restfulness which, in its essence, is divine. The perplexities, irritations and worries that have absorbed us pass like unpleasant dreams, and we wake to see with new eyes and hear with new ears the beauty and harmony of God's real world. The solemn nothings that fill our everyday life blossom suddenly into bright possibilities.

In a word, while such friends are near us we feel that all is well. Perhaps we never saw them before, and they may never cross our life's path again; but the influence of their calm, mellow natures is a libation poured upon our discontent, and we feel its healing touch, as the ocean feels the mountain stream freshening its

第23章 永远的朋友

我的幸福生活是因为有了许多人的帮助，如果我能将所有曾经帮助过我的人一一写出来，那该有多好呀！我在书中已经写了一些人，并为读者所熟悉。而另一些人，人们则可能不熟悉。虽然如此，但是那些因为他们的帮助而变得甜美、高贵的生命，将会永远记住他们。

人生中最值得庆幸的事情，莫过于结识一些益友，他们就好似一首首优美的诗歌，动人心弦，与他们握手时，你会感到不可言喻的心情。他们幽默风趣的性格，使我的愤怒、烦恼和忧虑一扫而光。当我一觉醒来时，就能耳目一新，重新看到上帝真实世界的美与和谐，看到化腐朽为神奇。

总之，身边有了这些良师益友，一切都令我感到欣慰。他们平静的面容和温柔的性格，哪怕我一辈子同他们只有一次相会，也可以化解我心头永不满足的冰块，犹如山泉汇入海洋，稀释了海水的浓度。

经常有人这样问我："难道没有人让你觉得厌烦吗？"我不明白这话是什么意思。我认为那些所谓的过于好奇的人和傻子，尤其是新闻记者，大概都是不怎么讨人喜欢的。我也不喜欢那些自以为是、喜欢说教、低估我的理解

brine.

I have often been asked, "Do not people bore you?" I do not understand quite what that means. I suppose the calls of the stupid and curious, especially of newspaper reporters, are always inopportune. I also dislike people who try to talk down to my understanding. They are like people who when walking with you try to shorten their steps to suit yours; the hypocrisy in both cases is equally exasperating.

The hands of those I meet are dumbly eloquent to me. The touch of some hands is an impertinence. I have met people so empty of joy, that when I clasped their frosty finger tips, it seemed as if I were shaking hands with a northeast storm. Others there are whose hands have sunbeams in them, so that their grasp warms my heart. It may be only the clinging touch of a child's hand; but there is as much potential sunshine in it for me as there is in a loving glance for others. A hearty handshake or a friendly letter gives me genuine pleasure.

I have many far-off friends whom I have never seen. Indeed they are so many that I have often been unable to reply to their letters; but I wish to

莎莉文年轻时照片，她对自己的未来充满了期待

力的人，他们就好像那些同你一起行走，但却故意缩小步伐来适应你的速度的人一样虚伪做作，让人不快。

我握过的各种各样的手就很能说明问题:有些人的握手显得高人一等；有的人郁郁寡欢，和他们握手就好像握住了西北风，寒冷刺骨；而另一些人则活泼愉快，和他们握手，让我觉得心里无比温暖。即使这只是一个孩子的手，但它确实能给我带来愉快，就像满含关爱的一瞥，让人感受到一种温情。一次真诚的握手，或是一封友好的来信，都能让我获得真正的快慰。

我有许多从未见过面的远方友人，他们的人数实在是太多了，以至于我常常不能一一回复他们的来信，我希望借此机会，衷心地感谢他们的亲切来信，可是这只言片语又哪里能完全表达我对他们的感谢之情呢!

我觉得我一生中最荣幸的事，是我能够认识许多智者，并且有机会和他们一起交流。只有认识布鲁克斯主教的人，才能领略和他在一起的雅趣。小

say here that I am always grateful for their kind words, however insufficiently I acknowledge them.

I count it one of the sweetest privileges of my life to have known and conversed with many men of genius. Only those who knew Bishop Brooks can appreciate the joy his friendship was to those who possessed it. As a child I loved to sit on his knee and clasp his great hand with one of mine, while Miss Sullivan spelled into the other his beautiful words about God and the spiritual world. I heard him with a child's wonder and delight. My spirit could not reach up to his, but he gave me a real sense of joy in life, and I never left him without carrying away a fine thought that grew in beauty and depth of meaning as I grew.

Once, when I was puzzled to know why there were so many religions, he said: "There is one universal religion, Helen-the religion of love. Love your Heavenly Father with your whole heart and soul, love every child of God as much as ever you can, and remember that the possibilities of good are greater than the possibilities of evil; and you have the key to Heaven." And his life was a happy illustration of this great truth. In his noble soul love and widest knowledge were blended with faith that had become insight. He saw

时候，我喜欢坐在他的膝上，一只小手放在他的大手心里。他生动有趣地给我讲上帝和精神王国的事，莎莉文老师则拼写到我另一只手上。我带着孩子的好奇和兴致听着，虽然我不能完全理解他所说的，但却体会到了生命的乐趣。随着年龄的增长，这种理解就更深了。

海伦·凯勒在布莱叶文打字机旁工作，撰写安妮·莎莉文·梅西的传记

有一次我问他："为什么世界上有那么多的宗教？"他说："海伦，世界上有一种无所不在的宗教，这就是对爱的信仰。用你的整个身心去爱上帝，尽你所能去爱上帝的每个儿女，而且要牢记在心，善的力量要远远大于恶的力量，进天堂的钥匙就掌握在你手中。"他的一生就是这个伟大真理的最真实写照。在他高尚的灵魂里，爱与渊博的知识以及信仰融合成一种洞察力，他看见了：

上帝无处不在，

使人获得解放，

获得鼓舞，

God in all that liberates and lifts,
In all that humbles, sweetens and consoles.

Bishop Brooks taught me no special creed or dogma; but he impressed upon my mind two great ideas-the fatherhood of God and the brotherhood of man, and made me feel that these truths underlie all creeds and forms of worship. God is love, God is our Father, we are His children; therefore the darkest clouds will break, and though right be worsted, wrong shall not triumph.

I am too happy in this world to think much about the future, except to remember that I have cherished friends awaiting me there in God's beautiful Somewhere. In spit of the lapse of years, they seem so close to me that I should not think it strange if at any moment they should clasp my hand and speak words of endearment as they used to before they went away.

Since Bishop Brooks died I have read the Bible through; also some philosophical works on religion, among them Swedenborg's "Heaven and Hell" and Drummond's "Ascent of Man", and I have found no creed or system more soul- satisfying than Bishop Brooks's creed of love.

I knew Mr. Henry Drummond, and the memory of his strong, warm hand-clasp is like a benediction. He was the most sympathetic of companions. He knew so much and was so genial that it was impossible to feel dull in his presence.

I remember the first time I saw Dr. Oliver Wendell Holmes. He invited Miss Sullivan and me to call on him one Sunday afternoon. It was early in the spring,

使人谦卑柔顺，

并得到慰藉。

布鲁克斯主教从来没有教过我什么特殊的信条，但是他将"上帝是万物之父"、"四海之内皆兄弟"这两种伟大的思想深刻在了我的脑海中，这正是一切信条和教义的基础。上帝就是仁爱，上帝就是慈父，我们就是他的儿女。尽管强权可能会在短时间内歪曲事实，但乌云终将会被驱散，正义永远会战胜邪恶。

我在这个世界上生活得很幸福，很少会想到身后之事，偶尔也不免会想起几位好友的在天之灵。时光流逝，虽然他们已经离开人间多年，但他们和我仿佛近在咫尺，如果他们什么时候拉住我的手，像从前一样亲热地和我交谈，我也不会有任何惊奇的。

自从布鲁克斯主教去世之后，我把《圣经》从头到尾读了一遍，同时还读了几部从哲学角度谈论宗教的著作，其中有斯威登伯格的《天堂和地狱》、德鲁蒙德的《人类的进步》，但我依然觉得，最能慰藉我灵魂的，还是布鲁克斯爱的信条。

我认识亨利·德鲁蒙德先生，记忆中他那热情而有力的握手令我久久难以忘怀。他待人热情、知识广博而又健谈，无论什么地方，凡是有他在场，

just after I learned to speak. We were shown at once to his library where we found him seated in a big armchair by an open fire which glowed and crackled on the hearth, thinking, he said, of other days.

"And listening to the murmur of the River Charles," I suggested.

"Yes," he replied, "the Charles has many dear associations for me."

There was an odour of print and leather in the room which told me that it was full of books, and I stretched out my hand instinctively to find them. My fingers lighted upon a beautiful volume of Tennyson's poems, and when Miss Sullivan told me what it was I began to recite:

Break, break, break
On thy cold gray stones, O sea!

But I stopped suddenly. I felt tears on my hand. I had made my beloved poet weep, and I was greatly distressed. He

总能笑声不断。

我还清楚地记得第一次见到奥利弗·温德尔·霍姆斯博士的情形。他邀请我和莎莉文老师在一个星期日的下午去拜访他,那是初春,我刚学会说话。我们一进门

海伦的成功离不开莎莉文老师的教育和帮助。在海伦的心目中,最亲爱的人正是莎莉文老师

就被带进了书房。他坐在壁炉旁边一张带扶手的椅子上。炉火烧得很旺,木柴劈劈啪啪地响个不停,他说自己特别喜欢沉思,正在回忆往昔的岁月。

"还在聆听查尔斯河的细语。"我补充道。

"是的,"他说,"查尔斯河引起我无数美好的回忆。"

书房里有一股浓浓的油墨和草革的气味,这使我知道这里一定全是图书。我本能地伸出手去摸索,碰到了一本装订精美的《坦尼森诗集》上。莎莉文老师告诉我书名后,我就开始朗诵:

撞击吧,撞击吧,撞击吧,

啊!大海,

撞击那灰色的礁石!

made me sit in his armchair, while he brought different interesting things for me to examine, and at his request I recited "The Chambered Nautilus", which was then my favorite poem. After that I saw Dr. Holmes many times and learned to love the man as well as the poet.

One beautiful summer day, not long after my meeting with Dr. Holmes, Miss Sullivan and I visited Whittier in his quiet home on the Merrimac. His gentle courtesy and quaint speech won my heart. He had a book of his poems in raised print from which I read "In School Days". He was delighted that I could pronounce the words so well, and said that he had no difficulty in understanding me. Then I asked many questions about the poem, and read his answers by placing my fingers on his lips. He said he was the little boy in the poem, and that the girl's name was Sally, and more which I have forgotten.

I also recited "Laus Deo", and as I spoke the concluding verses, he placed in my hands a statue of a slave from whose crouching figure the fetters were falling, even as they fell from Peter's limbs when the angel led him forth out of prison. Afterward we went into his study, and he wrote his autograph for my teacher and expressed his admiration of her work, saying to me, "She is thy spiritual liberator." Then he led me to the gate and kissed me tenderly on my forehead. I promised to visit him again the following summer; but he died before the promise was fulfilled.

Dr. Edward Everett Hale is one of my very oldest friends. I have known him since I was eight, and my love for him has increased with my years. His wise,

这时，我突然停止了朗诵，因为我感到有泪水滴在了我手上。是的，这位可爱的诗人竟然感动得哭了起来，我觉得不安，但他安慰我说没关系，并让我坐在靠背椅上，拿来各种有趣的东西让我欣赏。我还在他的要求下朗诵了《被禁闭的鹦鹉螺》，这是我最喜欢的一首诗。以后我又见过他好几次，我不仅喜欢他的诗，而且喜欢他的为人。

见过霍姆斯博士后不久，我和莎莉文老师又在一个晴朗的夏日，去看望了诗人惠蒂尔，地点在梅里迈克他幽静的家里。他儒雅的气质和不俗的谈吐给我留下了深刻的印象。他有一本凸字版的个人诗集，我读了其中的一篇诗歌《学生时代》。他很惊奇我能如此准确地发音，并说他听起来没有一点儿困难。我问了他许多关于这首诗的问题，并把手放在他的嘴唇上来"听"他的回答。他说，那首诗中的小男孩就是他本人，女孩子的名字叫萨利，还有些内容我已记不太清楚了。

我还背诵了《赞美上帝》，当我读到结尾一句时，他在我的手上放了一个塑像，是个奴隶的塑像。两条锁链从那蹲着的奴隶身上掉下来，就好像天使把彼得带出监狱时，身上的镣铐脱落下来一样。后来，我们到他的书房里去，他亲笔给莎莉文老师题了字，以表达对她的工作的钦佩，然后他又对我说："她是你精神的解放者。"他送我们到大门口，温柔地吻了吻我的前

tender sympathy has been the support of Miss Sullivan and me in times of trial and sorrow, and his strong hand has helped me over many rough places; and what he has done for us he has done for thousands of those who have difficult tasks to accomplish. He has filled the old skins of dogma with the new wine of love, and shown men what it is to believe, live and be free. What he has taught we have seen beautifully expressed in his own life-love of country, kindness to the least of his brethren, and a sincere desire to live upward and onward. He has been a prophet and an inspirer of men, and a mighty doer of the Word, the friend of all his race-God bless him!

I have already written of my first meeting with Dr. Alexander Graham Bell. Since then I have spent many happy days with him at Washington and at his beautiful home in the heart of Cape Breton Island, near Baddeck, the village made famous by Charles Dudley Warner's book. Here in Dr. Bell's laboratory, or in the fields on the shore of the great Bras d'Or, I have spent many delightful hours listening to what he had to tell me

额。我答应第二年夏天再来看他，但是天不遂人愿，我还没有来得及履约，他就与世长辞了！

我还有许多忘年交朋友，爱德华·埃弗雷特·黑尔博士就是其中之一。我认识他的时候只有8岁，随着年龄的增长，我越来越尊敬

海伦与爱犬在一起，手中拿着一本盲文书

他。他学识广博，富有同情心，莎莉文老师和我在艰难困苦时都得到过他的热心帮助，他那坚强的臂膀成为我们越过艰难险阻的强大援助。爱是无私的，除了对我们，爱德华博士对任何处境困难的人都能给予帮助。他用爱赋予了旧的教条以新义，并教导人们如何信仰，如何生活，如何追求自由。他言传身教，以身作则，爱国家，爱人类，追求勤勤恳恳、积极向上的生活。他不仅宣传和激励人们，而且还身体力行，是全人类的朋友。愿上帝保佑他！

我在前面写过第一次和亚历山大·格雷厄姆·贝尔博士见面的情形，后来我曾陪他一起度过了许多愉快的日子，有时是在华盛顿，有时是在布雷顿角岛中心他幽静的家中。这里离拜德克村非常近，这个地方因为查尔斯·达

about his experiments, and helping him fly kites by means of which to discover the laws that shall govern the future air-ship.

Dr. Bell is proficient in many fields of science, and has the art of making every subject he touches interesting, even the most abstruse theories. He makes you feel that if you only had a little more time, you, too, might be an inventor. He has a humorous and poetic side, too. His dominating passion is his love for children. He is never quite so happy as when he has a little deaf child in his arms. His labours in behalf of the deaf will live on and bless generations of children yet to come; and we love him alike for what he himself has achieved and for what he has evoked from others.

During the two years I spent in New York I had many opportunities to talk with distinguished people whose names I had often heard, but whom I had never expected to meet. Most of them I met first in the house of my good friend, Mr. Laurence Hutton. It was a great privilege to visit him and dear Mrs. Hutton in their lovely home, and see their library and read the beautiful sentiments and bright thoughts gifted friends had written for them.

It has been truly said that Mr. Hutton has the faculty of bringing out in every one the best thoughts and kindest sentiments. One does not need to read "A Boy I Knew" to understand him-the most generous, sweet-natured boy I ever knew, a good friend in all sorts of weather, who traces the footprints of love in the life of dogs as well as in that of his fellowmen.

德利·沃纳的书而出名。在贝尔博士的实验室，或在伟大的布拉斯道尔河边的岸上，我非常愉快地听他讲自己的实验，帮他放风筝。他告诉我，他很想通过风筝来发现控制未来飞船飞行的规律。

贝尔博士是个通才，精通各方面的科学知识，并且善于生动有趣地描述他研究的每一个课题。在他的解说下，那些抽象而枯燥的理论知识立即让人觉得趣味盎然。他的讲话能让你感到，哪怕只用一点点时间，你都可以想象自己也能成为一个发明家。他还表现得幽默而富有诗意，对儿童充满了爱心，当他抱着一个小聋儿时，常常表现出发自内心的真诚的快乐。他为聋人所做的贡献将永载史册，并造福于后世的孩子。因为他取得的个人成就和他对别人的感召力，我们将对他充满了敬爱。

住在纽约的两年中，我见过许多知名人士。虽然我此前久闻他们的大名，但却未曾谋面。我是在好友劳伦斯·赫顿先生家中同他们大多数人第一次见面的。能够到赫顿夫妇优雅宜人的家里做客，并参观他们的藏书室，令我感到十分荣幸。许多富有才华的朋友都为他们夫妇题词留念，以表达对他们的钦佩之情。对我来说，能在他们的藏书室中亲自阅读这些留言，实在是荣幸之极。

大家都说赫顿先生能够凭着他的人格魅力来唤起人们内心深处美好的思

Mrs. Hutton is a true and tried friend. Much that I hold sweetest, much that I hold most precious, I owe to her. She has oftenest advised and helped me in my progress through college. When I find my work particularly difficult and discouraging, she writes me letters that make me feel glad and brave; for she is one of those from whom we learn that one painful duty fulfilled makes the next plainer and easier.

Mr. Hutton introduced me to many of his literary friends, greatest of whom are Mr. William Dean Howells and Mark Twain. I also met Mr. Richard Watson Gilder and Mr. Edmund Clarence Stedman. I also knew Mr. Charles Dudley Warner, the most delightful of story-tellers and the most beloved friend, whose sympathy was so broad that it may be truly said of him, he loved all living things and his neighbour as himself. Once Mr. Warner brought to see me the dear poet of the woodlands-Mr. John Burroughs. They were all gentle and sympathetic and I felt the charm

想情操，人们不必读《我所认识的男孩》也能了解他。他也是我所认识的最慷慨、待人最宽厚的人。

赫顿夫人是一个能够共患难的真朋友，我思想中获得的许多最可宝贵的东西，都要归

《海伦·凯勒的故事》曾获奥斯卡纪录片奖，图为海伦领奖时的照片

功于她。我在大学的学习过程中所取得的进步，也都离不开她的引导和帮助。当我因学习困难而泄气时，她的来信会令我精神振奋，重新鼓起勇气。正是她让我真正体会到，只要征服了一个困难，随后的事情就会变得简单容易。

赫顿先生还介绍给我许多文学界的朋友，其中有著名的威廉·狄恩·霍威斯先生和马克·吐温先生。我还见过理查德·华生·吉尔德先生和艾德姆德·克拉伦斯·斯蒂曼先生。我也认识查尔斯·杜德里·华纳先生，他很会讲故事，深得朋友的敬爱，待人极富同情心，大家都说他是一个博爱的人。有一次，华纳先生带着"森林诗人"约翰·柏洛先生来看我。他们和蔼可亲，我非常钦佩他们在散文和诗歌创作上的才华，现在我又切身感受到了他

of their manner as much as I had felt the brilliancy of their essays and poems. I could not keep pace with all these literary folk as they glanced from subject to subject and entered into deep dispute, or made conversation sparkle with epigrams and happy witticisms. I was like little Ascanius, who followed with unequal steps the heroic strides of Eneas on his march toward mighty destinies. But they spoke many gracious words to me.

Mr. Gilder told me about his moonlight journeys across the vast desert to the Pyramids, and in a letter he wrote me he made his mark under his signature deep in the paper so that I could feel it. This reminds me that Dr. Hale used to give a personal touch to his letters to me by pricking his signature in braille. I read from Mark Twain's lips one or two of his good stories. He has his own way of thinking, saying and doing everything. I feel the twinkle of his eye in his handshake. Even while he utters his cynical wisdom in an indescribably droll voice, he makes you feel that his heart is a tender Iliad of human sympathy.

There are a host of other interesting people I met in New York: Mrs. Mary Mapes Dodge, the beloved editor of St. Nicholas, and Mrs. Riggs (Kate Douglas Wiggin), the sweet author of

海伦身穿格拉斯哥大学博士服

们在待人接物方面的魅力。这些文学界的名流在一起谈天说地，有时唇枪舌剑，有时妙语如珠，我总是跟不上它们的节奏。我就好像小阿喀留斯，迈着小脚紧跟着英雄阿留斯向伟大的命运进军。但是他们对我说了许多至理名言。

吉尔德先生告诉我，他是如何穿越大沙漠，在月夜向金字塔进发的。有一次他写信给我，特意在签名下做了一个凹下去的印迹，以便我能够感觉到。这让我想起黑尔博士给我写信时，也会把签名刺成盲字。我还会用唇读法听马克·吐温为我朗诵他的一两篇精彩的短篇小说。他的思想和行为都有些与众不同。在和他握手时，我能感觉到他的眼睛炯炯有神；甚至当他以特有的、难以形容的幽默声调进行讽刺挖苦时，你觉得他似乎就是那个温柔而又富有人类同情心的伊里亚特的化身。

我在纽约还见过许多有趣的人，《圣尼古拉斯报》受人尊敬的编辑玛莉·玛普斯·道奇女士、《爱尔兰人》一书可爱的作者凯蒂·道格拉斯·威

"Patsy". I received from them gifts that have the gentle concurrence of the heart, books containing their own thoughts, soul-illumined letters, and photographs that I love to have described again and again.

But there is not space to mention all my friends, and indeed there are things about them hidden behind the wings of cherubim, things too sacred to set forth in cold print. It is with hesitancy that I have spoken even of Mrs. Laurence Hutton.

I shall mention only two other friends. One is Mrs. William Thaw, of Pittsburgh, whom I have often visited in her home, Lyndhurst. She is always doing something to make someone happy, and her generosity and wise counsel have never failed my teacher and me in all the years we have known her.

To the other friend I am also deeply indebted. He is well known for the powerful hand with which he guides enterprises, and his wonderful abilities have gained for him the respect of all. Kind to every one, he goes about doing good, silent and unseen. Again I touch upon the circle of honoured names I must not mention; but I would fain acknowledge his generosity and affectionate interest which make it possible for me to go to college.

Thus it is that my friends have made the story of my life. In a thousand ways they have turned my limitations into beautiful privileges, and enabled me to walk serene and happy in the shadow cast by my deprivation.

格因女士。他们送给我一些富有情意的礼物，包括反映他们思想的书籍，给人启迪的信函，还有一些我爱不释手的照片。

可惜由于篇幅的限制，我不能介绍所有的朋友。事实上，他们那高尚纯洁的品质绝非我这笨拙的笔所能充分表达，甚至我在讲到劳伦斯·赫顿夫人时，也是心怀忐忑的。

在这里，我只想再提两位朋友，一位是匹兹堡的威廉·索夫人，我在林德斯特时经常去她家中做客。她总是乐意为别人做好事，自从我和莎莉文老师认识她多年来，她总是不厌其烦地向我们提出自己中肯的意见。

另外还有一位朋友（译注:指"钢铁大王"安德鲁·卡内基），也是我必须感谢的。他以强有力的企业领导才能而出名，他英明神奇的能力使他赢得了人们的尊敬。他对每一个人都很仁慈，默默地做着慈善事业。由于他的地位，我是不应该谈到他的，但是应该坦白地指出，正是有了他的热情帮助，我才有可能上大学。

就这样，朋友们创造了我的一生。他们竭尽所能地将我的缺陷转变成美好的特权，使我在已经造成的缺陷的阴影中，仍然能够安详而快乐地前行。

第二篇
假如给我三天光明

THREE DAYS TO SEE

Spend Your Days

All of us have read thrilling stories in which the hero had only a limited and specified time to live. Sometimes it was as long as a year; sometimes as short as twenty-four hours. But always we were interested in discovering just how the doomed man chose to spend his last days or his last hours. I speak, of course, of free men who have a choice, not condemned criminals whose sphere of activities is strictly delimited.

Such stories set us thinking, wondering what we should do under similar circumstances. What events, what experiences, what associations should we crowd into those last hours as mortal beings? What happiness should we find in reviewing the past, what regrets?

Sometimes I have thought it would be an excellent rule to live each day as if we should die tomorrow. Such an attitude would emphasize sharply the values of life. We should live each day with a gentleness, a vigor, and a keenness of appreciation which are often lost when time stretches before us in the constant panorama of more days and months and years to come. There are those, of course, who would

珍惜每一天

我们大家都读过一些激动人心的故事，这些故事的主人公只有有限而且特定的时间可活，有时长达一年，有时短到只剩下二十四小时。但我们总是有兴趣去发现那注定要死的人是如何度过他生命的最后几天或几小时的。当然，我说的是那些有选择自由的人，而不是那些活动范围受到严格限定的判刑的犯人。

这样的故事让我们思考，我们处在相似的情况下应该怎么办。作为终有一死的生命，在这最后的几个小时内，我们会有什么遭遇、什么经历、什么感受？回顾往事，我们将会发现什么快乐、什么悔恨呢？

有时，我会想到，过好每一天或许是一个非常好的习惯，就好像我们明天就会死去一样。这种态度非常尖锐地强调了生命的价值。我们每天都应该和蔼友善、精力充沛、充满向往地生活。随着岁月的流逝，这些品质常常也会一点点地丧失。当然，也有人愿意按照伊壁鸠鲁"吃喝玩乐"的信条去生活，但绝大多数人还是受到了必将来临的死亡的折磨。

adopt the Epicurean motto of "Eat, drink, and be merry", but most people would be chastened by the certainty of impending death.

In stories the doomed hero is usually saved at the last minute by some stroke of fortune, but almost always his sense of values is changed. He becomes more appreciative of the meaning of life and its permanent spiritual values. It was often been noted that those who live, or have lived, in the shadow of death bring a mellow sweetness to everything they do.

Most of us, however, take life for granted. We know that one day we must die, but usually we picture that day as far in the future. When we are in buoyant health, death is all but unimaginable. We seldom think of it. The days stretch out in an endless vista. So we go about our petty tasks, hardly aware of our listless attitude toward life.

The same lethargy, I am afraid, characterizes the use of all our faculties and senses. Only the deaf appreciate hearing, only the blind realize the manifold blessings that lie in sight. Particularly does this observation apply to those who have lost sight and hearing in adult life. But those who have never

海伦在汤玛森的陪同下参观农场

在这些故事中，注定要死亡的主人公往往在最后的时刻，由于某种命运的突变而得救，他的价值观也几乎从此被改变了。他对生活的意义和生命永恒的精神意义有了更深的领悟。我们常常可以看到，那些受到或曾经受到死亡威胁的人，都会从他们所做的每件事中发现芳醇甜美。

但是，我们大多数人都认为人生是理所当然的。我们知道，某一天我们一定会死去，但我们通常会把那天想得非常遥远。当我们身体强健时，死亡几乎是不可想象的，我们很少会想到它。日子无穷无尽地延续下去，于是我们每天干着一些琐碎的事情，几乎没有意识到我们对生活的倦怠态度。

我以为，同样的懒散也会作用于我们所有的本能和感觉，并形成固有的特点。只有聋子才会珍惜听力，只有瞎子才能体会到看见事物的巨大幸福，这种结论特别适合于那些在成年阶段失去了视力和听力的人。然而，那些从没有体会过失去视力或听力痛苦的人，却很少充分利用这些天赐的官能。他们的眼睛和耳朵漫无目的地看着或听着四周的景色和声音，毫无重点，不知道珍惜这一切。还是那句相同的老话：直到有一天失去了，才知道珍惜我们

suffered impairment of sight or hearing seldom make the fullest use of these blessed faculties. Their eyes and ears take in all sights and sounds hazily, without concentration and with little appreciation. It is the same old story of not being grateful for what we have until we lose it, of not being conscious of health until we are ill.

I have often thought it would be a blessing if each human being were stricken blind and deaf for a few days at some time during his early adult life. Darkness would make him more appreciative of sight; silence would tech him the joys of sound.

Now and then I have tested my seeing friends to discover what they see. Recently I was visited by a very good friends who had just returned from a long walk in the woods, and I asked her what she had observed. "Nothing in particular, " she replied. I might have been incredulous had I not been accustomed to such reposes, for long ago I became convinced that the seeing see little.

How was it possible, I asked myself, to walk for an hour through the woods and

海伦·凯勒用手指在浮雕上来回摸着，想"看到"上面描绘的古代场景

所有的感官；直到有一天生病了，才知道健康的可贵。

我常常想，如果每个人在他早期的成年时期曾经致瞎致聋，那将是一种幸事。黑暗会使他更珍惜视力，聋哑会教导他喜爱声音。

我经常询问我那些能看得见东西的朋友，问他们看到了什么。最近，我的一位好友来看我，她刚从森林里散了很长时间的步回来，我问她看到了什么，她回答道："没什么特别的东西。"如果我不是对这种回答习以为常，我都可能不相信，因为很久以前我就已经确信，能看得见的人却看不到什么。

我问自己，这怎么可能呢？一个人在森林里散步一小时，却没有看到任何值得注意的东西！而我自己，一个看不见东西的人，仅仅通过触觉，就发现了许多令我感兴趣的东西。我可以感触到一片树叶的完美对称。我充满欢喜地用手抚摸白桦树那光滑的树皮，或松树粗糙的树皮。在春天，我摸着树枝，满怀希望地摸索着嫩芽，这是大自然在严冬的沉睡之后苏醒的第一个征兆。我抚摸到了鲜花那令人愉快的天鹅绒般的花瓣，感觉到了它那奇妙

see nothing worthy of note? I who cannot see find hundreds of things to interest me through mere touch. I feel the delicate symmetry of a leaf. I pass my hands lovingly about the smooth skin of a silver birch, or the rough, shaggy bark of a pine. In the spring I touch the branches of trees hopefully in search of a bud the first sign of awakening Nature after her winter's sleep. I feel the delightful, velvety texture of a flower, and discover its remarkable convolutions; and something of the miracle of Nature is revealed to me. Occasionally, if I am very fortunate, I place my hand gently on a small tree and feel the happy quiver of a bird in full song. I am delighted to have the cool waters of a brook rush thought my open finger. To me a lush carpet of pine needles or spongy grass is more welcome than the most luxurious Persian rug. To me the pageant of seasons is a thrilling and unending drama, the action of which streams through my finger tips.

At times my heart cries out with longing to see all these things. If I can get so much pleasure from mere touch, how much more beauty must be revealed by sight. Yet, those who have eyes apparently see little. The panorama of color and action which fills the world is taken for granted. It is human, perhaps, to appreciate little that which we have and to long for that which we have not, but it is a great pity that in the world of light the gift of sight is used only as

的卷曲。大自然就这样向我展现了它的奇迹。有时，如果幸运的话，我把手轻轻地放在一棵小树上，还能感受到小鸟高声歌唱时的欢悦喜跳。我很高兴让小溪的凉水流过我张开的手指。在我看来，一片茂密的松针叶或松软而富有弹性的草地铺成的地毯，比最豪华的波斯地毯更受欢迎。对我来说，四季的兴衰更迭是一部令人激动

海伦与莎莉文、汤玛森合影

的、无穷无尽的、壮观而华丽的戏剧，它从我的指尖流淌而过。

有时，我的内心在哭泣，因为我渴望能看到这一切。如果仅通过我的触觉就能感受到这么多的愉快，那么通过视觉将会有多少美丽的东西展现出来啊！然而，那些看得见的人显然看得很少。在他们看来，充满世界的万花筒般的景象都是理所当然的。或许这就是人类共有的特性：对我们所拥有的却看不上眼，而对于我们没有的却渴望得到。然而，在光明的世界里，将视力的天赋仅仅看作是一种方便，而没有作为增添生活美满的手段，这是极其令人遗憾的。

如果我是一所大学的校长，我将开设一门强制性的必修课"如何应用你

a mere conveniences rather than as a means of adding fullness to life.

If I were the president of a university I should establish a compulsory course in "How to Use Your Eyes". The professor would try to show his pupils how they could add joy to their lives by really seeing what passes unnoticed before them. He would try to awake their dormant and sluggish faculties.

Perhaps I can best illustrate by imagining what I should most like to see if I were given the use of my eyes, say, for just three days. And while I am imagining, suppose you, too, set your mind to work on the problem of how you would use your own eyes if you had only three more days to see. If with the on-coming darkness of the third night you knew that the sun would never rise for you again, how would you spend those three precious intervening days? What would you most want to let your gaze rest upon?

I, naturally, should want most to see the things which have become dear to me through my years of darkness. You, too, would want to let your eyes rest on the things that have become dear to you so that you could take the memory of them with you into the night that loomed before you.

If, by some miracle, I were

海伦脱下右手手套感受植物和花朵

的眼睛"。上课的教授应该试图给学生展示如何观察那些在他们面前一闪而过的东西来增添他们生活的乐趣，尽量唤醒他们沉睡和懒散的天赋。

如果让我来用我的眼睛，哪怕只有三天的时间，或许我能以我想象得到的最喜欢看见的东西来很好地说清楚这个问题。而且在我这么想的时候，也请你思考这个问题。假如你也只有三天的时间来看世界，你该如何用你自己的眼睛？如果面对即将到来的第三个夜晚的黑暗，对你来说太阳将永远不再升起了，那么你将如何度过这插进来的宝贵三天呢？你最想让你的目光注视什么东西呢？

当然，我最希望看到的是多年来在黑暗中对我最亲切的东西，你也一定希望让你的目光停留在那些让你感到最亲切的东西上。这样，你就能把它们带进那正在逼近你的长夜之中。

granted three seeing days, to be followed by a relapse into darkness, I should divide the period into three parts.

The First Day

On the first day, I should want to see the people whose kindness and gentleness and companionship have made my life worth living. First I should like to gaze long upon the face of my dear teacher, Mrs. Anne Sullivan Macy, who came to me when I was a child and opened the outer world to me. I should want not merely to see the outline of her face, so that I could cherish it in my memory, but to study that face and find in it the living evidence of the sympathetic tenderness and patience with which she accomplished the difficult task of my education. I should like to see in her eyes that strength of character which has enabled her to stand firm in the face of difficulties, and that compassion for all humanity which she has revealed to me so often.

I do not know what it is to see into the heart of a friend through that "Window of the soul", the eye. I can only "see" through my finger tips the outline of a face. I can detect laughter, sorrow, and many other obvious emotions. I know my friends from the feel of their faces. But I cannot really picture their personalities by touch. I know their personalities, of course, through other means, through the thoughts they express to me, through whatever of their actions are revealed to me. But I am

如果出现某种奇迹，使我能有三天光明，随后又陷入一片黑暗之中，我将把这段时间分成三个部分。

第一天

第一天，我想看到这些人，他们的善良和友情使我的生活值得过下去。首先，我想长久地凝视我亲爱的老师安妮·莎莉文·梅西夫人的面容，当我还是一个孩子的时候，她就来到了我面前，为我打开了外面的世界。我不仅想看清她的脸部轮廓，这样我就能把它珍藏在我的记忆之中，而且我还要研究这张脸庞，从中找到富有同情心、温柔和耐心的生动证据，她就是以这种温柔和耐心完成了教育我的艰巨任务。我希望看到她眼睛里的坚强性格，它使得她在困难面前那么坚定。我要看她对所有人的同情心，她也经常如此对我显露出来。

我不知道通过"心灵之窗"，即从眼睛来看透一个朋友的内心意味着什么。我只能通过我的指尖来"看"一张脸庞的轮廓。我能够察觉到欢笑、悲伤和其他许多明显的情感。我是从面部的感触来认识我的朋友的，但我不能正确地凭触摸来描绘他们的个性特征。当然，我还要通过其他方式来了解他们的品格，例如通过他们对我表达的思想，通过他们对我表现的任何行为。

denied that deeper understanding of them which I am sure would come through sight of them, through watching their reactions to various expressed thoughts and circumstances, through noting the immediate and fleeting reactions of their eyes and countenance.

Friends who are near to me I know well, because through the months and years they reveal themselves to me in all their phases; but of casual friends I have only an incomplete impression, an impression gained from a handclasp, from spoken words which I take from their lips with my finger tips, or which they tap into the palm of my hand.

How much easier, how much more satisfying it is for you who can see to grasp quickly the essential qualities of another person by watching the subtleties of expression, the quiver of a muscle, the flutter of a hand. But does it ever occur to you to use your sight to see into the inner nature of a friends or acquaintance? Do not most of you seeing people grasp casually the outward features of a face and let it go at that?

For instance can you describe

海伦把食指放在小姑娘的嘴唇上，拇指放在她的喉部，靠这种方法来读唇

但我无法对他们有更深刻的了解。而要获得更深刻的了解，我相信通过看到他们，观察他们对别人表达出来的思想和情况的反应、通过注意他们眼睛和相貌的直接和迅即反应可以做到。

我对身边的朋友很了解，因为通过长年累月的时间，他们在各方面对我展现了他们自己。而对于那些偶然接触的朋友，我只有一个不完整的印象，这个印象还是我从一次握手、从我的指尖感触他们的双唇所说的话，或者是他们在我的手掌上轻轻地拍抚而得到的。

但是对于你们能看见的人来说，要很快地了解另一个人的本质是多么容易又多么令人满足的事情啊！你可以通过观察一些微妙的表情——一条肌肉的颤抖、一只手的摆动，很快抓住他的本质。但是，你曾经用你的双眼去看透一个朋友或熟人的内在本质吗？你们这些能看见的人，是不是偶然地抓住一张脸孔的外部特征就不再去想了呢？

例如，你们能精确地描述五个好朋友的面容吗？你们有些人能做到，但

accurately the faces of five good friends? some of you can, but many cannot. As an experiment, I have questioned husbands of long standing about the color of their wives' eyes, and often they express embarrassed confusion and admit that they do not know. And, incidentally, it is a chronic complaint of wives that their husbands do not notice new dresses, new hats, and changes in household arrangements.

The eyes of seeing persons soon become accustomed to the routine of their surroundings, and they actually see only the startling and spectacular. But even in viewing the most spectacular sights the eyes are lazy. Court records reveal every day how inaccurately "eyewitnesses" see. A given event will be "seen" in several different ways by as many witnesses. Some see more than others, but few see everything that is within the range of their vision.

Oh, the things that I should see if I had the power of sight for just three days!

The first day would be a busy one. I should call to me all my dear friends and look long into their faces, imprinting upon my mind the outward evidences of the beauty that is within them. I should let my eyes rest, too, on the face of a baby, so that I could catch a vision of

1913年，妇女们在美国首都华盛顿举行游行，要求修改宪法，赋予她们投票权。海伦参加了这次"投妇女一票"游行，热情地支持妇女争取选举权的运动。她们在1920年实现了自己的目标

许多人不能。作为一个实验，我曾问过那些相处多年的丈夫们，他们太太的眼睛是什么颜色的。结果他们常常显得非常窘迫，承认他们不清楚。而且，顺便说一句，妻子们还总是埋怨她们的丈夫不注意新衣服、新帽子和家中摆设的变化。

眼睛能看见的人，他们的眼睛很快就习惯了周围的环境。他们实际上只看到了那些惊人的和壮观的景象，然而，即使是那些最壮观的景象，他们的眼睛也是懒散的。法庭记录每天都表明"见证人"是看得多么的不准确。例如同一个事件要求"目击者"从尽可能多的方面去"看"，有些人看得比另一些人要多，但很少有人看到了他们的视线范围内所有的事情。

啊，假如给我三天光明，我能看多少东西啊！

第一天将会是非常忙碌的一天，我要把我所有亲爱的朋友都叫来，长久地凝视他们的面容，把他们内在美的外部迹象深深地铭记在我的脑海中。我还要让我的目光停留在一个婴儿的脸上，以便我能捕获一种热切期望的纯美的视觉，这是个人在意识到生活带来的冲突之前天真无邪的美的视觉。

the eager, innocent beauty which precedes the individual's consciousness of the conflicts which life develops.

And I should like to look into the loyal, trusting eyes of my dogs - the grave, canny little Scottie, Darkie, and the stalwart, understanding Great Dane, Helga, whose warm, tender, and playful friendships are so comforting to me.

On that busy first day I should also view the small simple things of my home. I want to see the warm colors in the rugs under my feet, the pictures on the walls, the intimate trifles that transform a house into home. My eyes would rest respectfully on the books in raised type which I have read, but they would be more eagerly interested in the printed books which seeing people can read, for during the long night of my life the books I have read and those which have been read to me have built themselves into a great shining lighthouse, revealing to me the deepest channels of human life and the human spirit.

In the afternoon of that first seeing day. I should take a long walk in the woods and intoxicate my eyes on the beauties of the world of Nature trying desperately to absorb in a few hours the vast splendor which is constantly

海伦坐在桌旁使用打字机，葆丽·汤玛森站在她身边，并在其右手中拼写

我还要看看我那忠诚的、令人信赖的狗的眼睛——那沉着机警的小斯科蒂·达基和那高大健壮、善解人意的大戴恩·赫尔加，它们的热情温柔和顽皮的友谊对我是如此巨大的安慰。

在这繁忙的第一天，我还要看看我家里那些简单的小东西。我要看我脚下地毯温暖的颜色、墙上挂的画，看看使这间屋子变成一个家的所有亲切而琐碎的东西。我的目光还要虔诚地注视那些我读过的凸字书，但我会更加热切地看那些视力正常的人看的出版物，因为在我生命的漫长黑夜里，我读过的书和别人为我读过的书已经筑成了一座伟大而明亮的灯塔，向我揭示了人类生活和人类精神的最深的航道。

在光明的第一天下午，我要在树林中远足，让我的眼睛陶醉在大自然的美景之中。在几个小时中，努力吸收那经常展现在视力正常的人面前的壮丽景观。在从森林回家的路上，我要走在农庄附近的小路上，这样我就能看到在田间耕作的温驯的马儿（或许，我只能看见一台拖拉机），看看紧贴着泥

unfolding itself to those who can see. On the way home from my woodland jaunt my path would lie near a farm so that I might see the patient horses ploughing in the field (perhaps I should see only a tractor!) and the serene content of men living close to the soil. And I should pray for the glory of a colorful sunset.

When dusk had fallen, I should experience the double delight of being able to see by artificial light which the genius of man has created to extend the power of his sight when Nature decrees darkness.

In the night of that first day of sight, I should not be able to sleep, so full would be my mind of the memories of the day.

The Second Day

The next day-the second day of sight-I should arise with the dawn and see the thrilling miracle by which night is transformed into day. I should behold with awe the magnificent panorama of light with which the sun awakens the sleeping earth.

This day I should devote to a hasty glimpse of the world, past and present. I should want to see the pageant of man's progress, the kaleidoscope of the ages. How can so much be compressed into one day? Through the museums, of course. Often I have visited the New York Museum of Natural History to touch with my hands many of the objects there exhibited, but I have longed to see with my eyes the condensed history of the earth and its inhabitants displayed there - animals

土生活的人们那安详的满足。而且，我将要为辉煌的落日景观而祈祷。

当夜幕降临时，我应该感受到双倍的愉快，因为能看到人造的光明，这是人类的天才创造出来的，以便在大自然进入黑夜时扩大他的视力。

在能看见的第一个晚上，我将无法入睡，脑海中充满了白天的记忆。

第二天

第二天——也就是光明的第二天——我会和黎明一道起床，亲眼目睹黑夜转成白昼的激动人心的奇迹。我要怀着敬畏的心情，仰望太阳唤醒沉睡的大地时壮丽的景观。

我要将这一天用来对整个世界的过去和现在作匆匆的扫视。我想看人类发展的进程，看时代变化的万花筒。这么多东西怎么能压缩在一天之内呢？当然是通过博物馆了。我已经参观过纽约自然历史博物馆许多次，用我的手触摸那里陈列的许多物品。但我渴望亲眼看到地球的简史，以及那里陈列的地球居民——在自然环境中展示出来的动物和人类，巨大的恐龙和剑齿虎化石。在人类出现之前，这些动物就在地球上漫游，后来人类以他小巧的身材和强有力的大脑征服了动物王国。还要观看动物和人类及人类工具的进化过程，人类曾用这些工具在这个星球上为他们建造舒适安全的住所，还有自然

and the races of men pictured in their native environment; gigantic carcasses of dinosaurs and mastodons which roamed the earth long before man appeared, with his tiny stature and powerful brain, to conquer the animal kingdom; realistic presentations of the processes of development in animals, in man, and in the implements which man has used to fashion for himself a secure home on this planet; and a thousand and one other aspects of natural history.

I wonder how many readers of this article have viewed this panorama of the face of living things as pictured in that inspiring museum. Many, of course, have not had the opportunity, but I am sure that many who have had the opportunity have not made use of it. there, indeed, is a place to use your eyes. You who see can spend many fruitful days there, but I with my imaginary three days of sight, could only take a hasty glimpse, and pass on.

My next stop would be the Metropolitan Museum of Art, for just as the Museum of Natural History reveals the material aspects of the world, so does the Metropolitan show the myriad facets of the human spirit. Throughout the history of humanity the urge to artistic expression has been almost as powerful as the urge for food, shelter, and procreation. And here , in the vast chambers of the Metropolitan Museum, is unfolded before me the spirit of Egypt, Greece, and Rome, as expressed in their art. I know well through my hands the sculptured gods and goddesses of the ancient Nile-land. I have felt copies of Parthenon friezes, and I have sensed the rhythmic beauty of charging Athenian warriors. Apollos and

历史的其他许多方面。

我不知道这篇文章的读者中，有多少人看过这个生动的博物馆所展示的千姿百态的事物的壮观景象。当然，许多人没有这种机会，但是我相信许多人的确有这种机会而没有利用。在那里，的确是使用你的眼睛的好去处，你们看得见的人将在那里度过许多颇有收获的日子。可是我呢，只能有想象中的三天光明的日子，只能匆匆忙忙地一瞥而过。

我的下一站将是大都会艺术博物馆。正像自然历史博物馆展示了世界的物质方面那样，大都会艺术博物馆将展示人类精神的诸多方面。贯穿人类历史全过程的那种对艺术表现形式的冲动，几乎就像人类对于食物、住所和生育的迫切需求同样强烈。在这里，在大都会博物馆那宽敞的展示大厅里，展现在我们面前的是古埃及、古希腊和古罗马的精神世界，它们是以艺术形式表现出来的。我通过我的手，清楚地了解了雕刻而成的古代尼罗河土地上的诸神，我抚摸了巴特农神庙中文物的复制品（译注：巴特农神庙是古代希腊雅典城内祭祀帕拉斯·雅典娜的神殿，由大理石建成，雕饰之巧世所罕见，是希腊古典建筑中的杰作），我体会到了向前冲锋的雅典武士的韵律之美。阿波罗、维纳斯和长有翅膀的胜利女神莎莫丝雷斯令我爱不释手。对于我来说，荷马那长满了胡须、布满了节瘤的面部雕像无比亲切，因为他也知道什

Venuses and the Winged Victory of Samothrace are friends of my finger tips. The gnarled, bearded features of Homer are dear to me, for he, too, knew blindness.

My hands have lingered upon the living marble of roman sculpture as well as that of later generations. I have passed my hands over a plaster cast of Michelangelo's inspiring and heroic Moses; I have sensed the power of Rodin; I have been awd by the devoted spirit of Gothic wood carving. These arts which can be touched have meaning for me, but even they were meant to be seen rather than felt, and I can only guess at the beauty which remains hidden from me. I can admire the simple lines of a Greek vase, but its figured decorations are lost to me.

So on this, my second day of sight, I should try to probe into the soul of man through this art. The things I knew through touch I should now see. More splendid still, the whole magnificent world of painting would be opened to me, from the Italian Primitives, with their serene religious devotion, to the Moderns, with their feverish visions. I should look deep into the canvases of Raphael, Leonardo da Vinci, Titian, Rembrandt. I should want to feast my eyes upon the warm colors of Veronese, study the mysteries of

么是失明。

我的手曾停留在栩栩如生的罗马大理石雕像和后世的雕刻上。我曾抚摸过米开朗琪罗（译注：佛罗伦萨著名

海伦在阿尔肯里奇周围散步

的画家、雕刻家、建筑师和诗人，意大利文艺复兴时期最杰出的代表人物）雕刻的鼓舞人心的英雄摩西石膏像，3我感受到了法国雕塑家罗丹的力量，对哥特木刻的虔诚精神感到敬畏。这些能用手触摸到的艺术作品，对我来说具有真实的意义，但这些艺术品即使是既可以观看又可以抚摸，我也只能是猜测那躲避着我的美妙。我能欣赏一只古希腊花瓶简单的线条，但我对它带有装饰的图案却一无所知。

所以，在我光明的第二天，我将努力通过人类的艺术来探究人类的灵魂。我将看到我通过触摸已经知道的东西。更加奇妙的是，所有的神奇世界将展现在我面前——从拥有平静宗教色彩的意大利文艺复兴前期作品到充满狂热梦幻的现代派作品。我将仔细欣赏拉斐尔、列奥纳多·达·芬奇、提香和伦布朗的油画。我要让我的眼睛饱享维勒内兹油画炽烈的色彩，研究埃

El Greco, catch a new vision of Nature from Corot. Oh, there is so much rich meaning and beauty in the art of the ages for you who have eyes to see!

Upon my short visit to this temple of art I should not be able to review a fraction of that great world of art which is open to you. I should be able to get only a superficial impression. Artists tell me that for deep and true appreciation of art one must educated the eye. One must learn through experience to weigh the merits of line, of composition, of form and color. If I had eyes, how happily would I embark upon so fascinating a study! Yet I am told that, to many of you who have eyes to see, the world of art is a dark night, unexplored and unilluminated.

It would be with extreme reluctance that I should leave the Metropolitan Museum, which contains the key to beauty- a beauty so neglected. Seeing persons, however, do not need a metropolitan to find this key to beauty. The same key lies waiting in smaller museums, and in books on the shelves of even small libraries. But naturally, in my limited time of imaginary sight, I should choose the place where the key unlocks the greatest treasures in the shortest time.

The evening of my second day of sight I should spend at a theatre or at the movies. Even now I often attend theatrical performances of all sorts, but the action of the play must be spelled into my hand by a companion. But how I should like to see with my own eyes the fascinating figure of Hamlet, or the gusty Falstaff amid colorful Elizabethan trappings! How I should like to follow each movement of the graceful Hamlet, each strut of the hearty Falstaff! And since I could see only one

尔·格列科绘画的神秘，从科罗的绘画中领略大自然的新视觉。啊！对你们能用眼睛去看的人来说，在那个时代的艺术中有多么丰富的意义和美丽啊！

在对这座艺术殿堂的短暂访问中，我没有资格评论那呈现在你眼前的伟大艺术世界的任何部分。我只能获得一个表面的印象。艺术家们告诉我，一个人要想真正而深刻地鉴赏艺术，就必须训练他的眼睛。他必须通过经验学会品评线条、构图、形态和色彩。如果我能看见，我将会多么愉快地去做令人如此着迷的研究工作！但是有人告诉我，对你们视力正常的许多人来说，艺术的世界是一个深沉的黑夜，未曾开发，也未曾照亮。

要离开大都会博物馆，我是多么不情愿啊！那里有美的钥匙，然而这种美又被忽视了。看得见的人不必去大都会博物馆寻找这开启美的钥匙，这相同的钥匙正在较小的博物馆，甚至小图书馆的书架上的书中等着。但是，在我想象的有限光明中，我当然要选择在最短的时间内打开最伟大宝库的钥匙的地方。

在我能看见的第二天晚上，我要在戏院或电影院中度过。即使现在我还经常去看各种戏剧表演，但需要由一个同伴将剧情写在我的手上。我是多么想亲眼看到莎士比亚戏剧中哈姆雷特的迷人形象，或者穿着伊丽莎白时代艳丽多彩服饰的生气勃勃的伏尔斯塔夫！我多想模仿优雅的哈姆雷特的每一个

play, I should be confronted by a many-horned dilemma, for there are scores of plays I should want to see. You who have eyes can see any you like. How many of you, I wonder, when you gaze at a play, a movie, or any spectacle, realize and give thanks for the miracle of sight which enables you to enjoy its color , grace, and movement?

I cannot enjoy the beauty of rhythmic movement except in a sphere restricted to the touch of my hands. I can vision only dimly the grace of a Pavlowa, although I know something of the delight of rhythm, for often I can sense the beat of music as it vibrates through the floor. I can well imagine that cadenced motion must be one of the most pleasing sights in the world. I have been able to gather something of this by tracing with my fingers the lines in sculptured marble; if this static grace can be so lovely, how much more acute must be the thrill of seeing grace in motion.

One of my dearest memories is of the time when Joseph Jefferson allowed me to touch his face and hands as he went through some of the gestures and speeches of his beloved Rip Van Winkle. I was able to catch thus a meager glimpse of the world of drama, and I shall never forget the delight of that moment. But, oh, how much I must miss, and how much pleasure you seeing ones can derive from watching and hearing the interplay of speech and movement in the unfolding of a dramatic performance! If I could see only one play, I should know how to picture in my mind the action of a hundred plays which I have read or had transferred to

动作、热忱的伏尔斯塔夫的每一个昂首阔步的举动！由于我只能看一场戏，这将使我面临进退两难的困境，因为我想看的戏剧有几十部。你们视力正常的人，可以看你们喜欢的任何一部戏剧。不过我怀疑，当你们全神贯注地观看一部戏剧、一场电影或任何奇观时，你们中间有多少人会意识到，并感激那使你们享受到色彩、优雅和动作的视力奇迹呢？

除了我的手能触摸到的东西之外，我不能享受那有节奏的动作所蕴含的美感。尽管我懂得一些节奏的愉快，因为当音乐通过地板振动时我经常能感觉到它的节拍，但我也只能是隐隐约约地想象一下芭蕾舞演员巴甫洛娃的优美。我能想象到，那有节奏韵律的动作一定是世界上最令人愉快的景象。我已经通过手指摸索到的大理石雕刻的线条轮廓来获得这样的感受；如果这种静态的雅致都是如此的可爱，那么，看见动态的美将会更加令人震惊！

我最珍贵的回忆之一，是约瑟夫·杰斐逊排练他心爱的角色瑞普·冯·温克尔时，在做动作和对白时让我摸他的脸和手。这样，对戏剧我只有这么一点点接触，我将永远忘不了那个时刻的愉快。但是，啊，我可能失去了许多，你们能看见的人从戏剧表演中看动作，倾听角色对白，将会得到多少快乐啊！假如我能看到哪怕是一部戏剧，我就会知道如何在我的脑海中描绘我曾经读过的或通过盲文书向我转述的上百部戏剧的动作。

me through the medium of the manual alphabet.

So, through the evening of my second imaginary day of sight, the great fingers of dramatic literature would crowd sleep from my eyes.

The Third Day

The following morning, I should again greet the dawn, anxious to discover new delights, for I am sure that, for those who have eyes which really see, the dawn of each day must be a perpetually new revelation of beauty.

This, according to the terms of my imagined miracle, is to be my third and last day of sight. I shall have no time to waste in regrets or longings; there is too much to see. The first day I devoted to my friends, animate and inanimate. The second revealed to me the history of man and Nature. Today I shall spend in the workaday world of the present, amid the haunts of men going about the business of life. And where can one find so many activities and conditions of men as in New York? So the city becomes my destination.

I start from my home in the quiet little suburb of Forest Hills, Long Island. Here, surrounded by green lawns, trees, and flowers, are neat little houses, happy with the voices and movements of wives and children, havens of peaceful rest for men who toil in the city. I drive across the lacy structure of steel which spans the East River, and I get a new and startling vision of the power and ingenuity of the

这样，在我想象中能看见的第二天晚上，戏剧文学中的许多人物会因我用眼睛看了之后，又都在我的睡梦中涌现出来。

第三天

接下来的早上，我再次欢呼黎明，迫切地要发现新的惊喜，因为我确信，对那些眼睛真的能看见的人来说，每天的黎明一定是一个永远重复的新的美景。

根据我想象中的奇迹的时限，这将是我能看见的第三天，也是最后一天。我没有时间浪费在后悔或渴望中，要看的东西太多了。第一天我献给了我的朋友们——有生命的和无生命的朋友。第二天向我展示了人类和自然的历史。今天，我将在当今的平凡世界度过，去那些为了生活工作而忙碌的人经常去的地方。在哪里能找到像纽约这样多的活动和条件呢？所以，纽约便成了我的目的地。

我从我在长岛森林山寂静的乡间小屋出发。这里，绿草、树木和鲜花环绕着整洁的小房，妇女和孩子们欢声笑语，实在是城里辛劳的男人们安宁的避风港。我驾车驶过那跨越伊斯特河的条带状钢铁桥梁，对人类智慧的创造力获得了一个新的令人震惊的视觉印象。繁忙的船只在河上往来航行——高

mind of man. Busy boasts chug and scurry about the river - racy speed boat, stolid, snorting tugs. If I had long days of sight ahead, I should spend many of them watching the delightful activity upon the river.

I look ahead, and before me rise the fantastic towers of New York, a city that seems to have stepped from the pages of a fairy story. What an awe-inspiring sight, these glittering spires, these vast banks of stone and steel-structures such as the gods might build for themselves! This animated picture is a part of the lives of millions of people every day. How many, I wonder, give it so much as a seconds glance? Very few, I fear. Their eyes are blind to this magnificent sight because it is so familiar to them.

I hurry to the top of one of those gigantic structures, the Empire State Building, for there, a short time ago, I "saw" the city below through the eyes of my secretary. I am anxious to compare my fancy with reality. I am sure I should not be disappointed in the panorama spread out before me, for to me it would be a vision of another world.

Now I begin my rounds of the city. First, I stand at

速飞驰的快艇和笨重的喘着气的驳船。如果我能看见的日子再长一些，我要花更多的时间看看这河上生机勃勃的景象。

海伦作为美国海外盲人基金会的代表，前往非洲访问

我向前眺望，纽约的高楼大厦在我前面升起，似乎是从童话故事中出现的一座城市。多么令人敬畏的景象啊！这些辉煌的尖塔，这些巨大的石头与钢铁的建筑群，就像诸神为他们自己修建的！这幅生动的图景是千百万人每天生活的一部分。我不知道到底有多少人会对它多看一眼？我以为恐怕会很少，他们的眼睛对这辉煌的景象只会熟视无睹，因为他们对此太熟悉了。

我匆匆爬上这些宏伟建筑之一——帝国大厦的顶端，因为在那里，不久以前，我曾通过秘书的眼睛"看"过下面的城市。我急切地把我的想象同现实作一番比较。我确信，我不会对展现在我面前的景色失望，因为对我来说它是另一个世界的景象。

现在，我开始周游这座城市。首先，我站在一个繁华的街角，仅仅是看着人们，希望通过审视他们来理解他们生活的某些东西。看到笑容，我就会高兴；看到严肃的决心，我就会骄傲；看到苦难，我就会同情。

a busy corner, merely looking at people, trying by sight of them to understand something of their live. I see smiles, and I am happy. I see serious determination, and I am proud. I see suffering, and I am compassionate.

I stroll down Fifth Avenue. I throw my eyes out of focus, so that I see no particular object but only a seething kaleidoscope of colors. I am certain that the colors of women's dresses moving in a throng must be a gorgeous spectacle of which I should never tire. But perhaps if I had sight I should be like most other women- too interested in styles and the cut of individual dresses to give much attention to the splendor of color in the mass. And I am convinced, too, that I should become an inveterate window shopper, for it must be a delight to the eye to view the myriad articles of beauty on display.

From Fifth Avenue I make a tour of the city-to Park Avenue, to the slums, to factories, to parks where children play. I take a stay-at-home trip abroad by visiting the foreign quarters. Always my eyes are open wide to all the sights of both happiness and misery so that I may probe deep and add to my understanding of how people work and live. My heart is full of the images of people and things.

海伦和保姆葆丽·汤玛森访问瑞典斯多克赫姆一所聋哑学校，海伦手中捧着一只鸽子

我漫步在第五大道上，把目光从聚精会神的注视中解放出来，不去留意特别的目标，仅仅看那川流不息的彩色万花筒。我相信那成群女人们的服装色彩一定是一种百看不厌的灿烂奇观。或许，如果我能看见的话，我也会像其他大多数女人一样，也对式样和剪裁时髦的服装感兴趣，而忽视了集聚的色彩斑斓。我也相信，我会成为一个习惯于浏览橱窗的顾客，因为看那陈列的无数美好的商品一定是一种享受。

从第五大道开始，我将环游这座城市——到派克大道去，到贫民窟去，到工厂去，到儿童游乐园去。我还将参观外国居民区，作一次不出门的国外旅行。我始终睁大眼睛，注视着所有幸福的和悲哀的景象，以便深入探究和进一步理解人们是如何工作和生活的。我心中充满了人和事物的形象，我的目光不会轻易放过任何一件细小的东西，力求触及并紧紧抓住所看见的每一件事。有些景象是令人愉快的，它让你心里充满喜悦，而有些则是悲惨的，对此我并不闭上我的眼睛，因为这也是生活的一部分，闭起双眼不看它们，就是关闭心灵与大脑。

我拥有光明的第三天行将结束了。也许还有许多强烈的愿望，我应花

My eye passes lightly over no single trifle; it strives to touch and hold closely each thing its gaze rests upon. Some sights are pleasant, filling the heart with happiness; but some are miserably pathetic. To these latter I do not shut my eyes, for they, too, are part of life. To close the eye on them is to close the heart and mind.

My third day of sight is drawing to an end. Perhaps there are many serious pursuits to which I should devote the few remaining hours, but I am afraid that on the evening of that last day I should again run away to the theater, to a hilariously funny play, so that I might appreciate the overtones of comedy in the human spirit.

At midnight my temporary respite from blindness would cease, and permanent night would close in on me again. Naturally in those three short days I should not have seen all I wanted to see. Only when darkness had again descended upon me should I realize how much I had left unseen. But my mind would be so crowded with glorious memories that I should have little time for regrets. Thereafter the touch of every object would bring a glowing memory of how that object looked.

Perhaps this short outline of how I should spend three days of sight does not agree with the program you

最后的几个小时去实现它们。但是，我怕在这最后一天的晚上又会跑到戏院，去欣赏一部欢快有趣的戏剧。这样我就可以欣赏到人类精神上的美妙韵律。

海伦正在留声机旁，通过触摸感受音乐

到了午夜，我摆脱失明的短暂时刻就要结束了，永恒的黑夜重又包围了我。当然，在这短短的三天时间里，我不能看到我想看的所有事情，只有在黑暗重又向我袭来时，我才意识到还留下多少东西没有看到。但我的脑海里充满了这么多美好的记忆，以致我没有什么时间来后悔的。此后，每摸到一件物品，都将带给我一个强烈的记忆，那东西看起来是怎样的。

也许，我这篇关于怎样度过这三天光明的简短概述和你们自己如有一天遭受失明之后所设想的不一致。然而，我确信，如果你真的面临那样的不幸，你的双眼一定会对过去从未看过的事情而睁大，为你今后的漫长黑夜储存记忆。你将会以过去从未有过的方式来利用你的眼睛。你所看到的每件事物对你都会变得珍贵起来，你的眼睛将会仔细端详每一件进入你视线范围之内的事物。然后，你将发现，一个前所未有的美丽新世界在你面前展开了。

would set for yourself if you knew that you were about to be stricken blind. I am, however, sure that if you actually faced that fate your eyes would open to things you had never seen before, storing up memories for the long night ahead. You would use your eyes as never before. Everything you saw would become dear to you. Your eyes would touch and embrace every object that came within your range of vision. Then, at last, you would really see, and a new world of beauty would open itself before you.

I who am blind can give one hint to those who see-one admonition to those who would make full use of the gift of sight: Use your eyes as if tomorrow you would be stricken blind. And the same method can be applied to the other senses. Hear the music of voices, the song of a bird, the mighty strains of an orchestra, as if you would be stricken deaf tomorrow. Touch each object you want to touch as if tomorrow your tactile sense would fail. Smell the perfume of flowers, taste with relish each morsel, as if tomorrow you could never smell and taste again. Make the most of every sense: glory in all the facets of pleasure and beauty which the world reveals to you through the several means of contact which Nature provides. But of all the senses, I am sure that sight must be the most delightful.

海伦在康涅狄格州韦斯特波特家中的图书室读盲文书

我——一个盲人——可以给那些能看见的人一个提示——给那些想充分利用视觉天赋的人一个忠告：善用你的双眼，就好像你明天就会失明一样。同样的方法也可以用于其他的感官：聆听悦耳的乐曲，鸟儿的歌唱，乐队强劲的旋律，就好像你明天就要失聪一样；触摸你想摸的每一个物体，就好像你的触觉明天就要失灵一样；闻闻花朵的芳香，品尝一口美味佳肴，就好像你明天再也不能闻到，再也不能尝到一样。

尽量利用你所有的感官吧！从各个方面尽情体会这个世界的快乐和美丽吧！这些感觉都是大自然恩赐给你的。但是我相信，在所有的感官中，视觉一定是最令人欣喜的。

附 录

第一篇　从黑暗走向光明

大学后的生活

　　我上面描述的都是大学一年级的生活，现在我来说大学二年级以后的情况。

　　《少女时代》这一部分，是由我在拉德克利夫学院读大学一年级时的作文汇集而成的。当时，在上柯兰老师的作文课时，我每个星期都写一篇文章。但我最初并没有打算将它们整理出版，直到《淑女报》的主编有一天忽然来访，他说："敝社社长希望能在我们的杂志上刊登你的传记，而且以连载的方式登出，请多多支持。"

　　当我明白对方的来意后，就以功课繁忙为由，婉转地拒绝了他，但他却坚持说："你不是已经在作文课上写了很多吗？"

　　我听到他这话时，吃了一惊："啊！你是如何知道这些事的？"

　　"啊，谁让我吃这行饭呢？"那位主编带有几分得意地笑着说。

　　紧接着，他又告诉我，只需将学校的作文稍加润色，就可以成为杂志需要的稿子，这做起来非常容易。于是，我只好答应以3000美元的价格在《淑女报》上连载《少女时代》的原稿，并在合约上签了字。说实话，我当时确实深受那3000美元的诱惑，忘了那份稿子只完成一半，更没想到要续写后半部分可能带来的种种困扰。当时，我的确有些得意忘形了。

　　事情就这样定了下来。刚开始的时候，一切进展得还算顺利，可是越往后写，我越觉得棘手了。因为我不知道该写什么合适，加上我又不是什么专业作家，当然也就不知道如何将现有材料进行适当的润色加工之后变成杂志社需要的东西，甚至对截稿日期的重要性也一无所知，可以说完全是个门外汉。当我收到杂志社发来的电报，例如"请立刻将下一章寄来"，或"第6页与第7页的关系交代不清，请立刻回电说明"等等时，我竟然不知道该如何做才好。

幸运的是，我的同班同学蕾诺亚介绍我认识了一个人，她对我说："他是房东的同班同学，他不仅头脑灵活，而且为人也很慷慨，富有骑士精神，对待他人也很和善。如果找他帮忙，他一定不会拒绝。"

就这样，我认识了梅西先生。梅西先生是哈勃特大学的教授，当时他正在拉德克利夫学院兼课，但我并不知道这事。听了蕾诺亚的介绍之后，我对梅西先生有了最初的完美印象，我从后来的交往中深切地体会到，正如蕾诺亚所说的，梅西先生不但聪明睿智，而且为人很热心。他知道了我的困难后，立刻看了一遍我带来的资料，然后非常快地帮我整理了出来。从此以后，我终于能按时交稿了。

梅西先生是一位杰出的文学家，他才思敏锐、感情丰富。对我来说，当时他既是好朋友，又是值得信赖的兄长，更是我碰到问题时不可或缺的咨询对象。如果我现在写的这部分文章水平比不上当年的，我一点也不觉得奇怪，因为这次缺少梅西先生帮忙了。

前面曾经说过，我在拉德克利夫学院求学时，觉得最大的困扰就是没有盲文书读，还有一个问题就是时间不够分配。当时，课外作业都是由莎莉文老师用手语来逐字逐句地告诉我的，所以我经常要学习到深夜，而其他人此时此刻早已进入梦乡了。虽然洛奇老师和维杜老师也在我的教科书上为我点字，但有一些老师直到上课也没有教我如何学习，所以我总是跟不上。

红十字会如今已为盲人出版了几千册盲文书，盲人可以读到许多的书！而我当时所有的盲文书加起来也不到30本，所以对我来说，每一本书都是无价之宝。我低着头，用双手"读"这些书，搜集论文材料，准备各种大大小小的考试。每当我读这些盲文书时，常常会想："现在我即使不用别人的帮助，也可以独自学习了。"这样我就会觉得非常欣慰。

在学习方面，我可以毫不费力地阅读和理解文学和历史。这一点或许和我少女时代的生活经历有关，因为在进大学之前，我早就接触过许多优美而富有想象力和知识性的文章。因此，我对这些课兴趣很高，成绩也很好。现在回想起来，我真的为自己的幸运感到庆幸。

我唯一觉得遗憾的是，自己没能和大学时代的教授们进行更多的交流。对我来说，大多数教授的讲课就像留声机一样，只能是机械性地听讲。虽然院长布里吉斯教授家就在我的边上，但我从没有主动去拜访过他。就连给我的毕业证签字的艾里华特博士，我也一直没有机会见。只有教我写作的霍布兰德教授以及教《伊丽莎白时代文学》的尼尔逊博士，还有教德文的帕德雷特教授等人，会偶尔请我喝茶，他们在学校外面遇到我时也非常亲热。

由于我的身体状况和别人不一样，因此我不能顺畅地和班上的同学玩在一起，不过大家还是通过各种方式来与我沟通。同学们经常成群结队地去外面的餐馆吃三明治、喝可可奶，他们常常围在我的身边，说一些有趣的事情，以此来逗我发笑。同学们还推举我当副班长。如果我不是因为必须在学习上要比别人花更多的时间，以至于感到很吃力的话，我想我的大学生活一定会像其他同学一样多姿多彩的。

一天，朋友们来找我出去玩。"海伦，你想去布鲁克林闹市区一个朋友家玩吗？"但我们后来却到了波士顿一间饲养"泰瑞尔"狗的宠物店。狗儿们都很热情地欢迎我，其中一条叫托马斯伯爵的狗对我尤其亲热。虽然这条小狗长得不是特别漂亮，但它很会撒娇，站在我身边时一副驯服乖巧样。当我伸手摸它时，它高兴得猛地摇摆着尾巴，还低声欢叫着。

"啊！托马斯伯爵，你是不是很喜欢海伦？海伦，你也喜欢这条小狗吧？"朋友们几乎同声问我，我非常爽快地回答说："是的，我很喜欢它！"

"那我们就把它送给你，作为大家送给你的礼物吧。"朋友们说。

托马斯在我身边直绕圈子，似乎听懂了大家正在谈论它。等托马斯伯爵稍微安静下来之后，我才说："可是我不喜欢'伯爵'之类的称呼，听起来好像高不可攀似的。"

我说完之后，小狗似乎在想什么，一声不响地静坐一旁，变得沉默起来。

"你们觉得'费兹'这个名字怎样？"这话刚说完，托马斯伯爵好像完全赞同似的，兴奋地在地上连翻了三个滚。于是，我就把这条小狗带回了康桥的家。

我们当时租了库利兹街14号楼的一部分。据说这栋楼房原本是高级住宅，位于一座美丽的小土丘上，它的周围全是葱郁苍翠的树木。虽然楼房的正门对着马路，但由于进深很长，所以马路上来来往往的车辆喧闹声几乎完全听不到。

楼房的后面有一个大花园，房主在花园中全种上了三色紫罗兰、天竺葵、康乃馨等花草，因此屋子里总是充满了花的香味。每天早上，那些穿着鲜丽衣服的意大利女孩就会来采摘花朵，拿到市场上去卖。我们经常在那些意大利少女们活泼爽朗的欢歌笑语中醒过来，实在是像住在意大利的田园乡村。

住在库利兹街期间，我们结识了几位哈勃特大学的学生和年轻讲师，我们相处得非常融洽，并成了很好的朋友。其中一位是菲利浦·史密斯先生，他现在担任华盛顿国立地质调研所阿拉斯加分所所长，他的夫人蕾诺亚是我最要好的同学之一。蕾诺亚对我非常友好，每当莎莉文老师身体不舒服的时候，她就替莎莉文老师帮我做功课，领我去教室。

约翰·梅西先生也是当时的成员之一，他一度是我生活和精神上的支柱，后来他和莎莉文老师结婚了。年轻人精力充沛，经常一口气走十多里的乡村小路，却一点儿也不觉得累。有时候我们骑着三座的自行车出去游玩，这一出去就是40里，一直玩到尽兴才回家。

那真是无忧无虑的年龄啊！做什么事情都觉得开心，玩什么东西都会高兴。大自然所有的一切在年轻人眼里是如此的美妙，秋天照射在树梢上的温暖的太阳、成群结队向南飞徙的候鸟、为雨季储藏食物而忙忙碌碌地搬运胡桃的松鼠、从树上掉下来的熟透了的苹果、河边草地上粉红色的小花，以及那碧绿的河水……所有这一切都是如此美妙，令人心旷神怡，陶醉不已。

在寒冷的冬天夜晚，我们会租一辆有篷马车，到处随便溜达溜达，或者去山上滑雪橇，或者到野外尽情玩耍，或者静静地坐在咖啡馆中喝那香浓四溢的咖啡，或者吃一顿美味可口的夜宵。我们的生活就像神仙般快乐。

在漫长的冬夜，我们有时候也会连续好几个晚上围坐在烧得很旺的炉火前，喝着可乐，吃着爆米花，随意畅谈，对社会、文学或哲学上的种种问题进行探讨；而且无论谈什么问题，我们总喜欢刨根问底。

一群年轻人开始懂得独立思考，并且富有强烈的正义感，对社会上的邪恶势力、黑暗面非常看不惯，大家在爱好和平、热爱人类这一点上是完全一致的。然而，这种纯理论的讨论并没有什么实际意义，也解决不了根本问题，它不过是一种建立在乌托邦上的理想。但是，也没有人敢提出不同的意见，因为那些冲动的激进分子正想找"叛徒"做决斗呢。

青春的光彩如此璀璨，令人不敢直眼逼视，那种毫无畏惧的精神也确实令人羡慕。

记得有一次，我们徒步去了一个很远的地方。那是3月，风还非常猛烈，把我的帽子都吹跑了。还有一次，大概是4月，我们也是徒步出门，忽然半路上下起了瓢泼般的大雨，我们几个人只好钻到一件小小的雨衣下躲雨。到了5月，大家一起到野外去采草莓，空气中飘荡着草莓的芳香。

唉！我现在还没有成为老太婆，怎么总是回忆过去的岁月呢！

4年的大学生活在这愉快的日子里眨眼就过去了，我们终于迎来了毕业典礼。当时曾有报纸报道过毕业典礼中的我和莎莉文老师，其中还有一家报纸登了这样一条消息：

"这天，毕业典礼的礼堂被挤得水泄不通。当然，在场的每一位毕业生都将接受毕业证书，但来宾的目光却聚焦在一位学生身上，她就是美丽而成绩优异的盲人海伦·凯勒。长久以来，不辞辛劳地协助这位少女的莎莉文老师也分享了她的荣誉。当主持人念到海伦·凯勒的名字时，全场响起了雷鸣般的掌声。这位少女不仅以优异的成绩完成了所有的大学课程，而且在英国文学上表现尤其突出，因此得到了老师和同学的交相赞誉。"

莎莉文老师很高兴我能在英国文学这科获得高分，这一点完全归功于她。不过，除了这两件事实之外，报纸上其他的报道都是胡说的。那天来的嘉宾并不像记者报道的那么多；事实上，专门来参加我的毕业典礼的朋友只有五六个。最遗憾的是我母亲因为生病而不能出席典礼；而且校长也只是做了例行演讲，他并没有特别提到我和莎莉文老师。不仅如此，其他老师也没有特别过来和我打招呼。另外，当我上台领毕业证时，也并未出现报纸上所说的"雷鸣般的掌声"。总之，毕业典礼并没有像报纸所描述的那样盛况空前。有些同学还因为莎莉文老师的遭遇而打抱不平，他们一面脱下学士服，一面气愤地说："真是太草率了，应该也给莎莉文老师颁发学位才对。"

毕业典礼之后，老师带我离开礼堂，直接乘车去新英格兰的连杉，那也是我们打算搬去住的地方。当天晚上，我和朋友们在奥罗摩那波亚加湖泛舟游戏，头顶着宁静祥和的星空，大家暂时忘却了人间的一切烦恼。

那家对毕业典礼夸大报道的报纸还说，连杉的房子是波士顿市政府送给我的，那里不但有宽敞的院子，而且屋子里放满了别人送给我的青铜雕塑，还说我有一间巨型图书室，它藏有几万册图书，说什么我坐拥书城，生活十分惬意。这简直是一派胡言。我和莎莉文老师住的，怎么是如此豪华的房子呢？

事实上，那是一栋很早以前就买好的老旧农舍，它四周有7英亩田地，它们被荒废许久了。莎莉文老师打通了挤奶场和存放陶器的储藏室，使之成为一个大房间，就充当我的书房。书房里大约有一百册盲文书，虽然相当简陋，但是我已经觉得很满意了。书房的光线充足，东西两边的窗台可以摆一些盆景，还有两扇落地玻璃门，可以眺望远处的松林。莎莉文老师还特意在我的卧室旁边搭建了一个小阳台，这样只要我高兴时就可以出去走走。就是在这个阳台上，我第一次听到鸟儿唱"爱之歌"。

那天，我在阳台上享受那和煦的微风，不愿进房间，呆了足足有一个多小时。阳台的南边长满了常春藤，它的枝叶绕着栏杆攀爬而上；北边则种着苹果树，每当苹果树开花时，那扑鼻的香味简直令人陶醉。忽然，我扶着栏杆的手感到了轻微的颤动，这种颤动的感觉就像是我把手放在音乐家的喉咙上那样。

这种颤动一阵接一阵，一会儿有一会儿停。就在某一次停顿的瞬间，一片花瓣掉落下来，轻轻地擦过我的脸颊，掉到了地上。我立刻猜想大概是鸟儿飞过，或者是微风吹过，所以花瓣才会掉落的。就在我猜测之际，栏杆又开始颤动起来。

"这究竟是什么？"我静静地站在那儿，神色专注地感受和思考着。这时，莎莉文老师从窗子里伸出手来，悄悄地暗示我不要动。她抓着我的手告诉我："正好有一只蚊母鸟停在你身边的栏杆上，你一动它就会飞走，所以你最好是站着不要动。"

莎莉文老师用手语告诉我说：这种鸟的鸣叫声听上去像"飞——普——啊——威，飞——普——啊——威"。我聚精会神地辨别这种鸟的叫声，终于感受到了它的节拍与情调，还感觉到它的鸣叫声正逐渐加大加快。

莎莉文老师再次给我传递信息说："这只鸟的恋人正在苹果树上与它应和。那只鸟儿也许早就停在那里了。哦，你看，现在它们开始二重唱了。"

停了一会儿，她又说："现在，这两只鸟儿已经在苹果花丛中卿卿我我地互诉衷肠呢！"

这栋农舍是我用糖业公司的股票换来的。这些股票是10年前史波林先生送给我的。史波林先生在我们最艰难的时候，对我们伸出了救援之手。

我第一次见到史波林先生时还只有9岁。当时他带来了童星莱特，和我们一起做游戏。当时，这位童星正参加电影《小公主》的演出。此后，只要我们有困难，史波林先生都尽全力予以帮助，而且他经常到帕金斯盲人学校来看我们。每次来的时候，他都会带一些玫瑰花、饼干、水果送给大家。有时他还请大家出去吃午饭，或者租一辆马车，带我们出去游玩，童星莱特也常常陪我们一起去。

莱特是一个活泼可爱的漂亮小女孩，史波林先生常对我们俩说："你们是我最心爱的两个小乖乖。"然后非常开心地看着我们一起玩耍。

当时我正在学习如何与人交谈，而史波林先生却总是不明白我的意思，对此我感到非常遗憾。一天，我特意在反复练习说"莱特"的名字，想给史波林先生来个惊喜。然而，无论我多么努力，就是说不好莱特的全名。我急得哭了出来。当史波林先生又一次来看我时，我迫不及待地给他展现我练习的成果。经过一遍又一遍的多次反复，我好不容易才让史波林先生明白了我的意思。我既高兴又感动，激动的心情至今都难以忘怀。

此后，每当我无法清楚地表达自己的意思，或者周围太吵闹了，史波林先生不能和我沟通时,他就会紧紧地抱住我,轻柔地安慰我道:"虽然我不太明白你的意思,可是我喜欢你,而且永远永远最喜欢你。"

史波林先生直到去世,都一直按月给我和莎莉文老师寄生活费。他在送给我们糖业公司的股票时,告诉我们可以在需要的时候卖掉它。正因为如此,当莎莉文老师和我第一次踏进这屋子,开始我们新的生活时,我们随时都能感到史波林先生与我们在一起。

我大学毕业的第二年,也即1905年5月2日,莎莉文老师和梅西先生结婚了。我长期以来一直盼望莎莉文老师能遇上一个好人,能有一个美满的归宿,所以对于他们的结合我由衷地感到高兴,并真心诚意地祝他们永远幸福。

婚礼在一幢漂亮的白色房子里举行,由我们的朋友爱德华·海尔博士主持的。婚礼之后,新婚夫妇去新奥尔良度蜜月,母亲则把我带回南部去度假了。六七天以后,梅西夫妇突然出现在我和母亲住的旅馆中,我们吓了一大跳。在南方的初夏美景中见到我最喜爱的两个人,真的让我喜出望外,如同做梦一样。

梅西先生告诉我:"这一带到处都飘荡着木兰花的香味,而且有最悦耳的鸟鸣声。"

这对蜜月中的夫妇,可能把啁啾鸟鸣当作是对他们新婚的最好祝福了。于是,我们四人一同回到了位于连杉的家。这时我隐隐约约听到一些流言蜚语,原来是那些好事之徒在无端地猜测说:"莎莉文老师结婚了,可怜的海伦一定很伤心,说不定还会吃醋呢!"甚至还有人因此而写信来安慰我。但他们一定没有想到的是,我不仅没有伤心吃醋,而且过得比以前更愉快、更充实。

莎莉文老师心地善良而高贵,梅西先生也待人和善热情,他讲的故事常常会引得我发笑,而且他经常教给我一些我应该知道的常识和科学知识,还偶尔和我讨论一些当前的文学动向。

有一段时间,因为打字机出了故障,我曾耽误了正常的写作速度,最后为了赶时间,梅西先生连夜为我打了40页书稿。当时,我应邀给《世纪杂志》写稿,主要是描述我身边发生的一些琐事,文章的题目叫《常识与杂感》。由于简·奥斯汀女士曾以同样的题目写过一本书,因此我的稿子结集出版时,就将书名改成了《我居住的世界》。我的情绪在写作过程中一直处于最佳状态,这也是我写得最愉快的一本书。我写到了新英格兰迷人的风光,也讨论了我所想到的一些哲学问题。总之,我把我所能思考到的事情都写出来了。

接下来的一本书是《石壁之歌》。这是一本诗歌集,其灵感来自于田园。一天,我们到野外去整修那古老的石垣,春天的气息和劳动的喜悦使我在心中孕育出一篇又一篇歌颂春之喜悦的诗歌。在整理这些诗歌时,梅西先生给了我极大的帮助。他毫不客气地指出了他觉得不满意的地方,当然也毫无保留地夸赞他欣赏的诗句。我们对每一篇诗歌都要经过再三吟咏,反复斟酌。梅西先生常说:"我们这么尽力润色,如果还有什么不好的地方,那也无能为力了。"

到了连杉之后,我们想到了父亲在亚拉巴马的农场生活,于是打算过朴实的田园生活,想养一些家畜,并种植农作物。起初,我们只有从康桥带来的那条名叫费兹的狗,但是搬到此地一年多之后它就死了。后来,我们又陆陆续续地养了几条狗。我们还去附近的养鸡场买了几只小鸡。大家都很热心地照料,可是没想到这些小鸡很不好养,不久全都死了。

由于我们觉得空几间屋子在那里太可惜了,于是想把它改成马厩养马。我们买了一匹野性未驯、凶悍无比的马,送马的少年在半路上就被摔下来两三次,可是他把马交给我们时却什么都没有告诉我们,我们当然也就不知实情了。第二天一大早,梅西先生牵出马来,套上货车,准备去镇上。但是刚出大门没多远,马儿忽然暴跳起来。梅西先生觉得奇怪,以为是马身上的马具有问题,就下车来查看。梅西先生刚把货车套具从马身上卸下来,马儿就人立起来,一声长嘶之后撒腿就跑了。两天之后,邻近的一位农夫看到一匹马身上套着马具在树林里溜达,就把它送了回来。

我们没有办法,只好将这匹失而复得的马卖给了专门驯马的人。由于那段时间我们比较拮据,就有人建议我们种苹果。于是我们又买来100棵果树苗,开始种起苹果来。到第五年头上,果树开始结果。我很兴奋,在笔记本上记下苹果的数量和大小。

一天下午,仆人神色不对地跑进来大声叫道:"不得了!野牛!野牛!"我们听了立刻跑到窗口去看,才知道并不是野牛,而是从附近山上下来的野鹿,而且似乎是全家都出来了。

一对鹿夫妇带着三只小鹿,在我们的苹果园里闲逛。它们在阳光下活泼跳跃的身姿实在太迷人了,以至于大家都看得出神了。然而,这群不速之客突然毫不客气地倒腾起来。等它们走后,大家这才缓过神来,赶紧出去查看"灾情"。

天啊!100棵苹果树只剩下五六棵了!就这样,我们的各种经营计划全都宣告失败。但是在我的记忆中,那段生活却既有趣又充实。

梅西先生在院子里用心栽培的苹果树长得倒很好,果实累累的。每到秋天果实成熟之际，我都会拿梯子去摘苹果，装满一个个木桶。当大家一起整理庭院时，我则耐心地捡起地上的枯树枝，打成一捆捆柴火。

梅西先生还想出了一个好办法，就是在沿着屋外通往山坡的路边的树上绑一些铁丝，这样我就可以扶着铁丝，独自一人走到森林里去。森林里面有高高的秋麒麟草，还有开着花的野胡萝卜。那条"铁丝小路"足有四五百米长，这就是说，不需任何人陪我就可以走那么远的路，而不必担心迷路。这件事对我来说非比寻常，即使现在想起来，我还是兴奋不已。

在一般人看来，有许多事似乎不值得一提，可是我却从中享受到了自由和快乐。我常常单独走出去晒太阳，心情也因此变得十分愉快。而这一切都是梅西先生赐给我的，我由衷地感激他。

住在连杉的那段时间是1905年至1911年。当时既没有汽车和飞机，也没有收音机，更听不到哪个地方发生战争，每个人都过着平静而悠闲的生活。活在当今世界，再回首往昔，真是感慨不尽，恍如隔世啊！

结识马克·吐温

早在1894年，当我还不甚懂事时，就已经对马克·吐温先生的大名有所耳闻了。随着年龄的增长，他对我的影响也越来越深，正是他教会了我人情的温暖和生命的宝贵。除了贝尔先生和莎莉文老师，我最敬爱的人就是马克·吐温先生。

我最早是在纽约的劳伦斯·赫顿先生家见到马克·吐温先生的，当时我才14岁。当我跟他握手时，我就有一种直觉："啊！这正是能给我帮助的那个人。"

那天，他幽默风趣的言谈令我非常开心；此后我又分别在赫顿先生和洛奇先生家见到过几次马克·吐温先生。如果碰到什么重要的事情，我们都会互相通信。

马克·吐温先生感觉敏锐，他善于理解残疾人的心理，经常给我讲一些感人的小故事，还有他自己亲身经历的、有趣的冒险故事，以此来鼓励我，让我从中看到了人生的光明。

一天晚上，马克·吐温先生在赫顿先生的书房当着众多的社会名流演讲，听演讲的人当中有后来成为总统的威尔逊。马克·吐温先生演讲的内容是关于菲律宾现状的。

他说："大约有600名菲律宾的妇女和孩子躲在某座死火山的火山口中，然而，冯斯通上校竟将他们全部杀死了。几天后，这位上校竟又命令部下假扮成敌军，逮捕了菲律宾的爱国志士阿基纳多等许多人。"

马克·吐温先生愤慨地痛斥这位嗜杀成性的残酷军官，并且非常感慨地说道："如果我不是亲眼见到，亲耳听到，我简直不敢相信世界上竟会有这种灭绝人性的家伙。"

对于一切非人道的事情，无论是政治事件或战争，也不管是菲律宾人、巴拿马人或任何落后地区的土著民族被残杀，马克·吐温先生都会极力反对。他不甘沉默，而是大声地抨击，这是他一贯的作风。他蔑视那些自我吹嘘的人，也看不起没有道德勇气的人。在他看来，一个人不但要知道是非对错，而且要毫不畏惧地指责伪善者的罪恶行径。因此，他总是毫不留情地向那些邪恶势力挑战。

马克·吐温先生一直都很关心我，任何事情只要与我有关，他必然会十分热心；而且他在所有认识我们的人当中，是最崇敬莎莉文老师的，因此他也一直是我们最亲密的朋友之一。

马克·吐温先生和他的夫人情意深厚，但不幸的是他夫人比他去世早，这使得他悲伤难抑，立刻觉得生活中好像少了许多东西。他经常对别人说："每当来拜访我的客人走后，我总是一个人孤独地坐在火炉前，尤其感到寂寞难耐。"在夫人去世后的第二年，他在一次谈话中说："去年是我这一辈子最悲伤的一年，如果我不是有许多工作来消磨时间，我快要活不下去了！"此后，他也常为自己没有更多的工作而觉得遗憾。

还有一次，我安慰他说："请不要想太多了，全世界的人都敬仰您，您一定会名垂青史的。萧伯纳将您的作品与伏尔泰的相提并论，连评论家吉卜林也将您誉为美国的塞万提斯呢！"

听了我这话，马克·吐温先生回答说："你不必说这些话来安慰我。你知道吗，海伦？我做任何事情都只有一个目标，那就是让人们发笑，因为他们的笑声会让我感到愉快。"

马克·吐温先生是在美国文学史上占有重要地位的文学家。不仅如此，我认为他还是一个真正伟大的美国人，因为他具有美国先民们特有的那种开疆拓土的精神，他崇尚自由平等，他的个性豪迈而爽朗，能够不拘小节，而且十分幽默。总之，他具有开国时代的美国人所有的优点。

在看过我写的《我所居住的世界》一书后不久，马克·吐温先生写了一封令我们又惊又喜的短信,说:"能否请你们三位立即来我家,与我共同围坐在火炉前,一起生活几天?"

于是我们三个人高高兴兴地整装上路。当我们抵达当地火车站时,马克·吐温先生派来接我们的马车早已在那儿等候多时。当时正好是2月,大小山头上全都覆盖着一层白雪,路上的树枝也挂满了冰柱子,从松林里吹来的风带有一阵淡淡的清香。

马车在曲折的山路上缓缓地行进。好不容易爬上一段坡路之后,一栋白色的楼房展现在眼前。接我们的人告诉我们,马克·吐温先生正站在阳台上等我们。马车终于驶进巨大的石门,他们又说:"看!吐温先生正向我们招手呢!"然后接着又说道:"吐温先生身穿白色的服装。他的白发在阳光下闪闪发亮,就像浪花拍打岩石激起的白色泡沫一样,充满了活力。"

我们舒舒服服地坐在烧得很旺的炉火前,室内飘着清淡的松香。我们喝着热腾腾的红茶,吃着涂有奶油的吐司,觉得舒适极了。马克·吐温先生告诉我,如果吐司上再涂一些草莓酱就更好吃了。

休息好了之后,马克·吐温先生主动向我们表示,一般的客人都喜欢参观主人的居处环境,他相信我们也不例外,因此提议带我们到各处去看一看。在主卧室的旁边是一个走廊形状的阳台,这是主人经常喜欢逗留的地方,阳光可以直射进来,里面栽了许多美丽的花草,充满了田野情趣。通过走廊就是饭厅,然后又是另一间卧室。我们随意走着,又来到一间放了台球桌的娱乐室,据说这是马克·吐温先生最常待的地方。马克·吐温先生领我们走近球台,亲切地表示要教我打台球。

我听了这话,就直觉地问他:"打台球必须用眼,恐怕我玩不了吧?"

他很快就说:"也是。不过,如果像洛奇先生或荷马先生这样的高手,他们即使闭上眼睛也照样能打得非常棒。"

接下来,我们走到楼上参观主人的卧室,欣赏那古色古香的漂亮花床。

太阳西沉之际,我们站在大落地窗前,眺望着外面的景色。

"海伦,你可以想象我们站在这里能看到什么景色。我们所处的这个丘陵被裹在一片银白色中,远处是一大片辽阔的松树林,左右两侧则是连绵不绝的山丘,山丘上面是断断续续的石垣。我们头顶上是略显灰暗的天空。整个景色给人一种自由的感受,它是那么的原始,让你觉得毫无拘束。你闻闻看,那阵阵松香是不是妙极了?"

我们的卧室紧挨着马克·吐温先生的,房间的壁炉上有一对烛台,烛台旁边有一张卡片工整地写明了房内放贵重物品的位置。他之所以这么做,是因为这里原来曾有小偷光顾,马克·吐温先生为了使自己不再在三更半夜受到打扰，就干脆指出东西的放置地点，想偷的人就自己去拿！这种做法倒是非常符合马克·吐温先生幽默的个性。

在进餐时，客人唯一的任务就是安心吃饭，而主人则担任娱乐宾客的角色。我们常常会感到吃了一顿丰盛的饭菜之后，如果不向主人道谢就会内心不安。可是马克·吐温先生却和常人的想法不同，他担心客人们在吃饭时气氛太沉闷，因此经常讲些笑话逗引大家。他在这方面的确很有天赋，说的每句话都那么生动有趣。他甚至经常站起来到处走动，一会儿走到餐桌的这一头，一会儿又走到餐厅的那一头。有时他会一面讲故事，一面走到我身后问我最喜欢吃什么。当他兴致来时，还会随手摘下一朵小花，让我猜是什么花；如果我碰巧猜中了，他就会高兴得大笑大叫的，简直像个孩子。

为了测试我的警惕性，马克·吐温先生会忽然偷偷地去另一个房间，他一边弹奏风琴，一边观察我，看我是否对琴声引起的振动有反应。后来莎莉文老师告诉我，马克·吐温先生那一边弹琴、一边观察我的样子非常有趣。

马克·吐温先生家的地面铺的是瓷砖，因此我对一般的声音没有什么感觉，但是音乐的振动会沿着桌子传给我，因此我有时很快就能察觉到。这时，马克·吐温先生甚至比我还要兴奋。

晚饭过后，我们坐在壁炉前闲聊，度过一天中最快乐的时光。每天早上约10点钟左右，仆人会来喊醒我起床，然后我就去给马克·吐温先生问好。这时，他多半是穿着漂亮的睡裤，半靠在枕头上，口述文章，由秘书速记下来。

一天，他刚看到我进房，就对我说："今天吃完午饭，我们一块儿出去散步，看看附近的田园风景，好吗？"

那天的散步令人非常开心。马克·吐温先生穿着毛皮做的厚厚的外套，戴着皮帽子，亲切地牵着我的手，一面走在曲折的小路上，一面向我描述沿途的景色。根据马克·吐温先生的描述，我知道我们正走在一条介于岩壁与小河之间的小路上，那里景色优美，令人心神陶醉。

在饱览小溪和牧场的美丽风景之后，我们又来到爬满了常青藤的石垣前，摸索石头上残留的岁月痕迹。

在走了一段较长的山路之后，马克·吐温先生感到有些累了，就请梅西先生提前回去，叫马车来接我们。梅西先生走了之后，吐温先生、莎莉文老师和我三个人打算走到位于山腰的大路上去，在那里等马车来接。可是我们所在的地方离山腰的大路还有一段距离，这中间要穿过一段窄路，而且它满是荆棘，还要穿过一条冰冷的小溪，最后是一片长满了青苔的滑溜溜的地面，我们有好几次都差点儿摔倒了。

"从草丛中穿过去的路越来越窄,你沿着它一直走,就会随着松鼠爬到树上去。"虽然马克·吐温先生走得很累了,但他仍然不失幽默的本性,依旧谈笑风生。

路真的越来越窄,后来几乎要侧身行走。我开始担心是否迷路了,但是马克·吐温先生安慰我说:"不用担心,这片荒野在地图上是找不到的。换一句话说,我们已经走进了地球形成之前的混沌中;而且我发誓,大路就在我们视线可及的那一头。"

他说的果然没错,大路确实离我们不远,可问题在于我们与大路之间横着一条小溪,而且那溪水还很深。

"如何才能渡过小溪呢?"正当我们无计可施之际,梅西先生与马车夫的身影出现了。

"你们稍等,我们来接你们。"

梅西先生与马车夫立刻动手拆掉了附近的一道篱笆,搭成一座临时小桥,我们这才得以顺利渡过小溪。

后来,我再也没有体验到这么愉快的散步了。当时我曾一度担心我们的冒险,但很快我就想,只要有马克·吐温先生在,那么即使真的迷路了,也会非常有趣的。这次散步也因此而成为我生命中一段珍贵的回忆。

我们在马克·吐温先生家住了几天。在临走的前一个晚上,马克·吐温先生为我们朗诵他写的《夏娃日记》。我伸出手去轻触他的嘴唇,清楚地感受到了他的音调,犹如音乐般悦耳动人,大家都听得出了神。当他念到夏娃去世、亚当站在墓前时,大家都流下泪来。

欢乐的时光总是过得那么快,我们不得不准备回家了。马克·吐温先生站在阳台上,目送我们的马车远去,直到我们走了好远好远,还能看到他在不停地向我们挥手。马车上的我们也频频回首,望着那逐渐变小的白色建筑,直到它在苍茫的暮色中变成一个紫色的小点。

"不知道什么时候才能再见到他。"马车上的人都在这样想。然而,谁也没有料到这竟是我们最后一次会面了。

马克·吐温先生去世之后,我们又再次来过这所住宅,但已经人事全非。那间带有大壁炉的起居室,因为没有人整理而显得冷清零乱,只有楼梯旁的一盆天竺葵还在开花,仿佛在怀念过去那段令人难忘的时光。

永不言输

我在大学读书时，就经常这样想："我努力汲取知识，就是希望日后能用得上，为人类社会做出微薄的贡献。这世界总会有一两件事情是适合我去做，而且只有我才能做的。但这又是什么事情呢？"

虽然我常常思考这一问题，可是始终没有找到答案。但令人感到奇怪的是，朋友们却替我想好了。

例如，有一位朋友就说："你不必勉强自己去接受大学教育。如果你将精力投入到与你有相同遭遇的儿童教育方面，对社会的贡献必然会更大，而且这也正是上帝希望你去做的事情。至于费用你不必担心，由我负责筹募。你觉得怎样？"

当时我回答说："我理解你的意思。但是在完成大学学业之前，我暂时还不考虑这件事。"

尽管我是这么说的，但这位朋友却不改初衷，不断地努力想说服我，因此他不停地对莎莉文老师和我进行疲劳性进攻。最后我们实在是穷于应付，干脆就不再和他争辩，而他竟然错误地认为我们是默许他了。于是在第二天一大早，我们还没来得及起床时，这位朋友就已经在前往纽约的途中了。他去纽约、华盛顿等地，遍访友朋，并宣称我计划投身于盲人教育事业，而且打算立刻操办此事。

赫顿夫人听到这一消息时，非常惊讶。她立刻给我写信，要我尽快赶到纽约去说明事情的真相。于是，我和老师不得不火速赶赴纽约，去拜访资助我的朋友们。洛奇先生由于当时碰巧有事而不能前来，就由马克·吐温先生代表他。大家为此事讨论了很长时间，最后马克·吐温先生下结论地说："洛奇先生明确表示，他不愿意在这种事上投一分钱。但那位先生却大言不惭地说，让海伦替那些盲童开办学校是上帝的旨意，可我怎么没有看到上帝的命令文件呢！而那位先生一再强调这是上帝的旨意，难道他身上带了上帝给他的委任状？否则他又如何知道，只有这件事才是上帝的旨意，而其他事情就不是呢？这话实在太令人难以信服。"

在我大学毕业之前，类似的事情发生过不止一次。有些人竟然建议我担任主角，到各地做旅行表演；也有人提出，由我出资，将所有的盲人都集中在一个城市，然后加以训练。我对提出这一计划的人说："你们的计划并不能使盲人真正独立。所以，很抱歉，我对此不感兴趣。"对方听了我的回答很生气，居然指责我是一个利己主义者，说我只愿意做对自己有利的事情。

幸亏贝尔博士、洛奇先生以及其他几位热心帮助我的先生都很开明和慷慨，他们给我最大的自由，让我去做我自己喜欢的事，却从不对我加以干涉。他们的做法不仅令我感动，也给我很大的启迪。我暗中下定决心："只要是真正对人类有益，而且又是我能做的事情，我都将竭尽全力！"

真正能为盲人做贡献的机会终于来了。那是我读大学三年级的时候。

一天，一位自称查尔斯·康培尔的青年找到我，说他父亲从帕金斯盲人学校毕业之后，在伦敦开办了一所致力于英国盲人教育的高等音乐师范学院，而他本人此行的目的，就是劝我加入"波士顿妇女工商联盟"，该组织以促进盲人福利为宗旨。我很快就加入了这个组织，我们还曾一同去议会请愿，要求成立特别委员会保护盲人的权益。这个请愿案最终被顺利通过，特别委员会也很快成立。于是，我的工作也就以特别委员会为起点，有了一个良好的开端。

在康培尔先生的领导下，我们先是调查了盲人能做的一切工作。我们为此还开办了一个实验所，专门教盲人做一些手工艺之类的副业。为了销售这些盲人制作的手工艺产品，我们又在波士顿开了一家专卖店。后来，在马萨诸塞州各地也开设了几家相同的商店。

搬到连杉之后，我更加认真地思考盲人的问题。据我来看，有两件最紧迫的事情：第一件事就是如何使每个盲人学会一种技艺，从而具备自食其力的能力。同时，为了方便盲人相互之间的联络，也为了方便职业调查，应该成立一个全国性机构；第二件事，就是把目前美国、欧洲等地现有的几种盲文统一起来，以提高盲人的教育水平。

有一天，纽约的摩洛博士在经过长途跋涉之后，来到我们委员会，并提出了预防失明的方法。他说："目前，在盲校中的儿童大约有三分之二是因为出生时，眼睛受病菌感染而导致失明的。如果我们在孩子出生之前先进行消毒和防范，那么像这种情况是绝对可以避免的。"

因此，博士极力主张婴儿在一出生时，就应该进行眼睛的消毒，而且他还认为应该在法律上明文规定这一点。为了达到这个目的，他希望我们委员会能积极推动社会舆论。

"既然你知道病因所在，为什么一直没有采取行动呢？"我们都不约而同地反问他。

他有点儿无奈地说："说实话，所谓病菌感染，是指这些孩子的父母曾做了不光彩的事情，以至于染上那种不可告人的病。连医生都无法公开说出这种情形，报纸和杂志也都避而不谈，我当然更没有办法，所以才来请你们提供帮助的。"

原来是有这种阻碍。当委员会的全体成员听了博士的说明之后，都同意尽力推展这项工作。

但正如摩洛博士所说的，事情可不如想象的那么简单，因为医生和大众传播机构都成见很深，不愿轻易打破习惯，而是尽力避免谈这类问题，因此他们都向我们表示无能为力。

这样过了两年，当我1907年前往堪萨斯市时，和一位眼科大夫谈到了这件事情。他说："这种事情在报纸上宣传效果最佳。你们何不去拜访《堪萨斯明星报》的总编辑？或许他会答应你们，在报纸上讨论关于盲童的问题呢。"

我立刻去拜访《明星报》的总编辑尼尔逊先生，但是他非常干脆地回绝了我的要求。当时我非常失望。

或许是我那沮丧的神情感动了他。他很快就改变了语气，说："这样吧，你们想写什么请尽管写，但是否刊载，由我们来决定，如何？"

我很快就写了几个真实的例子送过去。结果尼尔逊先生把这篇稿子登在《明星报》的第一版。我们这才度过了第一道难关。

同年，《仕女杂志》也刊登了关于同一问题的文章。我又接连写了好几篇文章，全国许多家报纸和杂志纷纷进行转载，讨论面由此扩大。此后，《盲人世界》、《盲人杂志》等专门讨论盲人问题的杂志也陆陆续续地创办了。

我还应邀在《教育百科全书》上发表了关于盲人的论文。我的工作量从此逐渐增加，稿约接连不断。我还得经常出席各种会议和演讲，我甚至有点应付不过来了。我的生活节奏也突然变得匆忙起来，常常是我急急忙忙地赶到一个会场，结束后回家，另一项邀请就已经在等着我了。有时，我在同一天之内要连着到五六个会场。

此外，信函也特别多，处理信函的时间也相应增加了。由于过度的劳累，老师和我都有些撑不住，身体也累垮了。

虽然我们忙得团团转，但经济上仍然感到很紧张，有一段时间连雇女仆的钱都没有。于是，莎莉文老师每天早上送先生到火车站后，回家时还要顺路去买菜。这时，我就在家里擦桌椅、收拾房间和床铺，然后去花园摘花插到花瓶里；或者去开动风车贮水，还要记住关掉风车，等等。我的工作很重,可这一时期的约稿和信函偏偏又特别多。

1906年,在州长的推荐下,我担任马萨诸塞州盲人教育委员会的委员。每次委员会开会时,莎莉文老师都要坐在我身旁,用手语为我传达会议的内容。我对开会的感觉,就是每位委员都喜欢做冗长而乏味的演讲,那些不着边际的质询和回答等官样文章,更是令人疲惫不堪,因此我担任这一职务四五个月之后就辞职不干了。然而,要想真正为盲人谋福利,又必须得借助社会团体的力量,因为只有这样做,才能唤起社会舆论的关注和支持。因此,我还是必须出入各种公开场合,例如去参加医生协会或其他协会的会议。为此,我必须努力练习演讲的技巧,以便在面对众人时更具有说服力。为了这个目标,我曾先后向多位老师学习表达的技巧,可惜的是效果都不甚理想。

就在此时,我遇到了波士顿的怀特先生。他精通音乐理论,在人类的发音机能方面深有研究。于是,我抱着碰运气的心理,去请他帮忙。"我也不知道自己能做到什么程度。不过对我而言,这也算是一种研究工作。我们不妨试试!"怀特先生很爽快地答应了我。于是,怀特先生从1910年起,每星期六都要来连杉,住在我们家,星期日才赶回去。他停留的这段时间,也就是我上课的时间。

我10岁的时候,莎莉文老师曾带我去找过豪拉先生,那是我第一次学习发音。当时,为了让我了解声音响起所引起的振动,豪拉先生抓起我的手放在他脸上,然后慢慢地发出"ARM"的声音,并要我尽量模仿。我们就这样反复练习,可是我太紧张了,勉强发出来的声音非常杂乱。

"把你的喉咙放柔和些,舌头也不必过于用力。"豪拉先生耐心地给我指正。他说,在练习发音前,应该先让发音器官变得发达,而且应该从孩提时代起就不断地练习,这样我的声音必然能够练得更美妙动听,同时也能够记住更多的单词。因此,我希望聋哑教育能及早教那些聋哑儿童练习发音技能。

怀特先生本来是抱着一试的心理来的,但他越教越感兴趣,结果连续教了我3年,而且其中有两年的夏天他几乎一直住在连杉。怀特先生的训练先从发音器官开始,然后练习发音,最后才教节奏、重音及声音的音质、音调。这样经过3年,我终于勉强可以在人们面前开口说话了。

莎莉文老师和我先是在新泽西州的蒙他克雷做了一次试验性演讲。那次演讲非常费劲,我现在回想起来仍然心有余悸。

我站在讲台上,全身一直颤抖着,一句话也说不出来。虽然早已拟好的讲稿就在我的喉咙里打转,可我就是发不出任何声音来。最后,我终于有了足够的勇气，使尽全力喊出声来，此时的我感觉自己就像在射出一发大炮。（但别人后来告诉我说，我的声音小得就像蚊子。）我毕竟不是一个肯轻易认输的人，我费了很大力气，终于完成了这次演讲。

从讲台上走下来之后，我忍不住哭出声来，懊恼地说："对我来说，讲话实在太难了。我这是不自量力，做不到的事情终归是没有办法的。"但事实上，我并没有因此而丧失信心；相反，我又重新鼓起勇气，开始更勤奋地练习。

现在，我终于可以在人们面前说话了，虽然我的声音并不怎么悦耳动听，但是和不会讲话相比，开口说话对我的工作进展帮助当然更大。至此，我的梦想总算部分实现了。

登上演讲台

我刚学会说话时，还不太敢去外面演讲，因为我经常不知道该说些什么。不过，我每次演讲时，总会有来自社会各阶层的听众，有老人，也有小孩，有富豪，也有穷人，甚至还有盲、聋、哑等身体机能残障的人。一想到有这么多听众和我一样是不幸者时，我就会极力想方设法去安慰和鼓励他们。

由于我和老师很受欢迎，因此我们才有了足够的勇气，开始到各处去做演讲。

莎莉文老师是一位天生的演讲家，她那生动的描述经常使听众们深受感动。尤其是在听完老师讲述如何苦心教导我的经历之后，几乎每个人都为之动容。莎莉文老师的演讲通常要花大约一个小时，这时我就静静地坐在一旁，读我随身带来的盲文书。

老师讲完之后，就轮到我了。会有人来引导我登上演讲台。我会先将手指放在老师的嘴唇上，向台下的听众证明，我可以通过老师的嘴唇动作知道她在讲什么；然后，我开始回答听众提出来的问题。这时，我一般都会借机鼓励他们，只要有信心、恒心和勇气，人类的潜能往往能达到我们难以想象的某种程度；同时，我也解释了人类应该相互帮助与合作的道理。

令我着急的是，虽然我已经有了一段时期的巡回演讲经验，可是在说话技巧方面我的进步却并不大。我觉得自己的发音不够准确，导致听众有时候根本不知道我在讲什么；或者是我说到一半的时候，会突然发出怪声来；有时，我的声音则显得单调而低沉。尽管我一再努力，想加以改善，但终究难以发出清脆悦耳的声音来。每当我想强调某句话，想让听众们都听清楚时，我的喉咙就更是和我唱反调，舌头也变得笨拙无比，几乎发不出任何声音。

这时，我当然又紧张又着急，可是越着急情况就变得越糟，可以想象我有多惨了！在这种情况下，我总会想到自己的演讲太蹩脚了，而且相信只要现场有一点儿声音，我的声音就会被完全掩盖，因此感到非常不自在。也正是因为如此，当我感觉演讲现场有椅子挪动，或者外面有车子驶过的声音时，我就会突然情不自禁地变得焦虑起来。但让我感动的是，听众们总是非常耐心地从头听到尾。每当我讲完之后，听众们不论听懂多少，总会用最热烈的掌声来回报我，有些人还特意上台来鼓励我。

我的演讲固然十分笨拙，但是莎莉文老师的演讲却非常精彩，大部分情况下她为听众讲述如何教育我的过程。由于她的口才很好，因此每个人都听得入了迷，有时连我都被老师的演讲所打动而忘了鼓掌。

我们最初只是在新英格兰及新泽西州的附近做演讲，后来范围逐渐扩大，到比较远的地方去演讲。1913年，我们去华盛顿演讲。我们抵达华盛顿时，正值威尔逊总统就职典礼的前夕，所以联合通讯社委托我为人们报道总统的就职典礼盛况，于是我得以亲历整个典礼的过程。

举行典礼的当天，天空云彩漂浮，这是最理想的阅兵天气。这天，华盛顿市区异常热闹，大家都跑到高处，希望能找到一个观看阅兵的最佳位置。行进中的军队雄赳赳气昂昂，士兵们全都精神抖擞，观众们也都为之精神一振。军乐队走在最前面，奏着雄壮的进行曲。

这一切是如此热烈，我当时不禁想："希望这些年轻可爱的士兵不要卷入到残酷的战争中去。他们只要身着整齐漂亮的军服，对着总统敬礼就好了。"

可是没过多久，第一次世界大战就爆发了。我反对战争，但是我却毫无办法！

唉！我怎么有能力阻止战争呢？

和贝尔博士交往

我在华盛顿的演讲究竟是安排在威尔逊总统就职典礼之前还是之后，我已经记不清楚了，但我永远不会忘记的是贝尔博士和我们当时一起度过的最愉快的一段时光。其实，那次在华盛顿我并不是第一次和贝尔博士同时登台演讲。当我还只有10岁时，就已经和贝尔博士一起出席聋哑教育促进大会了。

只要一说起贝尔博士，一般人就会联想到电话发明者，或者是致力于聋哑教育的大慈善家。可是对于我个人来说，他却是最亲密、最友爱的好朋友。真的，贝尔博士和我的交往历史最长，感情也最好。我之所以这么喜欢贝尔博士，可能是因为在我的生命中，他比莎莉文老师还要出现得更早些吧。

当时的我，仍生活在一片黑暗之中，而他却向我伸出了温暖友谊之手。也正是因为贝尔博士的帮助，安纳格罗斯先生才给我介绍了莎莉文老师。贝尔博士一开始就非常赞赏莎莉文老师的教育方式。他曾钦佩地对老师说："我认为你对海伦的教育方式，可以作为所有教育家最宝贵的参考资料。"

贝尔博士对聋哑教育的热心可以说众所周知，而且他这种热心还有家传渊源！原来，贝尔博士的祖父正是口吃矫正法的创始人，他的父亲梅尔·贝尔先生则发明了聋哑人教育的读唇法。

梅尔·贝尔先生很幽默，他从没因为自己对聋哑人的贡献而自命不凡，反而轻描淡写地对儿子说："这发明一点也不能赚钱。"

贝尔博士则一本正经地回答说："可是这种发明却比电话发明更重要。"

贝尔博士还是一个孝子，他们父子之间的感情很深厚，知道的人无不敬佩羡慕。如果一两天不见父亲，博士就会说："我得去看看我父亲，因为我每次和他聊天都会有收获。"

贝尔博士那栋位于波多马克河入海口河畔的楼房典雅而美观，景色非常漂亮。我曾见到他们父子俩并肩坐在河边，一边抽着烟，一边望着来来往往的船只，看上去非常惬意。当偶尔传来稀罕的鸟叫声时，贝尔博士就问："父亲，这种鸟叫声应该用什么符号代表比较好？"于是父子两人接着就会展开忘我的发音学研究。他们父子会对任何一种声音进行分析，然后将它转换成手语表达出来。或许是他们专门研究声音的缘故吧，因此他们父子二人的发音都非常清晰，也非常动人，听他们谈话可以说是一大享受。

贝尔博士对父亲非常孝顺，对母亲也是如此。当我认识他时，他母亲就已经患有严重的听力障碍，几乎快聋了。一天，贝尔博士开车带我和莎莉文老师去郊外游玩，我们采了许多漂亮的野花。返回的途中，贝尔博士忽然想到要把这些野花送给他母亲。

他俏皮地对我们说："我们就直接从大门冲进去，吓我爸妈一大跳。"

虽然他是这么说的，可是当我们下车之后，正要登上大门的台阶时，博士忽然抓住我的手说："我爸妈好像都在睡觉，请安静点，轻点儿进去。"

于是，我们三人都脚尖着地，悄悄地走进去把花插在花瓶里，然后又走出来。当时，博士的父母安睡的神态给我留下了非常深刻的印象。在两张并排的安乐椅上，博士的母亲伏在椅子的靠手上，看不到脸，只能看到一头银发，而他的父亲则仰头靠在椅背上，像君王一样神态庄严。

能结识这样一家人，我感到非常庆幸，我常常去拜访他们。老夫人喜欢编织，尤其擅长编织花草图案，她会抓着我的手，亲切而耐心地教我。

贝尔博士有两个年纪和我差不多的女儿。我每次去他家的时候，她们都把我看成自家人。

贝尔博士是一位杰出的科学家，许多知名科学家常常到他家来，如果我也正好在场的话，贝尔博士就会将他们的对话一一写在我手上。贝尔博士认为："世上无难事，只要用心学习，一定可以掌握。"因此，不管能不能听懂，我总是高兴地用心倾听他们的谈话，一点也不感到疲倦。

贝尔博士还是一位雄辩家。只要他进到房间，保证很快就能吸引所有人的注意力，而且每个人都很愿意听他讲话，这正是他不同于一般人的魅力所在。虽然如此，贝尔博士并不会因此而把自己的主观意识强加给别人；相反，他非常虚心，对于不同意见总是非常谦虚地说："哦，是吗？也许你的想法是对的，让我再好好考虑考虑。"

不过，贝尔博士也有一件事情是异常坚持的，那就是在聋哑教育方面，他坚持认为口述比手语更好，他说："当一个聋哑人用手语表达时，必然会引来一般人异样的眼光，从而产生隔阂，他们也因此而很难达到普通人的知识水平。"

也许有人不同意他的意见，但是我相信，每个聋哑教育工作者都不会不敬仰贝尔博士在聋哑教育方面所做出的伟大贡献。他没有任何野心，更不指望任何回报，而只是本着科学的态度，大力推广聋哑教育事业。他曾自费从事各项研究，还创办过学校，英国聋哑教育促进协会就是由他创立的。他因为发明电话而得到一大笔钱，但是他把这些钱捐了出来作为聋哑人奖学金。为了使聋哑儿童能像正常人一样说话，贝尔博士尽了最大的心力。

贝尔博士原来是苏格兰一个偏远地区的人，但他移居美国已经很久了，所以算得上真正的美国人。他的性格热情开朗，善良而亲切，因此深得朋友们的敬爱。在日常闲聊中，博士经常会把话题转到和科学有关的方面去。有一次，贝尔博士告诉我们，他很小的时候就想铺设海底电缆，但是直到1866年才梦想成真，而在这之前他的失败简直不计其数。当时我还只有12岁，所以觉得他的话就像神话故事般，听得着了迷；尤其当我听他说人们将能通过深海电缆和遥远的东方联系时，印象更是异常深刻。

贝尔博士还曾带我去了人类第一次将电话应用在日常用途中的那座房子里，他对我说："如果没有助手托马斯·华尔逊的帮助，电话的发明或许不会像目前这么完备。"

1876年3月10日，贝尔博士对正在另一个房间工作的华尔逊先生说："华尔逊，我有事请你过来一下。"这就是人类历史上第一次用电话时所说的话。突然听到这句话的华尔逊当时吓了一大跳。

听了贝尔博士的描述后，我说："第一次通话，应该说些更有意义的话才对呀！"

贝尔博士马上回答道："不，不！海伦，这个世界必将越来越繁忙，利用电话来传送的应该是'我有事请你来一下'这类有实际需要的话。"

除了电话，贝尔博士还发明了对讲机、感应天平等许多有实际用途的东西。如果没有贝尔博士发明的电话探针，大概谋杀加富尔总统的凶手至今还找不到呢！

在我的记忆中，关于贝尔博士的事情是如此之多，所以很难说得尽，尤其是他留给我的都是最美好的回忆。记得有一次，我们一同去匹兹堡观看烟火。当烟火冲上天空的一刹那，我们竟高兴得又笑又叫："啊！看哪！河水着火了！"

现在，我仍然可以很清楚地回忆起贝尔博士和他的女儿们一起坐在游艇的甲板上欣赏明月的情景。那天晚上，和我们一同住在船上的还有纽康博士，他兴趣浓厚地给我们大谈月食、流星及彗星等现象。

贝尔博士对我的关心比起我的父母来毫不逊色。他经常对我说："海伦，你还年轻，日子长着呢，你应该考虑你的婚姻大事。莎莉文老师总有一天会结婚的。到那时，又有谁来陪你呢？"

而我总是回答说："可我觉得自己现在很幸福啊！何况又有哪个人愿意

和我这样的人结婚呢？"

话是这么说，但我可以感觉得到，贝尔博士是真的为我的未来担心。当莎莉文老师和梅西先生结婚时，贝尔博士再次对我提起这件事："你看，我不是早就对你说过吗？但现在还不算太晚，你听我的话，应该赶紧成一个家！"

"我完全理解您的好意，可是如果一个男人娶了我这样的妻子，那不是太可怜了吗？而且我根本做不了什么事情，只会给丈夫增加负担。"

"也许你不能做很多家务事，但我相信会有心地善良的男孩子喜欢你的。如果他不计较这些，而愿意和你结婚的话，你会改变主意吗？"

正如贝尔博士所说的，我后来确实曾为结婚的事情动过心，这些就暂且不谈了。

我最后一次见到贝尔博士是1920年。当时，他刚从苏格兰回来，他对我说："虽然我算是回到了故乡，但我内心当中却有一种身处异国的寂寞孤独的感觉。"然后，他又谈到了飞机，显现出很感兴趣的样子，而且表示想研究飞机制造。据他预测，飞机作为交通工具的时代即将来临，纽约和伦敦之间在十年之内将会开辟出航线，而且在大型建筑的楼顶上将出现小型飞机场，就像现在每一户人家都有车库一样。贝尔博士还说，下一次世界大战将会以空中作为主要战场，那时候潜水艇在海上的作用将比巡洋舰还重要。

他还有一项预言说："学者们将来能发明出冷却热带空气的方法，或者是让热空气流到寒冷地带，然后让南北两极的冷空气流到热带，以此来调节空气的冷热，使地球的每个地方都适宜人类居住。"

我每次听到这些乐观的科学预言时，总是感到异常兴奋，但我绝对没有想到这些预言会那么快就应验。因此，当我6年后听说法国的学者能利用海洋调节气候时，真的是大吃一惊！

那次会面结束之后，我与贝尔博士挥手告别时，尤其觉得难分难舍。我似乎已经预感到这将是我们最后一次见面了。

我的预感竟不幸成真！1922年8月3日，贝尔博士离开了人世，遗体就葬在本市的雷山顶上——这地方还是他自己挑选的。记得有一次，他指着山顶说："海伦，那就是我长眠的地方。"他很坦然地说了这句话，随后还朗诵了一段布朗宁的诗句。

当我从报纸上得知贝尔博士去世的消息时，我清楚地意识到，我已经失去了我一生中最可贵的朋友。

当我们结束长途演讲旅行，疲惫不堪地回到连杉之后，我和莎莉文老师对未来都不禁感到茫然不安。我们的经济越来越困难了，洛奇先生以前会定期寄给我们生活费，老师结婚之后这笔费用就减少了一半。本来我们希望稿费能弥补一些的，但也不能如愿。

我们的贫困并不是秘密，因此有人主动表示愿意帮助我们，"钢铁大王"卡内基先生就是其中的一位。不知道他是从哪里得知我们的事情，当他于1911年知道我们有经济困难时，就对我的朋友法拉表示，愿意赠给我们一笔款项。法拉把这件事转告我，但是我请他在不失礼节的情况下替我婉言谢绝。

那时的我年轻气盛，心想即使不依靠别人，我也能生活下去。不过，虽然我拒绝了，但卡内基先生仍然非常客气地请我认真考虑此事，说只要我觉得有需要，他随时愿意赠送我一笔款项。

又过了两年，有一次我和老师去纽约，卡内基夫妇请我们去了他们家。卡内基夫妇都非常和蔼可亲，他们的宝贝女儿、人见人爱的美丽少女玛格丽特小姐当时还只有16岁。我们正在谈话时，她跑进房来，卡内基先生怜爱地看着她，笑着说："这就是我们家的小慈善家，她一天到晚就在我们耳边吵吵着，要我们去帮助那些需要帮助的人。"

我们一面喝着红茶，一面轻松地聊天。忽然，卡内基先生问我道："你现在还不愿接受我过去提的赠款之事吗？"

我笑着回答道："是的，我还不肯认输。"

"你的心情我可以理解，可是你有没有站在别人的立场想想呢？如果你能体会到对方遭到拒绝的感受时，你还会坚持自己的意见吗？"

他这些话使我感到很意外，因为我从来没想到大富翁也有他的义务。而他这么重视家人的感受和快乐，更是令我感动不已！随后，卡内基先生再次强调说，只要我有需要，就不要客气，随时可以向他开口。他还谈到了我和老师的演讲，问我们一般会讲些什么话题、入场券多少钱一张，等等。

"我这次打算以'幸福'为题发表演讲，入场券大概是1美元到1.5美元。"我这么回答他。

但是他却说："啊！这太贵了，我想如果是50美分一张的话，将会有更多的收入。对了！就应该这样，票价一定不能高过75美分。"

我和老师仍然在继续过着演讲的生活。那年秋天，由于老师做了一次大手术，身体太虚弱而不能再继续旅行演讲了。幸好我在夏天写了五六篇文章，因此在短时间之内还不必求助于人。就这样苦撑了一段时间之后，我不得不面临投降的困境了。那是第二年4月，我们去缅因州演讲。我们是自己开车进城的，天气突然变得很冷。当我第二天早上醒来时，发现老师病了，而且非常厉害。我们是第一次来这地方，附近也没有什么朋友，所以一时间不知该怎么办才好。最后，我好不容易才想到请旅馆的人派车送我们回家。

一星期后，我只好写信向卡内基先生求援。他很快就给我回了信，同时还附带了一张支票。他在信上说："说实话，我觉得命运对我太优厚了。你在人们的心目中是如此崇高而善良，竟愿意给我这种机会，使我觉得无比幸福。施与比接受更加幸福。因此，应该说感谢的是我，而不是你！"

于是，我和老师暂时不必为金钱而发愁了。然而，这时又发生了一件令我伤心的事——梅西先生和老师分居了。

梅西先生确实也很辛苦，但导致这种结果的，当然还有其他一些原因，我对此也就不便发表任何意见了。

投身反战运动

1913年秋天，我们又开始忙着进行访问和旅行演讲。我们在华盛顿乘过摇摇晃晃的乡村电车，在纽约还赶过第一班早车——这辆早班车每经过一处农舍，就要停下来收牛奶，所以一路上不知停了多少次。

我们到达得克萨斯和路易斯安那州的时候，刚好是洪水过后，所以路面上还有不少积水。我们虽然坐在车里面，但仍然能感受到滔滔洪水拍打着车厢。

忽然，一声巨响传来。乘客纷纷伸出头朝外看去，原来是一根浮在水面上的粗木头撞到了车厢。水面上漂浮着许多死牛死马的尸体，令人作呕。我们乘坐的那列火车，车头上拖着一株连根拔起的树木，竟然走了好长一段路。

邀请我们演讲的既有城里的学校、妇女团体，也有乡村和矿区的组织；有时，我们也去工业城市，为劳工团体做演讲。经过这样深入的演讲之后，对于人生我又有了不同的感悟，而且觉得自己过去的想法实在是太天真了。

过去我总是这样想：虽然我又盲又聋，但仍然可以过上相当幸福的生活，可见天下无难事，只要你愿意努力去做，那么所谓的"命运"也不会对我们造成什么损害。然而，我忘了一件最重要的事——我之所以能克服那么多困难，都是因为有别人的帮助。我是如此的幸运，出生在一个幸福的家庭，有疼爱我的父母，后来又有莎莉文老师以及许多好朋友的帮助，我才能接受高等教育。可是我起初并没有深切地体会到这些。现在我已经深深地懂得，并不是每个人都能成功地实现自己的愿望，环境的影响力仍然很大。当我见到工业区、矿区中那些贫苦的劳工后，尤其深刻地体会到了环境对人的巨大压力。渐渐地，这种想法变成了一种很深的信仰，但是我并没有因此而悲观失望；相反，我认为人类应该自助及互助的观念更强烈了。虽然现实环境有可怕之处，但人类应该保持希望，不断地奋斗；至于那些身处顺境的人，就更有义务帮助那些需要帮助的人。

1914年1月，我第一次有机会横穿美国大陆。这次母亲和我同行尤其让我高兴，这给我带来了不少方便。母亲很喜欢旅行，而我也终于有机会让她饱览东起大西洋海滨、西至太平洋海岸的美国大陆风光了。

演讲旅行的第一站是加拿大的渥太华，然后是俄亥俄州。中途曾转到英国伦敦，再回到密歇根州；随后是明尼苏达、艾奥瓦，就这样一路向中西部前进。

在旅行途中，母亲的兴致一直都很高，只是经常担心我会太劳累。母亲尤其高兴我们能到加州，因为她特别喜欢加州，尤其是旧金山的海滨。她经常在黄昏时分去沙滩上散步。她一再对我表示，加州的气候是如此的宜人，海边的景色更是让人流连忘返。

我曾和母亲一起坐汽船出海，于是她又喜欢上了那些尾随在船后飞翔的海鸥。她拿出食物来喂它们，引它们停下来。

母亲还是一个天生的诗人，她用吟咏诗歌般的语调为我描述了落日余晖照射之下的金门大桥。她以崇敬的口气告诉我，美国杉是"自然界之王"，因为它的庄严肃穆比山川大海还要令人折服。

现在，我一面写作，一面重温当时的喜悦，那点点滴滴的快乐重新又浮现在我的眼前：我仿佛又看到了"崖之家"，看到了我和母亲吃过早餐之后走出"崖之家"，来到奇岩林立的海边游戏，足迹踏遍那长满蓝色和黄色小花的美丽沙滩。

当我站在双子海岬享受大自然的清新空气时，母亲将我拉到她身边，无限感慨地对我说："看到如此宜人的景致，我过去的悲哀和不快全都不复存在了。"

在这个海岬上可以看到远处的城市，以及从海岬沿海岸一直延伸而至的繁华街道。我们还可以在海岬上看到街上的钟楼，渡轮每隔五六分钟就有一班从海港中鸣着汽笛，缓缓驶出。

我第二次横穿大陆的演讲旅行是1914年10月开始的，这次是秘书汤玛森女士陪伴我。

秘书的工作一点也不轻松，演讲的联系、预约，甚至于修改日程、处理善后等等，事无巨细都必须由秘书操办。这些事情有时非常麻烦，幸亏汤玛森女士很能干，她做起事来干净利落，处理问题也很有条理，还有余力照顾我的生活起居，整理内务。假如没有汤玛森女士的帮忙，我真不敢想象我们将会面临什么境况。虽然我们从卡内基先生那儿得到一笔赠款，但仍不能放弃认真工作的原则，更何况我们的开支也很大。

第一次世界大战爆发后，我们再也不能像以前那样随随便便地去各地旅行演讲了。只要一想到正在发生的战争浩劫以及它愈演愈烈的趋势，我也不能再像以前那样轻松地说出慈善的话来了。在这段时期，我经常因为梦见流血或残杀而惊醒。与此同时，一些出版社和杂志社纷纷向我约稿，希望我写一些比较时尚有趣的文章，然而，我满脑子都是枪声和军民遭受杀戮的惨状，又怎么会有心思去写这类文章呢？

当时，我最感到遗憾的是我收到了来自欧洲的几千封求援信，但我对此却无能为力。我这时其实也是自身难保，而且还要靠到各地旅行演讲来挣钱生活。

在这段时期，我们所属的社团开展了热烈的反战运动，希望能阻止美国参战。但是也有社团和我们持相反的立场，他们为了促使美国参战而不遗余力，其领袖正是以前的老罗斯福总统。

莎莉文老师和我都是坚定的反战人士，我们认为应该竭力避免让美国卷入到战争中去。因此，从1916年开始，我们就到堪萨斯州、密歇根州、内布拉斯加州等地进行反战演讲。但是我们的努力没有成功，这实在太可惜了。

我们去了每一个可能去的地方——有时在最豪华的大礼堂里，有时在临时搭建的帐篷里，极力宣传我们的观点。当然，有不少听众和我们产生了共鸣。但遗憾的是，当时的报纸大多并不支持我们的立场。

还有一些报刊态度转变，他们过去总是极力夸大其词，将我誉为"时代的奇迹"，或称我为"盲人的救世主"；可是现在，只要我的内容稍微涉及社会或政治，他们就视我为"左翼走狗"，对我大肆抨击。这实在是令人感慨万千。

听众中当然也有人不赞同我们的反战观点的；再加上社会正在热烈地传播战争思想，因此，全美各地参战思潮正在迅速弥漫。当时，我的失望真是难以形容！

1916年秋天，我心情沮丧地回到连杉的家中，想安抚一下自己那疲惫的身心。然而，即使在连杉也不能让人觉得愉快，因为汤玛森女士请假回了苏格兰，梅西先生也因为和莎莉文老师分居而离开了，只有女仆易安热情地迎接我回家。她重新整理和装饰了一下房子，并让我安静地等待园中的花儿绽放。她哪里知道，此时我毫无赏花的兴致。最后，我才想到打电话请母亲过来，这才使我得以排遣部分寂寞。

没过多久，莎莉文老师因为长期的疲惫忧愁交加，而再一次病倒了。她不停地咳嗽，医生建议她冬天搬到布拉西多湖畔去疗养。如果老师再离开的话，这个家也就散了，再也无力雇用易安了。可是我们又那么喜欢易安，不愿意她走，如果她走了，那么我们在连杉的生活必然会完全停顿。因此，我一直为这事而烦恼不安，以至于没有心思工作，甚至不能静下来好好思考。

这是我有生以来第一次感到人生的乏味。我常常恐惧地问自己："如果老师也像我一样有这种悲观的想法，该如何是好呢？"在我看来，如果这个世界没有莎莉文老师，将会多么寂寞无聊啊！假如她不在我身边的话，我一定什么事情也做不了吧？每当想到这里，我就更感到不安。而我之所以对一位青年产生感情，也正是在这种极其无助的情况下发生的。

一天晚上，我一个人单独在书房里思考问题。这时，那位暂时代替汤玛森女士的年轻秘书忽然走进来，用平静而温柔的态度倾吐了他对我的关怀。

我当然感到非常意外，但很快就被他的真诚感动了。他表示，如果我们能结合在一起，他将随时陪伴在我身边，为我阅读，为我搜集写作资料。总之，以前由莎莉文老师为我做的一切，他都能做。

我静静领会了对方这份爱意，心里情不自禁地升起了一阵难以言喻的喜悦。我几乎难以自持，全身颤抖。我从内心里已经想把这件事向老师和母亲公开，但他劝阻我说："我认为现在还不到时候。"

过了一会儿，他又说："要知道，莎莉文老师现在正生病，而你母亲又不喜欢我，如果这么突然地告诉她们，可以想象一定会遭反对的。我看我们还得慢慢来，以后再找机会告诉她们。"

此后，我们共同度过了一段相当美好的时光。有时我们肩并肩去森林中散步，有时则静静地坐在书房里，他读书给我听。

直到一天早上，我醒来后正在换衣服，母亲忽然火急火燎地跑进房来，问我说："报纸今天登了一则令人震惊的消息。海伦，你是不是已经答应和人订婚了？"

母亲说话时，双手在微微地颤抖。值此之际，我一方面因为没有心理准备而惊恐异常，另一方面又想替对方遮掩，于是就随口撒谎说："这根本是胡说八道。报纸上每次都会登一些荒唐可笑的消息，这事我可一点都不知道。"

我不仅这样回答母亲，对老师当然也不敢承认。母亲于是迅速辞退了他。现在想起来，我仍然觉得非常奇怪，不知道自己当时为什么要撒谎，结果使母亲、老师和那位年轻人都陷入痛苦之中。

我的恋爱就这样宣告结束了。

这一年虽然充满了烦恼,但毕竟熬过去了。

布拉西多湖的气候非常寒冷,老师的病情也没有怎么好转,因此12月底,老师就和汤玛森女士一起去了温暖的波多黎各,在那里一直住到第二年4月。在此期间,她们每个星期都要给我写信,信中常常会提到波多黎各美丽的风光和宜人的气候,还兴奋地描述她们从未见过的各种花草。

就在这时候,美国参战了!老师被这个消息吓了一跳,因此提前在4月返回连杉,不过老师的身体直到次年秋天才完全康复。因此,虽然人都回到了连杉,但我们仍然有一年多时间无法出去演讲。

没了工作,我们的存款当然在一天天减少。我们打算卖掉连杉的房子,另外再找一幢较小的房子。然而,真的要离开居住多年的地方,实在是令人难以割舍!屋内一桌一椅忽然间都变得那么亲切可爱,充满了感情。尤其是我常常在上面写作的书桌,还有书柜以及我经常伫立观看庭院的大落地窗、樱花树下的安乐椅等,更是让我难分难舍。然而,一旦离别的时刻来临,也只有洒泪挥别,将它们装在最值得怀念的记忆深处。

我们带着感伤与无奈,告别了这栋住了13年的房子。我心中唯一感到安慰的是,虽然不再住在那里,但那栋可爱的房子仍将为另一家人挡风遮雨。现在,这栋房子已经成了波士顿约丹士马狮百货公司女职工宿舍。房子虽然已经换了主人,但我对它仍然怀有主人的爱,因为那里有太多值得我回忆的往事,它装载了我人生中最精彩的10年。那里有我的欢笑,有我的泪水;更重要的是,它充满了生命的活力。

好莱坞的多彩生活

我们离开连杉,在国内旅行了很短一段时间后,最终决定在纽约郊区长岛的佛拉斯特丘陵地区住下来。我们在这块风景优美的地方买了一栋外面看上去很不错的小屋,它有着古城堡般的外表,到处都是凸出的棱角,我们给它起名叫"沼泽城"。这里的"我们",是指莎莉文老师、汤玛森、我,还有一只名叫"吉兰"的小狗。

经过长期的旅途奔波，我们都渴望过上安静的生活。我亲手在院子里种上了树。房子的二楼被隔出来一间，作为专属于我的小书房，房子的四面都有窗户。我开始学习意大利文，以便能读但丁作品的原文。可是，我们的新居还没有完全安顿妥当，就接到了一封十分意外的信。这封信是法兰西斯·米拉博士写的，他说他打算将我的《少女时代》拍成电影，而且希望我能参加拍摄。

接到信后，我心里充满了欢喜，因为我认为把自己的个人经历拍摄成电影，一定会激励那些遭遇不幸的人，而且能促使这个互相憎恶、充满暴戾的世界进行深刻的反省。所以，我怎么会放过这么好的机会呢？

改编后的电影叫《拯救》。现在想起来，我当年千里迢迢、不辞辛苦长途跋涉跑到好莱坞去拍电影的那股冲劲儿，真有点不可思议！或许是我当时太天真了，满以为自己的故事非常感人，观众在欣赏这部电影时必然会全神贯注，连呵欠也不敢打。正是那种过分的自信和自大，才使我毫不犹豫地接受了电影公司的邀请。

奇怪的是，我当时怎么没有想到，像我这样一个身有残缺的人，又怎么能担任电影的主角呢？因为一般的电影女明星都身材健美，而且长得如花似玉。而我却又肥又胖，长得也不漂亮，根本不能和一般的女明星相比。而且我还缺乏赚取观众眼泪、逗引观众发笑的表演技巧，我又凭什么去演戏呢？

不过，抛开这些不说，我在好莱坞的那段日子的确过得非常精彩。说实话，对于拍戏的那次经历，我毫不后悔。

我在好莱坞经历了许多以前从来都没有遇到过的事情，那种刺激的生活总是经常给我带来惊喜，甚至从来不知道走出大门后将会遇到什么事情。每当我漫步在开满天竺葵的小路上时，可能会有一位骑士突然从斜刺里冲出来；或者是当我走在马路上时，会遇到一辆卖冰的车子猛然四轮朝天；或者是在远处的半山腰上，不定什么时候会有一栋小木屋被熊熊烈火包围着……总之，来到这里之后，所有的见闻都令我感到新奇而有趣。

记得有一次，我们一行人顶着炎炎烈日，坐车到沙漠中去。阳光下的沙漠中稀稀疏疏地长有一些仙人掌和灌木丛。当我们来到一个小村落的拐角处时，忽然听到有人惊呼："看！印第安人！真正的印第安人……"

大家都很兴奋，立刻跳下车想看个清楚。果然，一个印第安人正站在那儿，边上没有任何其他人。我身旁的向导迈上前一步，请求印第安人让我摸摸他头上的羽饰，因为他的头上插了色泽艳丽的鹰羽，看上去非常神气。我惴惴不安地走上前去，并再次用手语和他打招呼。

出乎我们意料的是，这位印第安人竟然用流利的英语说道："尽管让这位女士摸好了，无论她摸多少次都没有关系的。"这时，所有在场的人都吓了一大跳。后来我们才弄明白，原来这是一位演员，他正在等摄影师，根本不是什么真正的印第安人！

汤玛森女士和我经常是天还没有亮就出去骑马。在露珠晶莹剔透的草原上，能闻到麝香草和尤加利树的清香。早上的微风是如此宜人，令人感觉非常舒畅！就这样，我在比佛利山的小路上度过了许多令人愉快的清晨。

以《少女时代》为剧本的电影《拯救》终于准备开拍了，导演是乔治·豪斯特·普拉特先生，他以《青鸟》一片而走红。首先是片头的拍摄，普拉特先生用敲打桌子的方式和我沟通。我们工作的过程通常是这样的：汤玛森女士看过剧本，并听完导演的安排后，再将这些写在我手上；当我完全理解之后，再根据导演的敲桌子声来表演。有时候，导演也会亲自在我手上写几句话，例如"不要害怕，关在笼子里的不是狮子，而是一只小金丝雀。知道吗？好的，请再来一次。"然而，导演越是这样关照我，我就越觉得紧张不安。

说实话，要想在摄影机前自然地表演真的不容易，因为不论是站着还是坐着，强烈的灯光总是会聚集在身上，所以总让人觉得全身热烘烘的，汗如雨下，可是还必须注意脸上的化妆不能被汗水弄花了，否则不是鼻尖太亮，就是额头反光，那样的话效果就会大打折扣，所以表演当中要经常补妆。

我一站到摄影机前就觉得全身不自在，可是导演却偏偏突然要求我笑，或突然紧锁眉头深思。但是我的表情怎么能转得这么快呢？因此，我有时听到指令后，只有茫然发呆，不知所措。

刚开始，大家都没有进入角色，所以许多地方还不很理想。幸好那位扮演我少女时代的演员很出色，当然她本人既不聋也不哑，但她却把这个角色演活了。为此我对她产生了强烈的好感，她也因为扮演我而很喜欢我。另一位扮演大学时代的我的女演员长得很美，笑起来尤其迷人。这位女演员起初闭着眼睛来表演眼睛看不见，可是她稍不注意就会张开眼睛，结果惹得场边上的工作人员哈哈大笑，这时她的表情实在是太滑稽了。不过这位女演员倒非常愿意扮演这个角色，而且她的演技也不差，尤其是在表演梦见希腊诸神时最为传神，这是我个人最喜欢的一场戏。

再下来，电影要介绍那些在我生命中有重要影响的朋友。可是那些曾给我很大帮助的热心朋友，例如亨利·庄梦德先生、马克·吐温先生以及布鲁克斯大主教等都已去世，而仍然活着的几位也都人老年迈，和我最初遇见他们时当然不同了。

当时，我曾写信给贝尔博士，他很快就回了信。他说："看了你的信，让我回想起当年在华盛顿的那位小姐。在我眼中，你一直是当年的那个女孩子。只要你乐意，我可以为你做任何事情。不过我现在身处异国，一时间还回不了美国。但你可绝不能忘了我！想起我们第一次见面时，我可不是一个71岁的糟老头子，那时我头上连一根白头发也没有，而你当时也才只有7岁。所以，如果真要拍写实电影的话，我想必须得由其他人来扮演。请你找一个没有白发的英俊青年扮演我，等拍到结尾部分时，我们再以目前的样子登场。这样前后一对照，是不是很有趣？"

看了信之后，我忽然想出了一个好办法："何不安排一个象征性的场景，来介绍我的朋友出场呢？这样做效果也许会更好些。例如，可以安排我在两边全都是洋槐的马路上散步，然后意外地遇见贝尔博士和庄梦德先生，大家一边聊一边散步，欣赏那美丽的湖光山色，这样就显得比较自然。"洋槐树荫对我这个又瞎又聋的人来说最合适不过了，我越想越觉得这是一个好办法。

可惜的是电影公司并没有采纳我的建议，而是安排了一个盛大的聚会场面，让所有曾帮助过我的人——包括那些已经去世的好友，还有我最怀念的已经去世20年的父亲——全都出现在宴会上。当然，布鲁克斯主教、霍姆斯博士、亨利·庄梦德博士等都各有"替身"。最让我感到欣喜的是，我又见到了将近20年不曾谋面的约瑟夫先生，和我刚认识他时相比，他甚至更活泼开心。

置身于这样一个场合，与这些既熟悉又亲爱的好友欢聚一堂，使我感到自己不知不觉到了天堂。不过，当我与他们握手时，觉得他们的手虽然都很温暖，但他们讲话的语气和神态却完全不同于我的朋友们；尤其是当他们突然开口对我说话时，我会有一种从梦中被惊醒的愕然。

在宴会结束时，我有一段台词："目前，全国约有8万盲人正处在悲惨的境地。他们孤苦无援，而我们社会现在却没有完善的制度来帮助他们……这世界上有多少人在从未体验到生之喜悦的情况下含恨而终啊！我们应该为这些人谋求更好的生活，让这个世界变得更幸福、更快乐。"

就在影片拍了大半之后，大家忽然发现它缺乏高潮，换句话说就是没有什么戏剧性。于是就有人说："海伦一生中没有过浪漫史，当然也没有伟大的恋人，她这一生太平淡了！"还有人提议："或者干脆替她创造一个恋人，让他们上演一段恋爱戏如何？现在的电影如果没有这些插曲，是注定不受人欢迎的。"但是导演从一开始就不赞同这些观点，他认为这不过是画蛇添足，反而会弄巧成拙。经过再三考虑，最后决定插演几场带有戏剧性的场面。

在加进去的几场戏中，我记得有一场是这样的：在一个名为"时间"的洞窟前，一位代表"知识"、脸色苍白的小姐在和一位代表"无知"、身材魁梧的大汉搏斗，结果"知识"获胜，抱起了幼小的海伦。

另一场戏，是莎莉文老师试过各种方法之后，年幼的小海伦仍然不懂她的意思，她黯然神伤，跌入了灰心失望的深渊中。此时，基督出现了，他对老师说："要帮助这个幼小的心灵，不要放弃她。"于是莎莉文老师再度鼓起了勇气。

不过，还有不少戏是有些牵强的。例如，一位伤心的母亲手擎火炬，为不幸的伤残者请命；又比如，四个大国的领袖聚集在法国，准备决定全世界人类的命运，这时海伦出现了，恳求他们不要发动战争。最后他们也觉得这场戏太牵强了，因此最终将它删掉了。

由于这部电影掺入了各种突发奇想，结果情节越来越离谱，变得没有真实感。尤其是结尾那场戏，我现在想起来都觉得可笑，因为那简直是异想天开。

他们让我扮成一位和平的使者，像圣女贞德一样，骑着一匹白马走在游行队伍的最前面。不料找来的那匹白马太冲了，跑起来时冲劲吓人。当时我一手握着喇叭，一手控制缰绳，有几次差点儿摔下来。因此我越来越紧张，全身直冒汗。而头顶上的太阳又火辣辣地照射下来，我额头上的汗水直往下淌，就连嘴里吹的喇叭都是汗水，咸咸的。我心惊胆战地骑了一段路之后，胯下的马忽然在没有任何征兆、没有任何命令的情况下人立而起，我立即被吓坏了。幸好旁边一位摄影记者眼明手快，他一步冲到马跟前拉住它，让它站稳了，我这才没有摔大跟头。

马戏团的客串演出

结果，我参加演出的这部电影虽然叫好，但票房收入却不怎么样。我重又回到佛拉斯特的住所，生活也由绚烂多彩归于一片平静，就这样过了两年宁静的日子。在此期间，我们当然也想方设法进行开源节流，因为朋友们只能给我赠送钱款，所以我必须考虑为莎莉文老师存储一笔养老金，否则一旦我比她先去世，她晚年靠什么生活呢？正是出于这种考虑，我们决定从1920

年起，去波多大厦的马戏团进行客串演出，结果这一下就是将近4年，直到1924年春。

当然，我们在这4年中间并不是持续参加演出。刚开始时，我们只是偶尔参加在纽约、新英格兰或加拿大的巡回演出。1921年至1922年，我们开始到美国国内各地表演。

我们参加马戏团演出这个消息传出去之后，曾遭到了某些卫道士的非议："看啊，海伦为了出名，竟然什么都干！"还有些热心人则写信劝我不要投身演艺圈。其实，我怎么是被名声所诱惑呢？我当然有自己的计划，这样做不过是依我自己的意愿去实行罢了，就连莎莉文老师也是经过我的多次劝说才同意的。

在我看来，和写作相比，这一工作不仅轻松得多，而且收入也相对要高些。这种演出名为巡回，但在一个地方往往要待一个多星期，而不像我们过去演讲，有时候一天要接连去好几个地方，因此饱受奔波之劳累；而且演讲的时候，往往每到一个地方就必须立刻上台，几乎没有时间歇口气。

在马戏团只有下午、晚上各一场演出，而且每场演出只有20分钟的时间。马戏团有一套管理制度，非常正规，生活也很正常。我们在这里完全有个人自由，而不必担心受观众的打扰，连以前演讲时观众要求握手的那种情况都很少发生。

从事这项工作，使我觉得身心都很愉快。不过，莎莉文老师似乎不像我这样坦然，从一开始她就感到别扭。这也难怪，因为我们的名字每次都是和那些特技演员、驯兽师、猴子、大象、鹦鹉等一起出现在节目单上，所以无论谁都会觉得不舒服的。但我觉得自己的表演没有任何低俗的地方，当然更没有什么不可告人的，因此心里觉得非常坦然。

和我过去在任何场合遇到的人相比，在这个圈子里遇到的人更容易引起我的兴趣。他们的性格大多豪迈开朗，为人热忱而讲义气，他们的举动常常让我大受感动。

总之，我在马戏团的这段生活的确非常快乐，台下的观众既亲切又热情，他们听到我说话时，无不表现出真正的赞叹。我们表演时，通常是由莎莉文老师讲述她对我的教育方式，然后由我做简单的自我介绍，最后由我来回答观众的问题。例如，观众最常提的问题有：

"你看不见钟表，是怎样分辨白天和黑夜的？"

"你是否打算结婚呢？"

"你的眼睛看不见，你相信幽灵吗？"

"你在梦里会见到什么？"

诸如此类，问题太多了，而且有些问题还非常滑稽！我一向很注意观众对我的反应，而且来这里的观众都坦诚热忱，当他们觉得我的话有道理或令他们开心时，他们就会毫不掩饰地鼓掌大笑，根本不掩饰自己的感情。也正因为如此，我总是非常轻松愉快地给他们最真诚的回答。

说起观众的反应，使我想起了另一个与之相反的极端。那次是在教会演讲。到教堂的听众和马戏团的观众层次当然不尽相同，心态也区别极大，但他们那种极其肃静的态度却使我手足无措。虽然我看不到听不见，不知道他们的表情，但是我能感觉到他们对我的话没有任何反应，台下完全是一片死寂；再加上讲台很高，因此我竟然错误地幻觉为只有我一个人在自言自语。

我到广播电台演讲时，也是一样的情况，四周都寂静无声，没有人走动，当然也没有鼓掌声，空气中也没有我已经习惯的烟味和发胶香味，我仿佛是在一个无人的世界里。

所以，我情愿在马戏团和观众打成一片。因为在那里，我至少感觉不到太拘束或太寂寞。

慈母离世

我一生中最悲痛伤心的事情，就是在一次演出前突然得知母亲去世的噩耗。当时，我们正在洛杉矶某地演出。父亲去世时，我只有14岁，那时候还不太了解生离死别的悲痛，因此不像这次一样伤心——当然，这也许是我和母亲在一起的时间较久，有很深的感情吧。

对我来说，在莎莉文老师来到之前，我对于母亲的记忆是一片空白，只知道母亲后来常说："你出生时，我觉得既骄傲又快乐。"

母亲的话一定不假，因为我患病以前19个月所发生的各种事情，她都记得非常清楚，总是细细地说给我听："当你学会走路以后，最喜欢去院子里追花中飞舞的蝴蝶，胆子比男孩子都要大，根本不怕什么鸡啊狗的，你还经常用胖胖的小手去抱它们。那时，你眼睛比谁都好，一般人不容易看到的针和小纽扣都可以很快找到，因此简直成了我缝纽扣的小帮手……"

这些事情母亲说了多少遍也不觉得厌烦。她还说，有一次我家里正在编一个三脚竹笼，竹笼四周有许多小洞。正在牙牙学语的我又好奇又兴奋，经常会爬到母亲膝盖上去,用不甚流利的儿语问:"还要多久能做好?"

母亲还说,我最喜欢壁炉中熊熊燃起的火花,经常不愿去上床睡觉,而是望着木材燃烧的火焰出神;如果我看到火苗向上窜出烟囱时,尤其会感到兴奋。

"那时,我们俩是多么快乐啊!"回忆完之后,母亲总是会这样满足地叹口气说。

当我不幸染上大病而变得又盲又聋时,母亲还只有23岁,年轻的她从此生活在痛苦和黑暗之中。由于天生内向谨慎,母亲很少有朋友。在遭此不幸之后,她的心情当然更惆怅寂寞了。我长大之后,总是尽量学会独立,而不希望让母亲为我担心。每次母亲和我外出旅行,或来连杉陪伴我时,也许会感到欣慰;然而,在更多的时候她必然会为我这个残疾女儿担心,甚至暗中饮泣!在最后几年,我似乎隐约感觉到母亲越来越沉默了。

母亲自己曾说,她早上醒来最先想到的事情,常常是和我有关;晚上临睡前,她也经常为我担心。虽然母亲的手有关节炎,写信非常困难,但她为了我还是不辞劳累地坚持用盲文写信给我。

母亲生了我之后,又生了一个妹妹,5年后又生了弟弟菲力普,他们的出生稍稍给母亲带来了一些安慰。父亲去世后,母亲独立承担着抚育弟弟妹妹的重任,生活非常艰苦。妹妹好不容易长大了,和亚拉巴马州的昆西先生结婚,母亲这才松了一口气。她会轮流到妹妹家或者我这里来,看望她的孩子们。

说实话,母亲年轻的时候对家务并不怎么感兴趣,但是出嫁之后,她不得不挑起一半的家庭重担,不但要监督工人劳动,还要帮着种菜、喂养家畜,而且还要自己动手制作火腿、熏肉等各种食物,孩子们的衣服也必须自己动手做。另外,母亲每天还要招待父亲带回家的客人。总而言之,凡是南方家庭的繁杂家务,母亲都得过问和操持。

母亲做的火腿和腌黄瓜是远近闻名的,只要吃过的人都会交口称赞,邻近的人经常会向母亲讨要一些带回家去。当时我年纪还小,根本不知道母亲的忙碌和辛劳,总是拉着她的裙角寸步不离地跟着她,但母亲从不会厌烦,而是默默地承受这一切。

像母亲这样敏感而脆弱的女子,是如何承受那么琐碎而繁重的家务的呢?莎莉文老师就经常觉得不可思议而夸母亲。更令人敬佩的是,我们从来都没有听过母亲说一句不满的话,她总是默默地劳作,似乎除了工作之外,还只有工作,而且一直做下去就是了。

母亲还是一个喜欢花儿的优秀园丁,她不但知道如何插苗播种,还知道如何养花种树。虽然浇水除草的活儿很劳累，但她非常乐意去做，一点也不觉得疲倦。母亲对花草的极端迷恋，当然也说明了她心思的优雅和细致。记得有一年初春，母亲移植了一棵蔷薇花，但没想到几天后来了寒流，那棵新移植的蔷薇花被霜寒冻死了，母亲在给我的来信中十分悲痛地说："我就像失去儿子的大卫王一样，忍不住失声痛哭。"

母亲还非常喜欢鸟儿。她每次来到连杉时，总是喜欢去附近的森林里散步，还会随身带一些食物喂鸟。她尤其高兴看到母鸟教小鸟飞翔的情景，有时一看就接连好几个小时，却毫不知觉。

母亲对时事政治也很感兴趣，她经常看书读报，憎恨政治舞台上那些伪善者和愚蠢者，常常讽刺地批评那些心怀不轨的议员和政客。母亲最欣赏的是那些头脑机智敏锐的政治评论家，托马斯·卡莱尔夫人就是其中一位，她曾和卡莱尔夫人有过信件往来。在作家当中，母亲偏爱惠特曼、巴尔扎克等人，他们的作品母亲会一再阅读，几乎能背下来。

有一年夏天，我们去帕蒙特湖畔山上的木屋避暑，那儿有我们非常喜爱的清澈的湖水、翠绿的树林以及幽静的羊肠小道。一天傍晚，我们坐在湖边的石椅子上，母亲看着那些在湖中划独木小舟玩耍的年轻人，突然心有所感，她心中那种莫名的消极情绪是我当时根本无法理解的。

世界大战爆发后，母亲绝口不提战争的事情。但是当母亲在一次外出途中见到一大群年轻人在野外帐篷中露营时，她不禁感慨地说："唉！这些活泼可爱的年轻人眼看就要被送到战场上去了，实在是太可怜了！有什么方法可以不让他们去呢？"说着说着，母亲的泪水不禁潸然而下。当母亲后来听到俄罗斯提出和平条件时，她评论说："一个国家有勇气说出'战争是人类的罪恶'，真是太伟大了！虽然远隔重洋，可我还是忍不住想伸手去拥抱它。"

母亲在世时还经常说，希望自己将来老了之后，不会给别人带来太多的麻烦，她情愿安静地离开人世。母亲去世的时候，正住在妹妹家，她安详而平静地离开了人世，没有惊动任何人，是后来被人发现的。

我是在上台表演前两小时才得知母亲去世的噩耗的。在此之前，我没有得到母亲生病的任何消息，所以没有任何心理准备。听到消息后，我马上联想到自己也要死了："啊！这时候我还能上台表演吗？"

我身上每一处几乎都想放声痛哭，但我还是坚强地挺住了。我在台上表演时，没有一个观众知道我刚听到这不幸的消息，这让莎莉文老师和我都感到很宽慰。我还记得那天有一位观众问我："你今年多大了？"

"我到底多大了？"我问了问自己这个问题，因为我感觉我已经很大了。不过我没有正面回答这个问题，只是反问他："你看我有多大了？"

观众席上发出一阵笑声。然后又有人问道："你幸福吗？"听了这个问题，我的眼泪几乎夺眶而出，但我还是忍住了，尽可能平静地回答道："是的！我很幸福，因为我信仰上帝。"

这一天的问答大致都是这样。回到后台之后，我心中的悲痛再也压抑不住了，全部倾泻而出，几乎无法动弹。虽然我知道总有一天可以在"永恒的国度"见到母亲，可是目前这个世界没有了母亲竟显得如此寂寞。无论何时何地，每一件事物都会唤起我对母亲的回忆。我无限思念地在心里呼唤："如果我能再次收到母亲写的盲文信，那该多好啊！"

直到第二年的4月，我去亚拉巴马州妹妹家时，我才不得不承认母亲真的已经离开了我。

亲爱的母亲，您为我操劳痛苦一辈子，现在您到了天堂，应该可以舒畅些了吧！

您该明白，我之所以会变成这样，完全是上帝的旨意。您应该得到平静了，这也将是我最感到安慰的。

为残疾朋友募捐

许多人都认为应该成立一个全国性的盲人机构，经过长时间的组织和策划，1921年终于成立了。宾夕法尼亚州盲人协会的会长就是该机构的发起人。在俄亥俄州举行的美国盲人企业家协会年度工作总结会上，正式通过了这项决议。

纽约的M·C·麦格尔先生是该协会的首任会长。刚开始时，麦格尔先生靠朋友们的资助创办并经营着协会，从1924年起，协会改变了策略，决定向社会筹募基金，因此希望我和莎莉文老师能够参加此活动。

为了募集一点钱而必须四处奔波，这对我来说，实在是令人不快。当我了解他们的计划时，虽然觉得他们是用心良苦，可是心里依然有点不太乐意。然而，我心里非常清楚，就当时的情况，如果没有社会的资助，任何慈善团体或教育机构都无法生存下去。为了所有盲人朋友的福利，我无论如何也得勉为其难，尽力去做。于是我便又开始出现在各式各样的高楼大厦之间，坐着电梯来来回回地去演讲。

这笔募集的基金，是用来协助盲人同胞掌握一技之长，使其能够自立，而且提供他们发挥特长的条件；另外，就是要帮助那些有一定天赋但家境贫困的盲人，让他们的才能得以发挥，譬如那些有音乐天赋，却买不起钢琴、小提琴等昂贵乐器的。事实上，被埋没的天才还真是不少。

从那时开始，大约花了3年左右的时间，我去了全国的每个角落，到访了123个大小城市，参加过249场集会，曾前后向20多万听众发表过演讲。此外，还动员了各种团体与组织，例如报纸、教会、学校、犹太教会堂、妇女组织、少年团体、少女团体、服务社团及狮子会等等，他们常常集中募款，赞助我们的协会。尤其是狮子会的成员，他们非常注重对残疾儿童的关照，同时他们对盲人也倾注了同样的关心，因而募款工作几乎成为所有会员的主要任务了。

俗话说："一个年过40岁的人，几乎所有的事情都经历过了，不会有什么值得高兴的事了。"但是上天似乎对我很厚爱，就在我40岁生日之后不久，连续发生了好几件事情，令我感到十分意外又喜悦。其中一件就是美国盲人事业家协会的成立；另一件是我们发起的募捐运动，得到许多人士的大力支持，成果显著；第三件喜事，正是由于美国盲人事业家协会的成立，使得那原本百家争鸣的盲文得到了统一。

喜事还不仅仅只是这些，第一座国家盲人图书馆成立了，政府还拨出一大笔经费用于出版盲文书籍。紧接着，各州的红十字会也都成立盲文机构，专门负责把各种书翻译成盲文。其后，我们又发起了为那些在第一次世界大战中不幸失明的战士们争取福利的运动。这样，我们长期以来的愿望终于得到了实现，我心里感到非常的宽慰。

1926年冬天，我们的演讲团来到了华盛顿，正好国会刚通过有关拨款筹建国家盲人图书馆以及出版盲文书籍的提案。听到这一喜讯，我们信心大增，对未来充满了希望。

有一天下午，我和老师去白宫拜会了柯立芝总统，他十分热情地接待了我们，然后又很认真地听了我们向他汇报的有关盲人协会的情况。最后他拉住我的手，放在他的嘴唇上，告诉我说："我认为你们做的工作非常重要，只要我的能力办得到，就一定会全力帮忙。"

这位总统真的是说到做到，他后来还成了盲人协会的名誉总裁，而且他本人也捐了不少钱给基金会。柯立芝夫人也一再表示要参加到我们的工作中来。这位第一夫人果真对聋哑残疾者非常热心，替他们争取了不少福利。

我们还曾拜访过盲人议员汤玛斯·希尔先生及赖辛浦夫妇，他们都十分乐意地伸出援助之手。另外，我的一位住在华盛顿的好友——贝尔博士的女儿艾露滋夫人也为我们向社会广泛呼吁，让我感激不尽。

在底特律，当地的残障者保护协会会长卡米尔先生，是我多年的好友，他不辞辛劳地向市民们反复宣传和说教，结果我们在该地只集会一次，便募集了4.2万美元。而且会后我们又陆续收到不少捐款，少的1美元，多的达4500美元，仅这个城市的收获就很可观了。

在费城的募款也很成功，募捐委员会的委员莱克博士，热心地向民众劝募，只用了一个星期的时间，就募集到了2.2万美元。圣路易斯、芝加哥、布法罗等城市的募集工作成绩平平，可是在罗切斯特这个小城市我们反而募到了1.5万美元之多。

一般来说，电影明星的生活比一般人要富裕得多，我想一定会得到他们的大力捐款，可事实上，结果令人大失所望。我前后寄了无数封信到洛杉矶，可回信却只有一封，是一位名叫玛丽·班克福的女明星寄回来的，其他信则如石沉大海一般，音信杳无。因此，我们格外感激玛丽及其丈夫道格拉斯·费蒙先生的好意。

在此次募集的旅行途中，我们曾到圣罗拉的农业试验场，那里的负责人是鲁沙·巴本克先生。许多过去无法生长的水果、花草、树木，他却奇迹般地让它们栽植成功了，他是一位了不起的农业家。巴本克先生不但对我们慷慨解囊，而且非常热心地领我们参观了他的试验场。他让我用手去摸他所培植的仙人掌，并且告诉我沙漠中生长的仙人掌有许多刺，如果家里栽植这种植物常会刺伤手，因此他加以了改良，我所摸的这种仙人掌就是没有刺的。果然，仙人掌摸起来光滑平顺，而且有水分充裕的饱满感觉，令我想象这东西吃起来一定很可口。

近两年来，我为了写书几乎很少外出去募捐，但我们的募集工作并没有结束，离原来的目标还相差150万美元，所以我整理完书稿后，就得再度出发。值得庆幸的是，我们前一阵的四处奔波总算没有白费，虽然两年内没有开展募款活动，但许多人已经知道我们在募集资金，因此仍有人陆续汇款过来。例如去年，大富翁洛克菲勒、麦克尔先生等人，都捐了不少钱来。迄今为止，捐款的人不计其数，无法在此一一列举他们的姓名，然而我们对每一位捐款的善心人都报以同样的感激之情，他们付出的爱心将温暖每个盲人心灵，而且将世代传承下去。

的确，募款本来就是将无数人奉献的点点滴滴累积起来，如果不是这么多好心人的帮助，我们的协会也就不能像目前这样照计划开展工作。汤玛森女士每次拆开信的时候，都会有支票从信封里掉出来。这些信件来自学生、劳工、军人等各种阶层的朋友；来自世界各地，包括德国、意大利、中国等，其中也有一些是与我们同样的残障者。

一天清晨，邮差送来了一封来自底特律的信，信的署名是"一位贫苦女工"，她捐了1美元。

孩子们也很热烈地参与进来，他们的真诚无邪之心令我感动得落泪。有些孩子亲自抱着沉甸甸的储钱罐，拿来放在我膝上，当场将其打开，数尽后将其捐出；有些孩子则给我写来了热情洋溢的信，告诉我，他们省下了父母给他们买可乐、冰激凌的钱，将其捐了出来。

记得我们在纽约的安迪集会时，其中有位残障的少年捐了500美元，而且还附上了一束美丽的玫瑰花。这位少年现在已经不在世了，而那束玫瑰也早已经枯萎，可他的一腔爱心之花却永远绽放在我心中的花园。

从黑暗走向光明

"我感觉你所接触的世界太小了，真是太可怜了！"常常有人会怜惜地对我这样说。我心想，这些人之所以这样说，是因为他们不太了解我的生活，他们也不知道我交了多少朋友，翻阅过多少本书，旅行过多少地方。当我听到有人说我的生活圈子太小时，我总是会忍不住暗暗发笑。

对于那些非盲文书报，我就请别人念给我听。例如每天的早报，就由老师或汤玛森女士先给我念标题，然后我挑出那些比较感兴趣的部分，请她再细读出来。一般的杂志也是这样，由老师或汤玛森女士念给我听，一个月下来，我平均要读七八种杂志。此外，我自己还经常阅读一些盲文杂志，因为那上面常常会转载一些别的杂志上的好文章。

有些朋友亲自写盲文信给我，另有些人则请别人代写信给我，因此我可以好好地享受书信中传来的友情。对我而言，我很喜欢读盲文，因为这是由我自己直接去感受的，而且印象也尤为深刻。

我有位好友，名叫爱特那·波达，对我特别好。当他环游世界时，随身带着盲文字板，每到一个地方，就把他的所见所闻写信告诉我。因此，我就如同跟着他在旅游一样，一起聆听着大西洋上冰山迸裂的响声；一同乘坐飞机越过英吉利海峡；一起在巴黎的茫茫大道上漫步；一块来到水都威尼斯，在皓月当空的夜晚，一边欣赏着月光下的威尼斯，一边静静地听着船夫唱意大利情歌。那是多么罗曼蒂克啊！

观看了维苏威火山与几千年前的罗马竞技场之后，我们又到了神秘的东方。我随着波达来到印度、中国，看到很多奇怪而又有趣的东西。抵达日本时正是樱花烂漫的季节，缤纷的樱花飘飘洒洒，构成一个奇异的景象，清幽的寺院里传出的钟声引发了我无限的遐想。

最有意思的是，波达竟然惊奇地对我说："你看呀！日本的妇女都背着孩子在大街上行走，而男士竟都穿着四寸高的木屐在马路上溜达，发出咯吱咯吱的声音。"

有波达这样的朋友，所谓形体上的不自由其实等于没有了。

在许多关心我的朋友中，威廉索夫人属于最为热心的人之一，时时都想着要帮助我。

威廉索夫人赞助过许多的慈善团体，凡是她指导的团体与我有关的，她捐的钱就特别多。当我们遇到一些对事情的看法，观点不一致时，她温和地对我说："虽然我不同意你的观点，但我们的友情是另外一回事，我们仍是好朋友。"果然，她会一如既往地关爱我。

佛兰克·克勃特是我大学时的同窗好友，25年前他创立了克勃特出版社，曾经出版过我的传记作品——《我生活的故事》。现在，我打算出该书的续集，佛兰克仍像过去那样全力支援我。事实上早在10年前，佛兰克就鼓励我写这本书的续集，而且就在我进行本书的写作时，也总是感到佛兰克似乎就在我的身边。

1912年的冬天，《青鸟》一书的作者梅多林克夫人到连杉来，她为人谦和，性格活泼，我们两人一见如故，非常投缘。她回法国后，还寄了卡片给我，在卡片上亲笔写着："为发现青鸟的少女求福。"

来连杉的名人还真不少，其中一位是诺贝尔文学奖得主——印度诗人泰戈尔先生，这位诗人个子非常高大，蓬松的头发呈灰色，与脸上的络腮胡连在一起，都分不清楚，他令我想起圣经上所记载的先知们的形象。我很喜欢泰戈尔诗集，看了很多他的作品，可以深深地感觉出他对别人的那份爱心。能够见到这位诗人，是我平生莫大的光荣。

当我向他说起我对他的尊崇与仰慕时，他说："我很高兴你能从我作品中，看出我对人类的爱，你知道吗?这个世界正在等待出现一位爱神，爱世人更甚于爱自己！"

泰戈尔先生谈到时局忧心忡忡，他用哀伤的语气提到印度、中国以及世界上一些强国的国际形势："欧洲一些国家强迫中国人吸鸦片，如果他们拒绝吸烟的话，国土就要被瓜分。在这种情况下，亚洲民族怎么能不做好准备以达到自保呢？英国就像一只秃鹰一样，已经把战火引到了太平洋的沿岸，在那里建了许多军事基地。而在亚洲各国中，日本已经能够站立起来了，但是中国恐怕要等到自己的城门被攻破，盗贼闯进家门时才会惊醒了……请记住：一个太爱怜自己的人，往往会导致自己的灭亡，能解救世人的，大概只有神的力量了。"

听了他的话，使我联想到甘地先生，因为他是一个不仅在嘴上谈"爱"，而且用自己的行动来实践的人。

艺术家们似乎对我特别的厚爱，如艾连塔利和约瑟·杰弗逊等优秀演员还特意为我表演了他们的拿手戏，他们让我用手指去触摸，以便感受他们的一言一行，一颦一笑，我异常兴奋，唯恐遗漏掉任何细节。歌唱家卡罗素、夏列亚宾等人，甚至允许我把手放在他们的嘴唇上，去"听"他们的美妙歌声。

我曾手抚着钢琴欣赏戈德斯基的演奏，轻轻地触摸海飞兹的小提琴去领会那美妙的琴音。当戈德斯基奏出肖邦的小夜曲时，我深深为之沉醉了，仿佛置身于热带海岛上。

有时候，我把手放在收音机的振动板上"听"音乐节目。在所有乐器中，我觉得竖琴、钢琴、小提琴的声音非常美妙。不过，我对于目前正开始流行的爵士音乐却不敢恭维，那种爆炸的响声，令我感到好像有什么东西正朝着我冲过来似的，每当指尖传来这种信息时，我便免不了产生想转身逃跑的冲动，似乎人类在原始时代就在体内形成的那种对大自然的恐惧感再度发生了。

对于实业界的名人，我曾拜访过电器发明大王托马斯·爱迪生先生。在我前往新泽西州演讲时，爱迪生先生热情地邀请我去他家。他给人的第一印象相当严肃。据他的夫人告诉我，爱迪生先生常把自己关在实验室内通宵达旦地工作，当他实验进行到一半时，最讨厌别人去打扰，甚至连吃饭也忘了。

爱迪生先生让我把手放在唱机上，然后很热切地问我听懂没有，可惜我实在听不懂。为了不让爱迪生先生失望，我试着把当时头上戴着的草帽靠近唱机，使声音在草帽上更加集中，但仍然无法理解。

一起进餐时，爱迪生先生对我说："你听不见声音也有好处，至少你会比较容易集中心思，不受外界的干扰，活在自己的世界里，不是很好吗？"我回答他说："如果我是像你这样了不起的发明家，我希望能够发明一种帮助聋子听声音的机器。"

他有点诧异地说："喔，你这么想吗?我可不做这种无聊的事情，反正人们说的话多半是些无关紧要的，可听可不听。"

我把嘴靠在爱迪生先生耳边，想直接对他说出我想要表达的意思，可是他却说我的声音像水蒸气爆炸时一样，让他无法分辨其中的意思，他说："你还是告诉梅西夫人，然后由她转述给我，她的声音像小提琴般悦耳。"我感觉他说的每一句话，都带有命令的味道。

汽车大王福特先生，是我在内布达斯加演讲时，才见到的实业界名人。

福特先生亲自带领我们到他的工厂里去参观，并且以谦和的态度向我们讲述了他成功的经历："开始时，我是想要生产一种连农夫都可以买得起的汽车，几经研究试验后，我对汽车就越来越内行了⋯⋯其实，有好的构想的人非常多，只是大多数人不知道如何去实践，因此有也等于没有了。"

在参观完福特先生的汽车工厂后，我有一个感想：如果把这个世界视为像福特工厂一样，用他们的方法来管理，是否会更有效率呢?那时，是不是每个人都可以缩短工作时间，却拿到更高的报酬呢?

如果人们一天中只需要工作几个小时，衣食住行都不成问题，还能有四五个小时的自由时间，这不是很好吗?但是我也知道这种想法只是理想中的状态，福特先生虽然是一个杰出的企业家，但他的管理方法未必适合整个世界，因为国家毕竟与工厂不是一回事！

那次拜见福特先生后，10年过去了，福特先生在一次盲人大会中捐了一大笔钱，他说在他的工厂里雇用了73位盲人，他之所以雇用他们，并非只是怜悯他们，而是因为他们在工作上表现得相当出色。我听到这些时，心里真有一种说不出的高兴。

当我感到自己的鼻子有些不舒服，心里时常阵阵不安时，我就知道我应该到纽约去散散心了。纽约市里有多种香味，可以刺激我那敏感的鼻子；我也常常喜欢到热闹嘈杂的地下铁路沿线去逛一圈。像这样到纽约去一趟，回来后我的活力又恢复了，因为我感觉到自己和其他人一样地活着。

从繁华的都市返回到宁静的田园，感觉到自己的家园格外亲切，虽然有人嫌弃它像个老鼠窝，但对我而言，它却是世界上最舒适的地方。

我时常自己从前门的梯子下来，沿着小径往前走，到尽头时一拐弯，就是我常散步的马路了。小屋的四周有宜人的景色，尤其是每年的6月，郁金香与风信子全都开了，我们就如同住在花海中的小岛上一样。在我走往小凉亭的马路两旁，种满了来自德国或日本的菖蒲花。6月真是个特殊的月份，连树木都伸展着它们的树枝，伸出的枝似乎想向我们诉说什么。我有时会感觉树木真的在对我说话："你们人类何时才能学我们这样站着不动呢?"有时"听"他们在说:"看那不安分的海伦,在花草丛中穿来穿去,就像一只风中的蝴蝶。"那横生的小树枝,似乎是对我指指点点的小手指。

我常想:"为什么人不会像树木一样,固定地站在某一个点上呢?树木虽然不会移动,不是照样能够生长得很好吗?甚至比人类活得更快乐、更长久呢!"

近来,我常会为了劳资双方矛盾对立以及国家之间的战争问题而失眠,我奇怪人类为什么把精力花在互相之间的战争上,而不投入到研究如何改善人类生活、迈向理想境界上去呢?如果能这样的话,这个世界不是可以更美好吗?不过我相信,这一天终将会来临的。

我希望世界能早一天实现和平,让人类生活得更加幸福,到那时候,人们就不必再去幻想死后能上天堂了。

最近,我常常独自坐在书房中思考:"如果当初豪博士没有设计这套教育盲聋者的方法,那么我的这一生将会是什么样的呢?"

据说在豪博士想要教育辅导劳拉时,当时的法律上还明文规定:盲聋者视为白痴。莎莉文老师在帕金斯盲校时与劳拉同室,所以对她的事情很清楚,而且第一个教莎莉文老师手语的,就是劳拉。

当莎莉文老师告诉劳拉,她将去亚拉巴马州,教一位又盲又哑又聋的女孩时,劳拉感到很高兴,同时又嘱咐她说:"别让这个孩子养成骄纵的性格,不能因为她身有残疾,就凡事顺着她,使她变得太任性。"

临走时,盲校的那些女学生们托莎莉文老师带给我一个洋娃娃,洋娃娃所穿的衣服是劳拉亲手做的。我就是从这个洋娃娃开始,学到"DOLL"这个字的。

我初到帕金斯盲校时,莎莉文老师带我去见的第一个人就是劳拉。当时劳拉正在房里做编织,由于她们很久没有见面,因此非常欣喜地接待了我们。劳拉还吻了我。可当我想伸手去摸她所编织的花边时,她就很快地把花边移开了,并且用手语对我说:"你的手太脏了!"

我想用手去触摸她的脸,她向后一躲,并暗示我的手太脏了。她问莎莉文老师:"难道你没教这个孩子要有礼貌吗?"接着,她很慎重地一字一句地对我说:"当你去访问一位女士时,举止不可以太随便。"

我一连碰了几个钉子后,心里很不痛快,索性就一屁股坐在地板上,可是劳拉不在乎,不迁就,立刻毫不客气地把我拖了起来。

"穿着漂亮的礼服,绝不可以坐在地板上,会把你的衣服弄脏的。你这个孩子太任性了,一点教养都没有!"

当我和老师告别出来,吻别时不小心踩到了她的脚,结果又被她训了一顿。事后劳拉告诉莎莉文老师："这个孩子好像任性了一点，但脑筋很灵活。"而我对劳拉的第一印象，觉得她冷酷无情，让人无法亲近。

其实劳拉与我有许多相似之处，因此，很多人总是拿我俩做比较。我们变成盲聋时的年龄差不多，刚开始时的行动都较粗鲁，不服从别人的管教；另外，我们两人都有着金发碧眼，又同在7岁时开始接受教育。但是我们的相同之处仅仅这些，劳拉比我用功得多。劳拉是个既聪明又善良的人，如果她当初也能和我一样，有一位如莎莉文这样的老师指导，那么她的成就必然会比我大得多。

想到这些，我就不得不为自己感到庆幸。可是当我又想到自己已经有40多岁，而且能够和常人一样的生活，但对那些仍处于黑暗中的人却没有做出一点贡献时，又不禁深感惭愧。

需要做的事情实在太多了，据调查，有资料显示在全国，除了年纪很大或卧病在床的人以外，有379人又盲又聋，正在等待有人去引导他们走出黑暗，其中有15人正处于学龄阶段，可是却没有学校收容他们。

常有人向我咨询："我应该如何来教育这样的孩子呢？"由于孩子们各自的智力高低不同，和所处的环境各异，因此我不能一味肯定地告诉他，是应该请家教，或者送到哪一所学校去。我们能说的是："在孩子的眼睛和耳朵的机能未完全丧失之前，要尽快送他们到附近的盲哑学校去，否则这样的孩子以后会难以进行学习。"

许多人对我们这样的人都感到好奇，借此机会，我顺便向大家说明一件事情，那就是即使一个人生活在黑暗或寂静之中，但他仍可以像常人一样进行回忆，也可以进行想象，过着属于自己的快乐生活。当然，他要尽量用他的方式去接触这个世界，不要封闭自己，处在这个世界之外。就我而言，我有许多朋友，他们都会热心地把他们耳闻目睹的经历和感受传输给我，因此，我一样生活得多彩多姿。

我永远也不会忘记朋友们对我的帮助，他们给了我许多的勇气与快乐。

不言而喻，身体上的缺陷终究会带来许多的不方便，这点我心里很清楚。我不敢说自己从没有过怨天尤人或感到沮丧的时候，但我更明白这样的想法没有任何好处，因此我总是会极力控制自己，让自己不要去钻这种牛角尖。

我用来自勉的一个目标就是：在我有生之年，要极力学会自立，在自己的能力范围之内，尽量不去给别人增加麻烦。用宗教上的话来说就是：带着微笑背起自己的十字架。这并不是向命运投降，而是勇敢地面对命运，进而设法去克服它。

这种事情口头上说起来非常容易，可要付诸实践的话，如果没有很深的信仰、坚强的毅力，加上温暖的友情和上帝的引导，恐怕就很难做得到。

现在回忆起过去，值得安慰的是，我至少可以做一只"只会模仿猫头鹰的鹦鹉"。所谓"只会模仿猫头鹰的鹦鹉"是什么意思呢？作家爱德华在完成《小洞的故事》这本书后，写信给他的一位朋友说："我的祖父养了许多鹦鹉，可是鹦鹉什么也不会，只会模仿猫头鹰鼓起翅膀的样子。来访的客人们总是会兴致勃勃地谈论起鹦鹉，并常追问它们会什么精彩表演。此时祖父就会一本正经地说：'快别这么说，否则我们的比利会不高兴的，是吗？比利，来，你来模仿猫头鹰给他们看吧！'我常常想起小时候的这段往事。现在我写了这本书，就像那只仅会模仿猫头鹰的鹦鹉一样。"

我也想自己就像是比利，因此很认真地模仿"猫头鹰"。我的能力有限，我所能做的只有这件事，就如同小鹦鹉比利一样。我在佛立斯特家中的书房写完自传的最后一行，由于手很酸，暂时停下来休息了一下。

这儿的院子里有落叶松、山茱萸，但是没有洋槐，至于为什么没有洋槐，我也不清楚。我的脑海中时常浮现出两边种满洋槐的小径，因为就在那条小径上，我度过了许多时光，同时享受了朋友们无限的温情，那里甚至可以说就是我的人生小径。现在，这些朋友们中，有的尚在人间的小径上行走，有的则已经去天国的花园里了，但我对他们的怀念是一样的。

平心而论，我过去看过的许多好书也都是我的良师益友，它们是许多智者的智慧结晶，我对它们都怀着敬畏与感恩的心情。

我的这本书不是什么伟大的作品，如果说它还有些价值的话，并非是因为我的才能，而是发生在我身上的那些不平常的事情。也许老天认为我是他的子女，进而能够肩负重任，希望由于我自身的盲聋，而能对其他人产生一点儿影响作用吧！

上天使我眼睛看不见，耳朵听不到，因而也就无法说话，是想通过我的这种残缺而给世上像我这样的残疾人一些启示。老天待我不薄，因为他为我送来了莎莉文老师，她带领我走出了黑暗而寂静的世界。

莎莉文老师自己的视力从小就弱，当她做我的家庭教师时，也仅仅能看到少量的光线而已。一个身体不太好的弱女子，远离自己的朋友，只身来到亚拉巴马州的一个小镇，不能不说是冥冥之中某种力量在支持她，使她有这样的勇气和决心。她为了我不辞辛劳，凭借她那微弱的视力，为我念了许多的书，这是我与这个世界接触的开始，也是最主要的桥梁。我与她非亲非故，她为我所做的这一切，岂能仅仅用"喜欢我"这句话来解释。

一直到现在，老师仍旧戴着一副度数非常高的特制眼镜来阅读，而那副眼镜是贝尔博士精心制造的。

我无法读自己的打字稿，这本书有关的修改工作，都是由老师用手语为我复诵。当老师帮我做这些工作时，贝尔博士一直伴在老师身边，检查她的视力，随时加以调整。

老师为了我，不惜付出自己的一切，她为什么对我这么好呢？

我始终认为，只要莎莉文老师有决心，她一定能轻易地成为妇女运动的领导人物，或者是一位知名的女作家。可是她却宁愿把她一生的精力花在我的身上。她的行为鼓舞了我，志愿报效社会，服务于社会。遗憾的是，我一直以来没有很好地报答老师的一片苦心。

最后，我要说的是，虽然我的眼前是一片黑暗，但因为老师带给了我许多的爱心与希望，使我的思想进入了光明的世界。我的四周也许有着一堵堵厚厚的围墙，它们隔绝了我与外界的沟通，但围墙里的世界却满是美丽的花草树木，我仍能够欣赏到大自然的神奇和伟大。我住的小屋虽然不大，也没有窗户，但在夜晚同样可以观赏到满天闪烁的星星。

我的身体虽然不能像别人那样自由，但我的思想却是完全自由的。让我的思想超出躯体，走向社会，沉浸在与人交往和沟通的喜悦之中，追求美好的人生吧！

第二篇　安妮·莎莉文老师的故事

厄运降临

　　1866年4月14日，安妮·莎莉文出生在美国马萨诸塞州一个名叫食禄岗的穷困农村。她的父母是爱尔兰人，1860爱尔兰闹饥荒，他们随着其他的逃荒者像澎湃的海浪般涌进了美洲新大陆。安妮的父亲托马斯很快就在当地找到了一份工作，在妻子艾利斯的操持下，日子过得还不错，最起码可以吃饱饭。

　　安妮是他们的第一个孩子，安妮出生后，牧师洗礼时问给婴儿取什么名字，艾利斯虚弱地微笑低语道："简。""简"是安妮的受洗名，但从一开始大家就叫她"安妮"。

　　安妮很受父母的宠爱，当她开始咿呀学语的时候，父母就在每天黄昏的时候抱着她，给她讲各种故事。晚饭后还要把她抱到膝上，逗她玩半天。临睡前，托马斯经常把安妮举过头顶，像荡秋千一样摇晃着，或者在屋内快步走，逗的安妮咯咯欢笑。

　　然而，这种好日子并没有过多长时间，幸运之神便不再光顾莎莉文家了，可怕的厄运开始降临到这个贫困之家。

　　厄运先从安妮下手。安妮还只有3岁的时候，就染上了一种疾病，眼皮上长满了小颗粒，异常的痒。安妮不停地用手揉，但是不见好转。情况一天比一天严重，但是托马斯夫妇没有钱给安妮治病，艾利斯只能从别人那里找来一些偏方，希望能治好女儿的眼睛。但是这些方法都没有奏效，反而加重了安妮的痛苦。

　　托马斯不忍心看到爱女遭受如此巨大的痛苦，只好带她去私人医院检查。医生诊断安妮患上了"结膜炎",还说这种病很容易在贫民区迅速传播,因为贫民区的卫生条件很差,加上营养不良,孩子的抵抗力差,只要是感染上这种病,眼睛就有失明的危险。

可怜的安妮正一步步走向黑暗。然而祸不单行,不久安妮的母亲就患上了专找穷人纠缠不放的绝症"肺结核",而她此时还患有身孕。也就是说,这个孩子尚未出生就有疾病。

1869年,安妮的小弟弟杰米出生了,当然又是一个多病的孩子,因为他遗传了母亲的体质,逐渐因疾病而致残。托马斯看到家庭的样子,开始失去信心,每天借酒浇愁,常常是喝得烂醉如泥地回到家中。安妮和杰米一点都感受不到父爱。

安妮的脾气变得越来越坏。她的母亲很快就被病魔夺走了生命,安妮的父亲托马斯请求他的亲戚帮他抚养安妮、杰米和另一个还在襁褓中的小女儿玛丽。

杰米和玛丽很快就有亲戚认养了,但是没人愿意领养安妮,因为她的脾气太坏了。经过一番推诿和讨价还价,安妮才被家庭条件最好的堂兄领回家,但安妮那仇视一切的暴躁脾气使堂兄很不喜欢她,他们相处得很不愉快。

几个月之后,堂兄实在是不能忍受安妮的任性和暴躁了,又提议召开家族会议。在这次家族大会上,安妮和弟弟杰米的命运开始发生了转变。

由于安妮的眼病非但没有好起来,反而越来越糟了;而且杰米的病也没有缓解,他们都需要花费昂贵的医药费,所有的亲戚都难以承受。于是大家一致决定把姐弟俩送到马萨诸塞州的救济院去,从此和莎莉文家族的人毫无关系。

救济院的生离死别

1876年2月,安妮和弟弟杰米被送到了位于德士堡镇的救济院。救济院的负责人很快就为安妮姐弟俩进行了档案登记,然后就把他们分别安置到男女宿舍。

"把这个男孩送到男宿舍,女孩送到女宿舍。"一位救济院的主管盼附道。

杰米听了号啕大哭,他恐惧地扑到姐姐怀里,紧紧地抱着她,大声喊道:"不,不,我不去。"

"不,"安妮也大声尖叫着,"他是我弟弟,我们必须待在一起,我们决不能分开。"

安妮紧紧地抱着杰米,心中升起从未有过的亲情,这是安妮多年来第一次关心"自我"以外的人。

那位主管被安妮的尖叫声和杰米的哭闹声吵得不耐烦了,最后同意了杰米可以和安妮待在女宿舍,但是他随后又补充道:"但他必须围上女孩子穿的裙子。"

杰米不久前才脱掉尿布包袱,现在又要他穿上裙子,他非常的不乐意,但是为了能和姐姐待在一起,他毫无选择的余地。

安妮泣不成声地说:"让我们做什么都行,只求你能让我们在一起,我们一定会听话的。"

救济院的管理人员无法割断这种手足之情,只好答应了安妮姐弟俩住在一起。

这所救济院虽然名为救济院,其实和收容无家可归的流浪者的收容所没有什么区别。无依无靠的老人、精神病患者、醉酒的男人都是这里的常客,而安妮和杰米现在就加入了他们的队伍。

安妮很不喜欢这里的环境。救济院的房子黑乎乎的,一个个生病的妇人躺在床上,有气无力地呻吟着等死。即使大白天耗子也敢出来到处乱跑。到处都显得阴森森的,让安妮感到很不舒服。不过除了这些之外,安妮还是觉得有些幸运,因为这里最起码可以吃饱,除了眼疾之外,她全身充满了活力。

救济院的多数人都不关心安妮姐弟,而安妮和弟弟杰米也不知道如何尊重比自己大许多的难友。但有两位老妇人成了安妮的好朋友,安妮觉得她们与众不同,因为她们至少还"活着"。其中一位瞎了眼的老妇人经常给安妮讲各种生动的故事,让安妮听得入了迷;另一位老妇人名叫马奇·卡罗,她患有严重的关节炎,几乎瘫痪在床上,连上下床或翻身都很困难。安妮经常帮助她,使马奇方便了许多。由于马奇的眼神很好,她又识字,她为安妮读了一本又一本书,使安妮从中获得了极大的乐趣,点燃了她读书的欲望。

安妮到处闲逛,一天,她发现一个大厅的橱柜里堆满了一大捆被老鼠啃过的旧杂志。杰米非常喜欢杂志上面的图片,安妮则被里面身穿各种艳丽服饰的女性所吸引。她常常将这些杂志捧得离眼睛很近,好看清上面的东西。

冬去春来，3个月很快就过去了，杰米的病情也日渐严重。安妮心疼地看着受到病痛折磨的弟弟，在心里祈祷上帝。她整天守候在杰米的身边，照顾他穿衣吃饭，还给他讲故事。但是安妮的这一切努力都没有用，就在安妮晚上实在支撑不住，靠在杰米床头睡着的时候，杰米安静地离开了人世。

当安妮醒来时，发现情况不对劲，但她又看不见任何东西。安妮急急忙忙地转向杰米的床，但是杰米的床已经不见了——原来救济院的人在杰米死后，将他的尸体连床一起推到太平间去了。

恐惧和忧虑使安妮吓得浑身颤抖。她摸黑走进太平间，伸手摸到了杰米的床。"杰米——"安妮失声哀号，惊动了所有的人。救济院的灯都亮了，人们跑了过来，看到安妮像一具尸体一样昏倒在地上。

这时，一双慈祥的手将安妮从地上抱起来。但是安妮误以为这人是想将她和弟弟分开，立即变得愤怒起来。她用尽全身的力气，死命地踢咬对方。那人想按住安妮，但是安妮的力气实在是太大了，经过一番争斗，那人只好让安妮重新躺在地上。

这一天成了安妮人生中最悲伤的日子。

她已经麻木了，连哭都不会了，只是静静地坐在那里。宿舍里一位善良的老妇人走近她，对她说："哭吧！尽情地哭吧，孩子。眼泪可以冲淡你的悲哀，哭吧，孩子！"然后她怜惜地抚摸着安妮的肩膀。

安妮似乎没有听进去，她痴呆地坐在床边，两眼发直，一眨不眨。"哭吧，人总是会死的。"老妇人缓缓地劝慰安妮。安妮悲从中来，泪水滚落而下。

向往光明

杰米去世之后，这个世界上只剩下安妮了，她成了救济院唯一的小孩，生活在众多的孤寡老人中间。她变得越来越孤独，视力也越来越弱了。同病房的老妇人知道安妮就要瞎了，抚摸着她的头说，"可怜的小东西，如果你要失明了，那你就什么也学不到了。"

听到老妇人叫她"可怜的小东西"，安妮从床上滚下来，大声哭喊道："我不想待在这儿。"她心想："我必须逃出去。"

但是，又有谁会来关心她这样一个可怜的小女孩呢？何况她又是个瞎子。安妮知道她可以去盲人学校，但怎样才能去这样的学校呢？她问自己。

巴巴拉神父的出现给安妮带来了希望。

巴巴拉是德士堡新来的一位神父，他负责主持女生宿舍每周六的祷告和星期天的弥撒仪式。但是良知还使他做了许多其他的事情，他经常到救济院来看望那些体弱多病的人，和他们说笑，减轻他们的痛苦。不久，他就开始注意到了安妮。

安妮也开始观察这位新来的传道者。每当他们的目光相遇时，安妮总是避开他的视线，不敢做任何奢望。但是即使这样，安妮仍然能够感觉到巴巴拉神父和蔼可亲的微笑。渐渐地，神父的笑容化解了安妮的恐惧心理，他们很快就成了好朋友。

巴巴拉神父不愿再让安妮待在救济院里。一天，他给安妮带来了一个意外的惊喜——他准备带安妮离开救济院，到马萨诸塞州罗威郡的天主教慈善医院，找他的朋友为安妮的眼睛做手术。

医生立即为安妮安排了检查，并且对神父说："我想应该可以治好她的眼睛。"接着他又重复说道："请放心，我们能治好。"

安妮的手术没过几天就做了。到了拆线的那一天，一群护士拿着药物和器械，跟着医生走进病房，神父也跟在后面。医生小心翼翼地拆开眼罩，慈祥地对安妮说："睁开眼睛。"

安妮听到吩咐，紧张得心都快要跳出嗓子眼了。可是当她张开眼睛时，看到的依然是一片模糊，甚至比原来的情况更糟。

这次手术没有成功。

"我不想回救济院去了。"安妮对神父说。

神父安慰安妮说还要做手术，安妮这才高兴起来。她第一次接触到有教养而且富有同情心的善良人，感受到了人间的温暖。

在接下来的日子里，安妮做了一次又一次的手术，但是先后六次都没有成功。医生们再也无计可施了，安妮的希望彻底破灭。

这时，巴巴拉神父要回家乡去了，安妮不得不再次回到救济院，重新回到了那个黑暗的牢笼。但是，安妮也更坚定了离开那里的决心。

我要上学

安妮想去上学，想离开救济院。她的想法遭到了人们的极大嘲讽，有人劝她趁早放弃这个念头。但是安妮不为所动，一直没有放弃心中的梦想。

安妮的执著终于感动了上帝。一天，一个考察团来到了救济院。原来，有人报告州议院，说这个救济院的条件非常恶劣，州政府这才派了人前来视察。考察团的成员到各病房巡视，查看这里的生活条件和设施。

有人告诉安妮，这个考察团的团长名叫弗朗·夏邦，也许他能帮助她。安妮立即记住了他的名字。当考察团视察的时候，安妮跟着他们，寸步不离，但是她不知如何开口求他们。

考察团很快就要离开了，安妮的时间也不多了。当考察团的所有成员全都离开救济院，大门缓缓关上时，安妮突然尖声喊叫，大声呼喊着团长的名字："夏邦先生，夏邦先生！"

众人一惊，夏邦团长回过身来，想看是谁在叫他。只见安妮磕磕绊绊地摸索着向他们走来，她的小手在空中抓舞着。

安妮走到大家身边，哭着说："我想去上学！请让我去上学吧！"

救济院的主管想把安妮推开，一个声音阻止了他："等等，是怎么回事？"

"我瞎了，看不见东西。"安妮紧张地说，"可是我想上学。我可以去盲人学校上学。"

"你在这儿多久了？"灰色人影问。

"我不知道。"安妮呜咽着。

"将近3年了。"旁边有人回答。

"我想去盲人学校。"安妮轻声地重复着。

"可怜的小东西。"有人说。然后问了一些问题，离开了救济院。

那天晚上，安妮哭泣着入睡。"也许有一天，"她想，"他们会把我带走的，就像带走杰米那样。"从那以后的几个晚上，安妮都是哭着入睡的。她确信自己已经完全失败了。

几天之后，女宿舍突然喧闹起来。一位老妇人步履蹒跚地跑进来问：

"安妮在哪儿？"

有人问："找她什么事？"

"赶快告诉她好消息，让她收拾好东西，她就要离开这里去上学了。"老妇人回答说。

安妮几乎不敢相信自己的耳朵。原来，夏邦先生回去之后，就帮助安妮注册入学了。这样，安妮就以慈善机构贫寒学生的身份，于1880年10月3日来到了帕金斯盲人学校，开始了她的学习生涯。从此，安妮朝着她生命中的第二个方向前进了。

第二次生命

帕金斯学校的生活对于安妮来说是全新的，但是它并不如安妮想象的那么美好。安妮现在已经14岁了，在学校算是大孩子，但她必须和比她小得多的孩子们一起学习，这就引来了他们的捉弄和嘲笑。安妮开始感到失望和困惑，又变得脾气暴躁，对任何人都充满了戒备。

但是帕金斯学校又是一个非常神奇的地方。在那儿，安妮发现了学习的奇妙。她学会了使用盲文来读和写，学会了用她的手指和嘴唇阅读，还学会了盲人书写的一整套方法。她在竭尽全力地学习。

在帕金斯学校，安妮和摩尔老师成了最知心的朋友。摩尔小姐是学校公认的美人，更加可贵的是，她对所有的学生都充满了关爱。当安妮和其他老师发生冲突，引起校长的不快时，是她化解了校长对安妮的不满，并且主动提出由她来教育安妮。

摩尔老师的宽容和关怀彻底改变了安妮。她不再撒野，并学会了沉默和谦虚。她开始爱身边的每一个人，喜欢和同学们在一起。这种改变还给安妮带来了其他的好处，当学校放寒假时，校方帮安妮找了一份打扫旅店卫生的工作，安妮十分珍惜这个机会，工作非常卖力。

安妮的努力付出得到了回报。旅店的一位房客见安妮虽然眼睛看不见，但是干的却那么认真，就对她动了同情之心。正好他有一位医术高明的朋友，他劝安妮去医治，但是被安妮拒绝了，因为一想到以前做过的六次手术，她就对自己的眼睛复明不抱有任何希望了。

但是这位热心的房客并没有放弃，安妮终于被他说动了。他们来到了他的朋友那里。

"我认为我们可以为你的眼睛做点什么，安妮。"医生对她说，"你需要进行两次手术。尽管你的视力不好，但你应该能够重见光明。"

最后一次手术之后，安妮躺在医院的床上，她非常害怕失败。她知道，当眼前的纱布绷带拿下去之后，她将能看见一些灰色的影子。

这一天终于来了。医生用剪子剪呀剪呀，最后纱布被剪开了，医生小心翼翼地将纱布轻轻移开。安妮微闭着眼睛呆了一会儿，然后慢慢地睁开双眼，期待着眼前出现灰色的形状。

呵，她真的看见了明亮的光线，比以往所看见的任何东西都要明亮。一束光线从窗子里照射进来。

"我看见窗户了，"安妮激动地叫道，"外面有树，还有河流，我能看见它们了，我能看见这一切了。"

尽管安妮见到的还不是十分清晰，就如同隔着一玻璃杯水，但她毕竟能够看见了，这就足以慰藉所有的人了。安妮当然更是欣喜若狂。

新的转折

复明之后的安妮学习进步更快了。她跟劳拉·布里奇曼学会了手语。劳拉两岁时就因病而成为聋哑人，后来进了帕金斯学校，一待就是近40年。在学校创始人豪博士的教育下，劳拉懂得了手语，这在当时是个奇迹。安妮常常找劳拉聊天，渐渐地也对手语达到了熟练的程度。

安妮喜欢到处转。一天，她去法院听了关于德士堡调查的公众听证会。当时人们认为法院是一个充满了污秽的地方，而安妮竟然敢去这种地方，真是胆大包天。校长安纳格罗斯知道后非常恼火，所有人也都觉得安妮玷污了学校的名誉，于是决定送安妮回德士堡的救济院。

这时，霍普金斯太太挺身而出，留下了安妮。霍普金斯太太是学校的义工，早年丧偶，中年丧子，安妮正好和她死去的孩子年龄相当。她眼看着安妮将要受到惩罚，就提出当安妮的监护人，并保证不会让安妮再犯同样的错误。安妮这才得以留下来，从此也有了一个"家"，受到了霍普金斯太太无微不至的照顾。

1886年6月，安妮即将从帕金斯学校毕业。这些年来，她看到了那么多新鲜事物，学到了那么多知识，也做了那么多事情。转眼之间，她不再是个小女孩了，已经长成了一位亭亭玉立的女郎，现在她就要离开帕金斯学校了。但是像她这样一个半盲的姑娘能靠什么维生呢？当然，她可以去饭店洗盘子，去旅店擦地板，但她怎样才能运用所受到的良好教育呢？难道她就命中注定一辈子都毫无用处吗？

8月底，安妮在她朋友的一所海滨寓所里度过了离校前的最后一个暑假。在那儿，她收到了校长安纳格罗斯先生写来的一封信，问她是否愿意去亚拉巴马州照顾一个盲女孩，给这孩子当家庭教师。

安妮见到安纳格罗斯先生之后，安纳格罗斯先生对她说："听说这是一个7岁的女孩，名叫海伦·凯勒，她是个相当任性的孩子。她在家里总是按自己的意愿行事，父母也总是迁就她，觉得对不起她。"

安妮露出了微笑。她记得自己7岁时也相当惹人讨厌，但她也清晰地记得，当时自己是多么的孤独。

"她像我所认识的人一样健全。"安妮对自己说，"海伦·凯勒需要什么呢？正是正确的训导和无限的慈爱和关怀。"

艰辛而伟大的教育

就这样，安妮于1887年3月3日抵达了亚拉巴马州海伦·凯勒的家，受到了凯勒夫妇的热情欢迎。

"感谢上帝！终于有人肯来帮助我可怜的小东西了。"凯勒夫人说。

安妮听到她这样的话后，立即脸色骤变，回转身来说："今后再也不要让任何人这样叫她'可怜的小东西'了。"

安妮见到海伦的第一印象，就觉得自己好像是见到了一个小霸王。凯勒家的人都纵容着她，让着她，不敢违逆她的意愿。其中凯勒夫妇尤其如此，生怕他们的宝贝女儿受到任何委屈。安妮心想，要想打开海伦·凯勒思维的阀门，自己首先必须学会和她的父母相处，尽管这是一件艰苦的工作，但在她与学生开始交流之前，她不得不先做好这项工作。

"很快，我就清楚地知道只要海伦待在这个家中，就什么事情都做不成。"安妮在信中告诉安纳格罗斯先生。于是，在她的要求下，她和海伦搬到了花园的一所房子里，那儿离海伦的父母约有一英里远。正是在这个新的地方，安妮初步"制服"了海伦，使海伦那粗暴不羁的性格得到了改变。

与此同时，安妮开始一步步教海伦拼写字母，还教会了海伦如何模仿她，如何拼写单词。直到1887年4月的一个早晨，安妮终于开启了海伦蒙昧的心智，使海伦知道了世界上每一样东西都有名字。

安妮这样写道："1887年4月5日的早上，海伦在洗脸的时候，先指了指盆里面的水，然后又拍了拍我的手，我明白她是想知道'水'这个单词，我就在她的手上拼写了一遍'w—a—t—e—r'（水），就没有再多想它了。直到早餐时，我突然想到，也许'水'这个新词可以帮助海伦弄清楚'杯子'和'牛奶'的难题。我立即带着海伦来到水房，我一边抽水，一边让海伦拿着杯子对着喷水口。冰凉的水从水井中涌了出来，装满了海伦手上的杯子，瞬间就从杯子里溢了出来，在海伦的手上倾泻而下。我抓住这个机会，在海伦的另一只手上拼写'w—a—t—e—r'（水）。第一遍我写得很慢，第二遍就写得快了些。这种水流过她手的冰凉感觉和单词联系在一起，是如此之近，几乎让她震惊。海伦手中的杯子跌落在地上，她一动不动地站在那里，脸上出现了一道异常亮丽的光彩。她连着拼写了好几遍'水'，然后高兴地蹲在地上用手捶打地面。接着她又指着水泵和架子，问它们的名字。突然，海伦转过身来问我的名字，我在她手上拼写了't—e—a—c—h—e—r'（老师）。在回家的路上，海伦显得异常兴奋，她问我她所触摸到的每一样东西的名字，我告诉了她。就这样，在短短的几个小时之内，海伦的词汇量又增加了30多个。"

安妮和海伦的单词游戏从此宣告结束了。安妮流下了激动的泪水。而海伦·凯勒也生平第一次不再孤独地沉湎于黑暗的世界中了，此刻，安妮的兴奋丝毫不亚于海伦。

毕生的奉献

在接下来的十几年中,安妮一直致力于对海伦的艰苦教育。她凭着极大的毅力和耐心,在没有任何经验可以借鉴的情况下,尊重海伦的孩童天性,不断地摸索,成功地对海伦进行教育。由于她的努力,海伦从一个懵懂无知、心智未开、蛮横撒野的疯丫头,渐渐转变成了一个知书达理、思维活跃、富有才华的少女,并且考进了拉德克利夫学院。安妮对海伦的教育工作暂时告一段落。

海伦进大学之后,安妮并没有离开海伦,她继续留在海伦身边,辅助海伦的大学学习。1904年6月,海伦和其他95位年轻姑娘从拉德克利夫学院毕业。举行毕业典礼的那一天,海伦走到安妮身边,将荣誉献给了自己最亲爱的老师安妮·莎莉文小姐。

海伦结束大学生活之后,在安妮的陪同下,开始了一系列演讲和写作活动。海伦的演讲极大地启发了大众,使人们开始关注残疾人的生活;她的作品也给了美国甚至全世界一种新的启示。海伦的声名日益显著,成为美国乃至全世界最著名女性。马克·吐温就曾说:"19世纪有两个最值得关注的人物,一个是拿破仑,另一个就是海伦·凯勒。"而作为培养海伦的安妮·莎莉文,却一直默默无闻地居于海伦的背后,为海伦的发展贡献自己的力量。

1920年,陪伴了海伦33年的安妮渐渐老了,再也无力随同海伦到各地演讲,她原本就视力不佳的双眼也因为过度疲劳,完全失去了光明。16年后,为海伦费尽心血的安妮终于油灯耗尽,在人们的惋惜声中与世长辞,享年70岁。

《大美百科全书　海伦·凯勒传》

海伦·凯勒（Helen Keller），1880年6月27日出生，1968年6月1日去世，美国作家兼演讲家。虽然她生理上患有残疾，但她一生所取得的成就却给数百万人以启迪。

海伦·凯勒出生于美国亚拉巴马州的塔斯坎比亚，原名叫海伦·亚当斯·凯勒（Helen Adams Keller），她的父亲亚瑟（Arthur Keller）是美国南方联邦的一位老兵，母亲是凯蒂（Kate Adams Keller）。

海伦出生19个月之后，因为患急性充血而失去了视觉和听觉，而且由此变成了哑巴。海伦的父母向波士顿的帕金斯盲人学校寻求帮助，学校派了安妮·莎莉文（Annie Sullivan）小姐到凯勒夫妇家帮助小海伦。莎莉文的祖辈是从爱尔兰移民到美国的。

在莎莉文的启发下，海伦到了7岁时，很快就知道"每件事物都有名字"。在莎莉文的教导下，海伦依靠触摸的方式学会了聋哑语言。她还通过布莱叶盲文学会了阅读，并利用特殊的打字机写东西。1890年，海伦在波士顿霍勒斯曼盲人学校女教师沙拉·富勒（Sarah Fuller）小姐的指导下学会了说话。1896年~1900年，在莎莉文的陪伴下，海伦到剑桥女子中学读书，上完了所有的课程，然后由莎莉文小姐在下课之后重复上课的内容，并以触摸的方式和海伦进行讨论。经过私人辅导之后，海伦通过了拉德克利夫学院的入学考试，并于1900年入学。莎莉文小姐陪她上每一堂课，还帮助她做各门功课。海伦上课时用的课本是用盲文印刷的，她还用自己的打字机回答考试卷。除了在课堂上听讲之外，海伦和老师之间也有专门的讨论。

1904年，海伦从学校荣誉毕业，但令她感到遗憾的是，莎莉文的角色并没有得到认可。此后，海伦和莎莉文到波士顿的郊外定居，由她们合著而成的海伦自传《我生活的故事》（The Story of My Life），成了广为传颂的名著。

1905年，莎莉文与哈佛大学一位风度优雅的讲师约翰·梅西（John

Macy）结婚。当时，梅西承诺他们生活的一切都将以海伦为主。在梅西的影响下，海伦成了一位斗志昂扬的社会主义者和积极的妇女参政运动分子。她努力改善自己的声音，虽然她的声调很古怪，但是能听懂。在梅西遗弃她们之后，一位名叫葆丽·汤玛森（Polly Thompson）的年轻苏格兰女子于1914年来到她们身边，为她们当秘书兼管家。

海伦的经济紧张，生活时常入不敷出，后来接受了卡内基基金的终身捐赠。她经常到各地做巡回演讲，写过几本书，并以她的一生经历为题材，拍了一部电影。她甚至还到杂耍马戏团做了两年的客串演出，她这样做的目的，一方面是为了养活自己，另一方面则是为了她所献身的事业——激发世人对生理残疾患者问题的重视。1924年，海伦开始为刚刚组建的"美国盲人基金会"筹募基金，这项工作后来一直成为她生活的重心。1927年，海伦出版了《我的信仰》（My Religion）一书，书中讲述了她皈依斯维登堡教派的经过。1930年，她又出版了第二本自传性作品《中流》（Midstream）。这时，视力原来就不好的莎莉文完全丧失了视力，并于1936年去世。但是，在汤玛森的帮助下，积极乐观的海伦仍然能够过自己的正常生活。她不仅前往日本旅游访问，并成为美国华盛顿特区家喻户晓的人物。后来，海伦和汤玛森迁往美国基金会在康涅狄格州为她们建造的房子。

第二次世界大战之前，海伦已经成为一位激烈的反法西斯主义者。在战争期间，她支持美国参与到战争中去，并经常接受邀请去军队医院探望访问。战后，她与汤玛森代表海外盲人环游世界。1960年，汤玛森去世。海伦也在一年之后第一次中风，但她一个人又独自生活了7年，最后在康涅狄格州的西港逝世。这位美国女英雄的骨灰盒与莎莉文和汤玛森的骨灰盒被并排安放在华盛顿特区的国家大教堂中。

译后记

美国著名文学家马克·吐温曾说:"19世纪有两位伟大的人物,一位是拿破仑,一位是海伦·凯勒。"作为一个盲聋哑残疾人,海伦·凯勒的一生给我们留下的,不仅仅是她与身体机能障碍做斗争、并最终取得成功的传奇经历,她那永不言输、执著奋进的光辉人性更使她成为激励一代又一代青年的楷模。

正是这么一个被禁锢在盲聋哑世界的残疾人,却克服了常人难以想象的困难,考入了哈佛大学拉德克利夫学院,成为人类历史上第一位获得文学学士学位的盲聋哑人。不仅如此,她还通过自己的努力,终生致力于救助残疾人的事业,建立了许多慈善机构,并获得总统自由勋章,这是美国公民的最高荣誉。

海伦·凯勒不仅用自己的行动证明了人类战胜疾病的能力和勇气,还将自己的经历写了下来,给世人以宝贵的启迪和借鉴。海伦的一生著述颇丰,共有十多部作品。这些作品虽然篇幅比较短,但都体现了海伦对光明和自由的向往与渴望,表达了她内心的痛苦和幸福,蕴藏着巨大的精神财富。

《我生活的故事》是海伦·凯勒在老师安妮·莎莉文的帮助下,于1902年完成的处女作,书中所展现出来的顽强品质和毅力,无不震撼着每一位读者。此书刚一出版,就被誉为"文学史上的一大奇迹。"美国著名文学家黑尔博士也曾这样评论说:"1902年文学上最重要的两大贡献,就是吉普林的《吉姆》和海伦·凯勒的《我生活的故事》。"

该书出版后,不仅在美国引起了巨大的反响,一百多年来,许多国家也翻译出版了各种不同的版本,世界各地的读者更是深受其影响和激励,踏上了成功的人生道路。在我国,该书也有许多种译本,尽管如此,我们还是不揣浅陋地将其翻译出来,希望能给读者提供有益的帮助,同时也希望读者给我们提出批评和指正。

本书除了将《我生活的故事》重新翻译之外，还收入了海伦·凯勒的著名散文《假如给我三天光明》，以使读者对海伦·凯勒的一生及其出色的文学才华有全面而清楚的了解。

在此后记当中，我们希望用美国总统富兰克林·罗斯福的夫人的一段话来做结尾："人类的精神之美一旦被认识，我们就永远不会忘记。凯勒小姐的生活和生活乐趣，给我们这些没有那么多困难需要克服的人上了永远难忘的一课——我们希望这本书有越来越多的读者，并让她的精神传播越来越广。"